DIRK BOGARDE

Cleared for Take-Off

VIKING

VIKING

Published by the Penguin Group
Penguin Books Ltd, 27 Wrights Lane, London w8 5tz, England
Penguin Books USA Inc., 375 Hudson Street, New York, New York 10014, USA
Penguin Books Australia Ltd, Ringwood, Victoria, Australia
Penguin Books Canada Ltd, 10 Alcorn Avenue, Toronto, Ontario, Canada m4v 3b2
Penguin Books (NZ) Ltd, 182–190 Wairau Road, Auckland 10, New Zealand

Penguin Books Ltd, Registered Offices: Harmondsworth, Middlesex, England

First published 1995
1 3 5 7 9 10 8 6 4 2
First edition

Copyright © Dirk Bogarde, 1995

The moral right of the author has been asserted

Typeset by Datix International Limited, Bungay, Suffolk
Printed in England by Clays Ltd, St Ives plc
Set in 10.5/14pt Monophoto Bembo

A CIP catalogue record for this book is available from the British Library

ISBN 0–670–86505–2

Contents

Author's Note

I'm beginning to forget.

Which seems a very good reason to bring this six-volume ego trip to an end.

After the first effort, *A Postillion Struck by Lightning*, I never remotely thought that I'd write another book. Neither did anyone else. But fate, or whatever one chooses to call it, deemed otherwise, and I sprinted away with delight.

But now the time has come to call a halt; as far as autobiographical work is concerned. Enough is enough. It is not at all easy. I keep reminding myself that each book has to be integral, a book to read separately, alone and entire. To that end I have dealt here with some familiar (to some readers) situations but have gone into deeper detail where, before, I feared to disturb the past too much. For obvious reasons I have changed names and even place names when I felt it essential.

So, as always, to my editor, Fanny Blake, who has tried to control my excesses, and to Mrs Sally Betts, who has set them down with perfect clarity, my profound gratitude and thanks.

D.v.d.B.
London
26 June 1995

Come of Age

Brussels was liberated by Chris and me on a Monday. I know this because I wrote it down in my pocket diary as we bumped across tramlines and cobbles in the jeep. I wasn't driving; Chris, my RAF counterpart, was doing that. Bert Cobb, his batman-driver, was slumped anxiously in the back seat, distastefully ducking the bunches of garden flowers and reaching hands of the screaming, delirious population. It was Monday, the fourth of September.

Sunlight exploded like shell bursts through the dense leaves of the plane trees along the road. People were cheering, waving, singing, shouting, hugging each other. Arms and legs flailed as people scrambled wildly to try and get up on to, or into, the jeep, and Bert Cobb kept scowling and pushing them off. He said they were all bloody barmy, as barmy as the lot in Paris. They had no self-respect or control. Last month in Paris they'd been 'right loony'.

On *that* day in Paris the Germans were still banging away. Bullets whined and zinged all about us like mad hornets, chipping the façades of buildings, shattering windows, clanging into the huge brass monuments to past wars. Brussels, it had to be said, was marginally less hysterical because the Germans had pulled out. Marginally. Everyone had gone crazy. If not quite barmy.

A woman in a light flowery summer dress, her hair piled high, suddenly grabbed Chris's arm to pull him towards her. For a kiss, I suppose? The crowd around her cheered and Chris lost control of the jeep and we idled into a tree. We were only meandering along anyway, in the crush. People chucked more flowers and, for some

I

reason (I suppose because it was September), apples and grapes at us. Bert Cobb threw them back. Furiously.

The woman was shouting above the noise. Had we seen her husband anywhere? He was 'formally' dressed for his office. He would have been very easy to see in a Lanvin suit. She had seen him climb on to a tank, but couldn't get up on to it with him because of her high heels. He had a rosebud in his buttonhole. She directed us, in perfect English, towards a quieter side street. She was running beside the jeep so I just pulled her up next to me, and her hair spilled down. People still ran alongside, but it was not as dense a crowd as in the big square.

Chris muttered he'd murder for a cold beer, and was there a bar anywhere? She replied no, but there was a very good restaurant she knew off the avenue Louise which was very chic. Chris didn't mind about the chic part, did it have beer? Bert Cobb sat hunched indifferently, his .303 across his knees. He didn't care about beer, being 'TT'. The restaurant *was* extremely chic: lace curtains, crystal, white cloths, little pink lamps, polished wood, deep carpet. People sat murmuring quietly at the tables or else along the walls on crimson plush banquettes. They hardly looked up at us; when they did it was under lowered lids, then the eyes slid away and they went on murmuring to each other. We were dusty, untidy, un-shaven, booted. Chris and I carried the Un-Expired-Portion-of-the-Daily-Ration: two tins of bully-beef, four slabs of cookhouse bread wrapped in the *Daily Mirror*. Bert Cobb had exactly the same, but stayed outside to 'mind the jeep and keep an eye on things'. He had Rose's lime juice in his water bottle. Against scurvy. So we didn't argue with him.

The maître d'hôtel came silently towards us, smiling smoothly, eyebrows raised in polite enquiry. The woman, who now looked pretty dishevelled, demanded a table in a clear, cool voice, and a 'bottle of Krug and three glasses'. She made it obvious that she was used to ordering things and knew her way about perfectly well. I remembered that her lost husband wore a suit by Lanvin. She wasn't the kind of person you messed around with and the maître d'hôtel didn't. We moved to a table at the back. A huge, aged woman with rouged cheeks and feathers raised her glass to us as we passed, gently inclined her head. Pearls gleamed. Everyone was very calm, polite, well bred, discreet. No fussing or staring. You would never know we'd just won this part of the war that morning.

I put our tins on the table with the bulky package of bread, and when the champagne arrived the woman, who had introduced herself as Madame Alexandre Malfait and told us that her husband was 'in steel', gave the tins to the maître and told him to deal with them. He accepted them with well-concealed distaste but as if they were tins of beluga. We toasted each other. We toasted Belgium. The Allies. Churchill, Eisenhower and The End of the War by Christmas. I don't really know why it is, but all wars, it seems, are supposed to be 'over by Christmas'. They never have been. Of course we couldn't possibly tell her that we were actually on our way north to Arnhem in Holland, where a gigantic operation was about to take place which would quite certainly mean that the war *would* be over by Christmas. No doubt about it. So Chris and I, with a secret smile to each other, made the toast feel private and, somehow, real. We drank to Arnhem.

Instead I asked her if she knew a little town called Courtelle, it was near Louvain? My recent ancestors all came from there and my father had suggested that, when the time came, I should go and 'liberate' it, which seemed quite a pleasing idea to me.

Madame Malfait got tremendously excited to think that I was 'really, *au fond*, one of us!' and threw her arms round my neck, which made some of the clients at last raise their eyelids and then look away. She said that I simply *must* go and 'liberate' them all, as soon as it was possible, but that, as far as she knew, Liège and

Louvain were still occupied. At that point the maître d'hôtel arrived bearing, himself, a huge silver platter to present for our inspection. Then everyone turned round in their seats to watch.

The tins of bully-beef had been sliced as thin as cigarette cards, decorated all about with transparent rings of tomato and gherkin and little puffs of parsley. It looked extremely pretty, and Madame Malfait asked that it should be carried to the other clients, because it must be the first bully-beef they'd ever seen in this restaurant, certainly since the war. So it was carried from table to table, presented with a little flourish, and everyone murmured and clucked; heads were bobbing and glasses raised, because, as Madame said, even though this was a very famous black-market restaurant, it must be the first liberated, unrationed, un–black–market meat they had ever seen.

So we invited everyone: Chris got up and made a little speech in French to take some as a symbol of liberation day, although I don't think anyone really knew much about that. So they all did, and there were cries of '*Vive Churchill!*' and '*Vive les alliés!*' and '*Vive Fray Bentos!*', and the room had suddenly become very jolly. We were so fed up with the U-E-P-O-T-D-R that we let them have it all and stayed happily with the wine. Madame Malfait kept the chunks of cookhouse bread in the *Daily Mirror*, and we were all a bit tiddly when we got bowed out because she had ordered another bottle of Krug and we hadn't had any breakfast.

Bert looked pretty fed up and complained it was obvious who the driver would have to be: 'Old muggins'. And wasn't it a blessing that he'd stayed with the jeep? Otherwise we'd *all* have been pissed as farts and someone could easily have made off with everything. 'Legless!' he grumbled. 'In the middle of a total war.' Madame Malfait hugged us all and cried a bit, and said she simply had to go and find her husband somehow, and waving the packet of bread above her head she pushed into the still-laughing crowds.

'Not a bad swap,' said Chris. 'Two Krug for two tins of bully.' Had I got my map ready to drive out of the city? Could I read the map references and so on, and get to the flying-strip which was our next rendezvous? That's all it was, just a map reference. Six figures on the paper, in a totally blank area, all white. It had to be blank because the airstrip had to be bulldozed and got ready, so the terrain had to be board flat. And it was.

It was raining by the time we got there. Well, it would be, wouldn't it? It seems to rain all the time in Belgium. Anyway, we got there. The earth was all torn and ripped up by the tyres and tank tracks and the huge field near Saint-Thomas-le-Grand was a sea of mud, sloshy and puddled, and had a flapping mess tent, latrines and a cookhouse tent. We set up our tents in a far corner and Ernie Ball, *my* batman-driver, had got the office-truck safely settled and camouflaged. That evening, sitting in a damp cluster in the truck with a half-bottle of Geneva gin, some sodden biscuits and two tins of looted sardines, we heard that Louvain was liberated. Then pretty soon all Belgium was free, our airstrip had started to function and we were preparing for the battle of Arnhem.

But there was a bit of a lull, owing to the weather, so I decided that we might go up to Courtelle to see if there were any ancestors hanging about. I rather liked the idea of swanning up to the family château and liberating them all. Fearfully romantic. Chris said that he was game, and Bert Cobb said that he bloody *had* to come so he could drive when we got pissed and legless, what with all the celebrations and that, and whatever I may think, there was a War On Still, and our services (as photographic interpreters, 39 Wing, Royal Canadian Air Force) were essential, so he'd come and keep an eye on us.

Well, we got to Courtelle and it was really just a long, straight road running through turnip fields and as flat as a breadboard. The long street bore my family name on blue enamel signs, so we'd obviously come to the right place. It was lined on either side with red-brick, high-gabled villas, with fretwork balconies and neat lace curtains. There were neat little gardens with neat little gnomes in them, and neat everything. Very tidy and silent. There was no one much about. Chris thought that they were all probably stunned with relief now that the Germans had gone. Then we reached a big square with more gables and civic buildings with towers and turrets, lots of cobbles, and a few shops, very silent looking, and beyond the square the spire of a high church.

And that was that really. No one cheered, no one was about, a man wobbled past on a bicycle and didn't even bother to look at us. I said to Chris that perhaps he thought we were Germans and that the war was still on. Chris said that was pretty damn silly because we had a Union Jack stuck on the windscreen, not a swastika or the SS sign, and anyway we were in khaki and RAF blue and not field grey, and then we saw a scowling woman standing with folded arms in a shop doorway sheltering from the rain, with a small child clinging to her skirts, and a bedraggled bunch of flags dripping above her head. So they *did* know about the Liberation. I called out to her politely and asked her for directions to 'the château' and she stared with eyes wide with sudden terror and swiftly dragged the child with her into the shop and shut the door.

Chris wondered if I *had* got the right town. The locals weren't exactly friendly. Then it dawned on me that they were probably all Flemish and didn't speak French. *I* didn't speak Flemish. Chris asked why the hell hadn't I thought of that before we started out? We were all soaking wet and cold, now he'd probably get flu just before the Big Day. Meaning the drop on Arnhem. He reversed angrily, nearly making Bert Cobb fall out of the jeep. We shot into a narrow, walled lane which was too twisty to turn in and too dangerous to reverse in safely, so he drove towards a cluster of old barns just as an aged man came hobbling out of a doorway with a sack over his shoulders, wooden clogs on his feet and a battered brown uniform cap with 'Palace Hotel' in faded gold lettering on the rim.

We stopped beside him and I risked French, because I reckoned that if he worked in an hotel somewhere he probably understood French; which he did, because in reply to my question, 'Where is the château?', he shrugged and asked which one. Château de Bois Moulin or Château Belair? I said I was looking for the van den Bogaerdes, and told him why. He shook his head and asked whose son I was.

'I am the grandson of Aimé van den Bogaerde. He was born here, I believe?'

For a tiny moment there was a flicker of light in the oyster-dead eyes. Slowly he removed his gold-braided cap, took my hand in his writhen one and raised it to his lips. He said that he had been my grandfather's groom, as a boy. He replaced his cap, shook his head and murmured something inaudible.

Chris said for Christ's sake, let's stop whinnying on. He'd get pneumonia. But the old man said that Bois Moulin was the place and it was right ahead, beyond the farm. Across the barnyard I saw the high-pitched slate roof, the high, pink-brick walls with white dressings, the tall, shuttered windows. It looked forlorn and closed up in the fine rain. Rooks cawed in the great trees all around it. It stood on a slight hillock, and down below it lay a long, dark lake, spanned by a white iron bridge, a graceful arc. There were some ducks sadly bobbing about, and the paths along the lake were overgrown and sere with weeds and dead leaves and fallen boughs. There was no sign of life anywhere. The old man in the Palace Hotel cap watched us curiously and then said that there was no one at the house. They were in Brussels. Chris muttered very sarcastically, 'Just leave your card, why not?'

The old man shrugged, and asked if I was part of the family. And I said again that I was, and he just said everyone was away, they would not welcome intruders.

'Bugger that for a lark!' said Chris, spinning the jeep round and we raced off, as fast as we could, through the farmyard, and that was how I 'liberated' my ancestral château.

I felt tremendously cheated, but no one had seemed very interested. Perhaps their war had been particularly harsh. We drove on in the gathering dusk and steely rain back to the airstrip which was the map reference in the middle of acres of beet fields. There were no sorties being flown that week because of low cloud, I hadn't found my 'relations', Chris was shivering, and thought he might easily have a temperature. And that was that.

Somehow I had had a lyrical, theatrical vision of it all being very different indeed. I had imagined (in those drifting moments just before sleep) that we would have been received with enthralled rapture by a flag-bedecked town, that all the dignitaries would have hastened to welcome us: the mayor, the mayor's wife even, my long-lost family – I didn't know how many, but masses of them – the priests, and perhaps even the bishop or someone tremendously grand, with a crozier and pointed hat, acres of lace and flowing vestments. We'd have been taken in a procession (I was certain it would have been a formal procession) all the way to the great church with the high spire where all my relatives would have been laid to rest (after all, they ran the town). Then after a solemn mass, with censors and altar boys flying about, we'd be led down into the huge tombs under the altar: arches and pillars and flaming torches, and under the most enormous and elaborate tomb, perhaps with my great-great-great-great-grandparents, lying side by side in stone, with ruffs, clasped hands, and their pointed feet lying on little stone dogs, would be marvellous family treasure! Then the bishop, or maybe the senior member of the family, would give a signal to four strong townsmen, and I would be brought respectfully to the side of the tomb as the great stone lid was jemmied open, so that I could pay my respects to the dusty relics of my ancestors and their fortunes. But instead of dusty relics from the Middle Ages, all there would be in the tomb would be the *entire* contents of all the town's wine cellars, hidden during the German Occupation! Bottles and bottles of Krug, Lafite, Château-Yquem and so on (I was, at that time, a bit hazy about my wines, and these were the ones which most loudly beckoned). My 'imagining' continued with a tremendous kind of bacchanalia under the soaring arches in the flickering light of the flares.

But, of course, it wasn't ever like that, and perhaps just as well. I imagined it all so completely, and in such detail, that finally I almost came to believe it had actually taken place, the bishop, the Krug and all.

Years later I found my way back to Courtelle once again. I was working on a film in Louvain. Some thirty years later it was still raining. The town had grown larger, there was a little supermarket in the square, light industry had spread everywhere, but the château was still beyond the barns, the lake still dark and sad, the graceful bridge still arched across it, and the rain dripped forlornly from all the great trees on either side. There was no one living in sight.

Sloshing back to my hired car, I turned to look for one final time at the tall, elegant, slate-roofed, pink-brick building. In a ground-floor window a lace curtain flashed closed. I had been observed as an unwelcome trespasser. It was the nearest, and only, contact I ever had with the ancestors. I drove back to Louvain. I had met no one, seen no one, the old man with the Palace Hotel cap had obviously long since been laid to rest.

Aged twenty-three, in that wet September of 1944, I did, I confess, feel a very strange pull towards roots which I had never really accepted as being mine; but in a short time, a matter of a week or so as it happened, all thoughts of ancestral belonging were exploded in the wreckage and carnage of the disaster at Arnhem.

Chris and I quickly realized that there would not be 'peace at Christmas'. It was not now even certain that there would be peace in the foreseeable future. Then on Christmas Eve I was sent by HQ, with Ernie Ball (to share the driving), through a silent, almost empty, terrified Brussels. A very different city from how it had been in September. Now it was grey, abandoned, shops shuttered, a few anxious people about who no longer blew kisses but shook their fists and shouted abuse or even spat. I wondered about Madame Malfait and her Lanvin-suited husband. We had failed them all. The Germans had broken through in the Ardennes and now retribution and reoccupation faced a horrified population who had counted so joyfully on our summer liberation.

We were, Ernie Ball and I, on our way down to a grubby town called Charleroi; from there we had to find the HQ of an American Army Group and advise them on the very alarming situation – if they were still there. Following the military signs we reached the small, silent town of Dinant and drove right past the huge gates to a château which was their HQ. In the pelting rain, and, I confess, a nervous panic, we somehow had missed these, and bucketed on down a deserted road to a river bank. The river was swollen with brown December rain, curdling and swirling, dragging bits of branch and stuff past us, and there, before our appalled eyes in the spumy rain, only half hidden in scrub and some sagging camouflage nets, crouched three gigantic Tiger tanks, gleaming wetly on the opposite bank. Gun barrels pointing straight, it would appear, at our tinny jeep. I had never felt so exposed in my life. Really silly and petrified. I wrenched the jeep round into an amazing circle, skidding and lurching in the mud, and tore away bouncing and jumping over the mortar holes which scuffed and pitted the road.

Ernie Ball was hanging on to the edge of the windscreen loudly calling out Hail Marys at the very top of his voice – so she would hear him the better over the roar of the jeep and the belting rain? I knew now that he had to be a Catholic, and devout at that if he really thought that there would be any divine help coming our way. Although, oddly, perhaps there was. Perhaps these hysterical 'Hail Mary full of grace's bounced us back to the great brick gates we'd earlier passed? Because twenty minutes after leaving what seemed to be instant obliteration at the riverside, I was confronting a tall American general, in the pillaged library of the château, a Christmas tree in a corner. I suppose he was a general. I never understood the Yanks' insignia, or all the medals they wore like stamp collections on their chests. But he seemed to be the boss, and although he looked about my own age, he did have grey hair at the temples and was frantically chewing gum.

When I told him I was from 2nd Army HQ, that the Germans had broken through in the Ardennes, and that there were already three huge Tiger tanks across the river just down the road, that the bridge at Dinant, as far as I could tell, was still intact, he simply spat out his gum, shouted, 'Oh! My! Oh! My! *Sheet!* Let's get outa here!', and screamed orders to evacuate and destroy all papers to two white-faced captains.

I told him that I was there to brief him on the latest German positions and he pointed out, very reasonably under the circumstances I thought, that I already had. If they were twenty minutes down the road he really didn't need to know anything else, but I should go get some 'chow' because it was 'up'. In a short time the whole hideous red-brick château had exploded with hurrying men, clattering boots, and boxes and piles of papers being carted about in extreme haste. In general you could say there was a subdued, almost contagious, sense of panic, but we finally all sat down at a long table set about with dishes and bottles and guttering candles, with great platters of food and chunks of bread, crates of Coke and jugs of milk, and plates of steaming waffles, and a huge round platter of hot tinned salmon, piled like a small Fujiyama, a wavering plume of steam rising from its peak. There was more food on this table that evening than Ernie and I had seen in a whole month in our mess. Maybe the Hail Marys? Then, to my veiled surprise, great slurps of *hot* marmalade were poured over the mountain of pale-beige salmon and everyone scooped it up. They ate hugely. I contented myself with waffles and hot maple syrup and wondered how we'd ever get back in the hostile dark. But a plump, jolly major from Cincinnati said it was too darned late to move about, they'd be leaving at first light, so grab a 'corner, kiddo' and get some shut-eye.

As the grey dawn of Christmas Day filtered through the rain, it revealed the great gravel forecourt of the château crammed with revving trucks, jeeps and half-tracks. Blue exhaust smoke loitered and wavered in the wet, sullen air. We shook hands, called 'Good luck!', then drove away through the dank morning and the dead, shuttered, deserted town of Charleroi, cobbles glinting in the white dawn.

Later the tramlines of the Brussels suburbs threaded through empty, closed, dead streets, and eventually, much later and without trouble, we reached HQ in a school in a small industrial town called Eindhoven, just over the border in Holland. This was where we had pulled back to after the catastrophe of Arnhem, to regroup, bind our wounds, bury our dead, when we could, and await events. We'd lost this part of the war. The agony of Arnhem burned deeply into each and every one of us who had survived. It was now a question of sitting it out for the winter, and just waiting. No one was quite sure what for, but it was going to be a long and cruel wait.

★

We struggled through a bitter, wretched winter. I saw *The Merry Widow* every night for two weeks and became word-perfect. Still am. *I'm going to Maxim's, where fun and frolic beams* . . . It was about the only decent thing that ENSA, the forces entertainment brigade, ever sent us.

Chris and I got billeted on a pleasant elderly couple in a spick and span little house next to HQ and were very comfortable. There was very little food, so we drove into Belgium and bought jeep-loads of vegetables and coffee beans and stuff, and, apart from the odd bomb and a couple of furious Messerschmitts who flew low and strafed us from time to time, we managed pretty well. I got sent up to a Division in the front line for a while, which was unnerving, mainly because the major-general, a civilized, erudite man, had a tiresome predilection for slender young officers and fancied me like anything. His ADC, a tall, elegant, very handsome young man, who had been an actor, called Peregrine, alerted me to this rather worrying problem the day I arrived in the compound of divisional trucks parked under some frozen apple trees. He lay, supine, in his truck, the epitome of grace and beauty smoking a Balkan Sobranie with a gold tip: his curly hair haloed by a huge lynx collar, his leather jerkin lined with mink; his boots shone like polished conkers. He said that there was a stalled German train across the orchard on a bit of bombed railway track which was stuffed with loot that the Germans had tried to get back to Germany. But we had got there first. Most of it was luxury stuff: furs, silks, scents, wines, pictures and so on. Everyone in the division had managed to supply himself with something 'to keep the cold out'.

Peregrine shook his head sadly at me and said, '*Far* too pretty, Ducky. "Uncle" will be after you in a flash. At the moment he's gobbling up half the Highland Infantry, but he'll make a beeline for you. What on *earth* are you here for?' He yawned indifferently.

When I told him, he smiled kindly, said that I really wouldn't find much to do, there would be no one to brief about mine-fields, sunken lanes, lines of fire, marsh or gravel, or 88-millimetre emplacements. No one actually *did* anything in the division. Patrols were about their limit, with the odd recce up to the Rhine. They were, as we all were, waiting. The débâcle at Arnhem had stopped them just before they could cross the river. Too tiresome, utterly boring, fearfully bad for morale, and did I know that dinner in the mess was madly formal every night? That I was not to be surprised to see that the mess-waiters were all in very tight-fitting, lime-green, sateen uniforms, with the divisional crest on their pockets. We would also have *all* the divisional silver on display. It gave them something to do, cleaning it.

He also pointed out that just because Uncle might make a grab for my genitals, it did not mean that he was not absurdly, even hideously, brave. If we had to go up to the river, to Driel just across from the ruins of Arnhem, a most unsalubrious area he assured me, I would most likely be asked to join him, and Uncle, in the Bren carrier and we would not, at *any time*, wear helmets. This was considered 'common' by Uncle, and not the behaviour of a gentleman. I would not, said Peregrine, be told of this strange piece of information. It would be supposed that I would auto-matically know.

As I was from 2nd Army HQ, and one of Monty's 'little fellows' – this was said sarcastically, but obviously I had been checked out thoroughly – and as I would have to present myself at the general's truck, with my information on the area and the 'guff' (as he called it) for the patrols to use on my updated maps, it might be sensible for me to wear my bathing-trunks. I suppose I looked slack-jawed.

'*Under* your uniform of course. You have *got* a pair, I suppose?' In mid-December, with icicles hanging feet long from the roof of his truck, with the ruts in the field as hard as cast iron, a fog as thick as butter-muslin, the frost white as icing sugar, I simply shook my head. 'Oh, never mind. Mine will probably fit you. Got masses of them. They *must* fit tightly. Part of my survival kit. Remind me before you troll off. He'll be *most* attentive at first. Listen to all your info. Read your maps with you, heads together, then he'll lean closer and closer, and amazingly you'll find his hand on your thigh and he'll say, because he *always* does, 'Now you *will* be kind to me, won't you?', and you either close your maps or open your flies. That is strictly up to you.'

In shocked, spinster-like silence, I sat rigid.

'The bathing-trunks . . . most useful. They just stop him getting too frisky, d'you see? If he *should* get into your trousers, he finds the rebuff. Simple. You don't have to say a word. Thank God you aren't wearing a kilt. Any particular choice of colour? Red, white, a nice pair in yellow here? Satin elastic. Very *firm* and secure. Try the white? Match your face.'

That was my introduction. Peregrine was absolutely correct in every detail, he knew the drill exactly. He'd been through it constantly with many young officers 'up there on a visit'. The general was nervously rebuffed. He was furious. Sulky. I was therefore placed, at dinner, far below the salt, and miles from the candle-stuffed candelabras on the mess table. I ate my late-served meal – I was always the last – in the dark.

'Now see what a silly you have been,' said Peregrine the next day. 'You'll be classed as "difficult and uncooperative" and get sent back to base. Not a good recommendation. He's *frightfully* close to Monty. I mean, ducky, all you had to do was comply politely, takes a couple of seconds, he doesn't want much, and then you'd be golden boy and go on delicious trips with him and eat your dinner in the light. And it is *frightfully* good food. From Fortnum's. Silly billy! As soon as someone else catches his eye you'll be off the hook. They never last, and he really does like the butch ones best. Miners, drivers, weightlifters, labourers.'

But I hung on to my virtue and froze to death for a few more days, then got banished from the mess (my tent space was needed very suddenly) to be billeted on a Dutch farmer and his plain daughter, where I slept in the attic on my camp bed along with two old men, the girl, two dogs and a goat. When the tiles rattled off, and flew into the orchard, as they frequently did, with a salvo of shells whanging across the river to 'keep our heads down', I sometimes regretted that I had not been just a little friendlier to my major-general. However, after a month of this punishment I was sent back to Eindhoven and Chris and the friendly people in their neat little house next to HQ.

Peregrine, to my amazement, later got married to a girl I knew very well in the theatre. They had a blissful life together in Connecticut, until he died, suddenly and without fuss, on a flight from New York to Palm Beach. Not so long ago.

The winter dragged on, and then, almost suddenly, there were yellow crocuses in the little front gardens, and the sky changed from beaten pewter to baby blue. And on my birthday exactly, just before noon, we crossed the Rhine in an amphibious vehicle. I was twenty-four. Almost grown up. The water was swollen with melting ice, swirling and raging with little white-capped waves. Bullets whizzed about our heads, so we lay crouched behind piles of ammunition boxes, tinned rations and god-knows-what-else as they zinged into the water with definite hisses, or else screamed over our heads. Someone said not to worry about them. They were all badly aimed and right off course. They appeared to be dead *on* course from where I lay. But they would, because I couldn't swim.

'Werewolves. The kids and raggle-taggle fighting to the death for Hitler,' said Chris dismissively.

But I noticed that he was crouched as low as I was. I didn't think it was really the most glorious way of marching on the conquered enemy.

Actually, to be absolutely fair, they weren't conquered yet. It was only March. There were still a few weeks to go. But amidst the cracking of bullets, the stench of cordite, and smoke from burning buildings on the German bank I didn't have much time to consider anything serious apart from the fact that I was a non-swimmer and that I didn't really want to drown on my twenty-fourth birthday.

Ernie Ball was crouched, I remember, at my side, frantically telling his wretched rosary. Lying there, Chris's backside in my face, Ernie at my side, bilge water under my belly, I remembered that I had made a strict pact with myself, when I was seventeen, busy making birdcages and arranging rocks and plants in my vivarium, that if at twenty-one I had not made it as a 'star' – I did, actually, mean Clark-Gable-Cary-Grant-Gary-Cooper-stuff – I'd simply go and hang myself from a convenient banister. The fact that at twenty-one I was on punishment jankers scrubbing out the officers' lavatories at Wrotham Camp, or somewhere, hit me a cruel, bitter blow when I remembered it, pouring Brasso into an old toothbrush.

But then everything I had planned in the halcyon days of my early youth had come to nothing. Whoever, least of all my poor mother on her birthing-bed, imagined that on my twenty-fourth birthday I'd be lying on my belly crossing the Rhine under enemy fire?

But I was growing up quickly. Reaching man's estate the hard way. Germany saw to that. Being a member of the Occupying Powers, even a modest member like me, gave one a feeling of undreamed-of power. They were our captives, these grovelling creatures standing sullenly at the roadsides, or in their fields, hands shielding their eyes from the lowering sun. After France, a comfortable, tumbling, untidy, joyful nursery of a land, Germany was stricter. Tidy, prim, trim, a billiard table of neat efficiency. Patches of dark pine woods, ribbed fields, pretty toy-town cottages. No men to be seen. Or if there were, they were very old. 'All dead or fighting us,' said Chris. We drove, Bert and Ernie in the office-truck, Chris and I in the jeep, a simple convoy of two, through once-enemy territory. No one threw a grenade, stretched piano wire across the road, set off a mine. We sailed through our part of Occupied Territory. Then, on the second day, a strange straggle of men and women in striped prison pyjamas, draped in old blankets or sacks, came towards us across the fields, arms outstretched. The first DPs we had seen: displaced persons, people suddenly let free, or escaped from the camps. We were not absolutely certain about the camps yet. We had heard growing rumours long since, and a place called Auschwitz had been discovered by the Russians in Poland in January – we had seen these strange complexes on our aerial photographs, but had not been a hundred per cent convinced. Now we met the appalling, shattering evidence. The extermination camps existed; here were a few of their relics: French, Russian, Italian, Dutch, deportees or prisoners, or just Jews ... haggard, hysterical, shaven-headed, weeping creatures crying out to us in a babel of tongues. Begging for food, clutching our hands, kissing the jeep bonnet, sobbing in gratitude, urinating down their legs as they stood, from sheer joy.

Even Ernie and Bert were mute. Shocked, unnerved. We sent them gently on their way explaining that the main body of the army was still ahead for them, that there would be people to help them, we could not feed them, that Paris had *not* been destroyed, that Amsterdam was whole, that the Russians were almost in Berlin. We were silent for a very long time after they had trudged away in the fading light. No one had ever warned us to expect this terrible sight. It was the first one, but alas! not the last.

Ernie broke the handle off the coffee pot one day. We decided that at the next farm we would 'liberate' one. Liberating, or 'swanning', was merely a euphemism for simple looting. Nervously, hands on holsters, we swung into the yard of a farmhouse. Closed shutters, closed doors, no signs of life. No hens scratching, barns empty – but, after forcing the door, embers glowing in the stove, a cat hiding under a chair. The hideous feeling that unseen eyes were watching from somewhere in the darkened house. Feet, our booted feet, clumping on board floors. Chris found a coffee pot on the stove, emptied its dark contents into the yard. Ernie and Bert collected a couple of jars of pickled things from a shelf and we drove away. Our first attempt at looting. It was a pleasing coffee pot, grey enamel, with little blue daisies on the lid. But I never really liked it. We used it constantly, but it was always an unpleasant, rather guilty, reminder of something better forgotten. Ernie reported the pickles were sour and he hated gherkins, so they got chucked away and Bert had refused to eat any because he was certain they had been poisoned.

Four days later we drove into the huge barracks at the airfield on the heath outside Lüneburg, and set up our tents: the last stop, we felt convinced, before Berlin. One morning we decided to visit a camp which had just been abandoned by the Germans. They had pulled back, leaving us to deal with the camp and 'some cases of typhoid'. Apparently it was a vast place, and Chris felt certain that he would find a pair of Zeiss Ikon binoculars there. The few Germans who remained were, apparently, unarmed. I said I'd go with him, to see if I could get some jackboots. I rather fancied myself in a pair. We had no other reasons at all for going to the place, apart from the fact that Chris had 'liberated' a very smart pale grey Opel car two days earlier and felt a 'run would be fun'. It was. *Huge* fun. All in the high, clear April sun, birches greening in the woods, birds singing, fat clumps of primroses everywhere, little crystal streams running among mossy boulders and king-cups. We had some bottles of liberated beer, and the unexpired-portion-of-the-daily-ration again. We planned to have a picnic somewhere in the warm spring sun, by a stream, before we reached the camp. We had a map, but strangely enough the Germans had never feared an invasion as we in England had. We'd removed all our signposts. They had left theirs intact. We gratefully followed the black and yellow signs to Bergen-Belsen.

Where we lost our boyish laughter for ever.

Sitting on a hillock outside my tent, looking down at the smouldering ruins of the mess tent which the pilots of 39 Squadron had set alight as a gigantic symbol of success on the night of Unconditional Surrender, we watched the sparks spin and eddy up into the blue night sky.

'It's all over. I've never felt so totally useless in all my life,' I said.

Chris drained his mug, dribbled the dregs of his drink into the heather. 'You won't be demobbed yet, chum. *I* will. I had a year before you came in. What in God's name will I do, I wonder? You'll be on your way East within a month.'

Down on the field, beside the drifting smoke and the sparkling wire skeletons of the mess armchairs, the pilots of 39 Squadron were singing mournfully – '. . . *my owwwn Lili Marlen-e . . . my owwwn Lili Marlene . . .*' – voices blurred by drink and extreme weariness. They had been flying non-stop since last June. I knew, of course, that Chris was right, that the war was not yet over for me. I was too young. My demob number had still a year or so to go; also, I was a Specialist and that meant I'd be kept as long as 'the emergency', as it was idiotically called, continued. The Japs by no means beaten yet, and the next job on my agenda, I was certain, was to join the others who had already started work on

Operation Zipper: the fall of Singapore. So I'd be in a war for quite a while yet.

But that evening I felt drained and gutted. Older than anyone in the whole world. Chris, Ernie and Bert would all pretty soon go back to the UK. I'd be, as I had been before, another 'draft of one'. Bound for somewhere in the East. I can remember, now, the enormous wave of self-pity which engulfed me sitting on a long, un-barked, felled pine. This quite amazing friendship we had all forged would end. Just as the war had ended in Europe. Suddenly. With little warning, everything was over. An appalling emptiness sagged through my body.

I reached for the bottle of looted schnapps and poured some into my tin mug. 'I feel bereft,' I said. 'Everything suddenly coming to an end. Not grinding to a halt. Just *ending*. Bosh! Like that.'

Chris grinned. I remember how his glasses glittered in the light from our exposed (for the first time in the war) hanging hurricane lamp. 'Don't whine, chum! That's not in order. It's all over and we are both here to *see* it over. Hell of a lot of us aren't.'

That sobered me up. Chris wondered if it had been worth the effort. If it had done us any good, shaken us up, made us wiser, older. Or would we have been better off if it had never happened and we'd just been left to idle gently into middle age and senility instead of being made too aware too soon? I said, I remember, that it was all too difficult to answer. I'd have been better off without *some* things. The last few weeks for one. We neither of us spoke of Belsen. We *never* spoke of it ever again to anyone. I didn't feel that seeing that, smelling that, had made me wiser or more adult. But perhaps it had? I knew that he and I, and the others there that April day, would never be quite like anyone else. We'd always be apart. We had a terrible comparison now to set against everything and anything which might happen to us in future. But I didn't think that dry-mouthed fear, generally, was something which I had a desperate need of in the process of 'growing up' or in adulthood. Here I was, twenty-four, and still blindingly aware of sheer funk, the terror of hearing bullets being fired *at* you, the draining relief when you heard the crack of their missing you. The tearing, hissing of shrapnel shards raining down in whispering death through the standing corn like lethal hail, the first bodies, in the early weeks, swinging and bobbing in the shallow water as the tide nudged them gently up the litter-strewn sands, politely returning them to the living. I just wondered, looking back, if all these images, and many more, were actually necessary to growing up? Well, perhaps they were. But one amazing, to me, fact did emerge, sitting up on the log pile listening to the drunken, happy Canadians dancing and singing below. I had survived. Against all odds the late developer had managed to get through. Largely intact. At least physically. And now I remember saying aloud, 'Yes, I *do* feel it was important for us to go through all this awful stuff.'

'We'll be altered now, for ever. Won't we?' Chris poured another generous schnapps, spilling some over his fist, shoved the cork back into the bottle, ramming it home with a hard thrust of the heel of his hand. 'Well, just *remember* that, chum,' he said. 'Be bloody grateful we made it. I reckon you've had a better education out here, for the rest of your life, than any school or university could have given you. What you've learned here will help you get through the next phase. Got it? You really can say, I think, that at long last you have come of age! Important!' He raised the tin mug in a mock salute. 'Here's to Tokyo ... Singapore, Rangoon, or wherever you go, anyway: all stations East. And the best of luck.'

'I'll need it. God! I really don't feel that I am ready for that yet ... haven't got my breath back. Not ready, quite. Not yet, Chris ... that's my worry ...'

'Balls! You *are*. Quite ready. Ready, and cleared for take-off.'

He was smiling, took a swig of his schnapps, wiped his lips with the back of his hand. 'All ready and correct! Good luck!' he said.

There was a fading burst of maudlin singing down by the smouldering ruins of the mess. This part was over now.

Coming to Terms

My name was Pip in those days. There was no pixie-like reason for
this. It was not a diminutive of 'Phillip' or 'Paul' or 'Peter', and
nothing whatever to do with *Great Expectations*. It was just brutally
slung at me by an exhausted instructor in Le Cateau Lines, Catterick,
where I had been sent to join the Royal Corps of Signals. I can't
imagine why, can't now, couldn't then. Maddened by my calm,
bovine, agreeable incomprehension of anything whatsoever to do
with valves, wires, wireless, frequencies, transmissions or the total
absurdity of Morse code, indeed anything remotely connected to
the business of my becoming a little Signaller, the unhappy man
suddenly hurled his piece of chalk, the book of instructions, a
duster and, finally, his cap at me and roared for quick delivery
from my dumb bewilderment. 'You bloody give me the *pip!*' he
yelled.

And of course it stuck. I was 'Pip' from then on and carried the
unlikely name from Catterick Camp until the day I shuffled
wretchedly down the gangplank of the *Monarch of Bermuda* in
Liverpool back from Singapore for demob. With a pork-pie hat, a
speckled cotton and wool suit, and a travel warrant for Haywards
Heath, I was dispersed into civilian life, and anonymity, like a fart
in a colander, overwhelmed, overlooked in the vast wilderness of
an exhausted and grubby peace. After that last scene on the log-pile
on Lüneburg Heath, having drained the schnapps bottle and sol-
emnly shaken hands, Chris and I, without fuss or friction, dwindled
into being the strangers we both were long before we had been
joined together by someone high up at 2nd Army HQ.

After over a year of intensive work, with an office-truck, a batman-driver each, a couple of tents and the full details of Operation Overlord, the invasion of Europe, and Operation Neptune, the Normandy landings, the job was now finished and so was the extraordinary relationship with which the intensity of that time had suffused us both. Suddenly it was all over.

It was an odd feeling. Hard now to explain that relationship: tighter, closer, more profound, more trusting than any marriage. We had tremendous security, no sexuality, nothing remotely romantic. We hardly even knew each other; never discussed our families, our backgrounds, or who and what we had been before the war. The individuals we were before we joined the forces, and APIS, had never even existed. We did the job we were assigned and trained to do. When it ended, then so did we: as a team.

But, like cards in a pack, pages in a book, bricks in a wall, we were close. Just before complete limbo finally claimed us we did both attend an exhibition of our paintings, which we had been permitted to do by the Air Ministry, held at Batsford's. It was the first big exhibition of war paintings from Normandy and as such, from the point of view of novelty rather than any excellence, it was a great success. We had painted, Chris and I, in the odd lulls which do arrive strangely in a war: if the weather precluded flying sorties for us to work on, or if exhaustion had finally taken its toll (which it did from time to time) and we had to clear off and relax. Although relaxing in and beyond (on occasion) minefields, or sitting silently, working intently amidst the unburied dead, or in the wreckage of some fought-over, shattered village, was hardly a jolly form of relaxation. But we drew and painted, and *that*, more than anything, was the relaxation. The calm and joy of holding again a pencil or brush drained stress, renewed lost energy, calmed us.

At the exhibition, in worn uniforms and modest medals, we

were warmly received, and felt pretty good. Chris was over-whelmed by the fact that Peter Ustinov had wandered in, bulky in a drab raincoat, looking rather like a hippopotamus. He poked about, didn't sign the Visitors' Book, and never made the second floor, which saddened us. But the confetti of little red stickers everywhere from others, denoting a sale, cheered us considerably.

Four days later I left on the *Carthage* as a draft of one bound for Bombay and the Far East in general, and Chris limped off to his early demob. We did meet once again after I got back to the UK and was starting to try and break into the theatre; for lack of any other job for which I might be qualified. He had married, a nice little bright-eyed dunnock of a girl; I think she had been a nurse, or had nursed him, I'm hazy about that. They had a pleasant flat in a house in Surbiton overlooking the river, and he'd been very clever about painting designs on some bedsheets and she had made them into curtains. Material was still on coupons. I remember we had a simple, uneasy little supper: Algerian wine, candles, and Margaret had found some off-ration stuff. There was a little desultory chat on the 'Remember that awful day at Tilly-sur-Seulles?' or 'Do you ever see Ronnie, or George or Jack?' line. Margaret naturally wearied of this. So did we. It was all over and done. We had nothing left to say. We exchanged telephone numbers (he was by this time very successful in some form of commercial art) and parted on the steps of the Victorian house, his clever curtains bellying in the half-open bay window. I turned at the corner, looked back. They waved brightly, gratefully free of me, and went in. I can't remember that we ever met again.

He was older than me – wiser, too – older by about four years or so, calm, quiet, wry, funny. He was of average height, had granny-glasses, thinning blondish hair, thin almost to the point of bald in front, a friar's fringe round his ears. He had a slight limp, the result of a vicious bout of polio contracted in Malta during the siege. He always said that he had fallen madly in love with his nurse there, but that she didn't reciprocate. I suppose that was a nursing hazard? He was neat in his RAF uniform, wore his cap at a slightly rakish tilt, had a little medal – a distinction for something he never discussed, but every time he washed his uniform, which he did for any important engagement, like the liberation of Paris and Brussels, he'd douse the lot in a barrel of petrol and stink for days. And no one went near him with matches or lighter. But he always, most carefully, removed and pocketed his medal ribbon. So it must have been important to him.

He was so much cleverer than I was, so much wiser, so good at his job – and a far better painter – that I frequently wondered how we ever stayed together for so long and under such gruelling conditions – because they *were* gruelling. In the UK things weren't so bad: we had beds in different rooms in a hideous house built for, or by, a pickle millionaire on the Thames at Medmenham. This awful house, together with Benson, the airfield near Oxford, and Southwick House outside Portsmouth were the boundaries of our world and entire existence.

Among these three places our lives were conducted at top pitch. Abroad, after the landings, living together was tougher. We each, thank God, had a tent – pitched under trees in orchards, woods; or else camouflaged with branches or nets – sparse: a hurricane lamp, camp bed, sometimes an ammunition box in which to keep the Bovril, biscuits, books, *Oxford Book of Modern Verse*, a Dickens of some sort, paperbacks of Waugh, Isherwood – that sort of stuff. If it rained, which it often did in the first weeks of the landings, Chris's tent leaked. So he heaved his camp bed into my tent and snored. It was not altogether attractive, but comforting. He read a great deal. Sometimes I used to read aloud, which he liked, until he slept. We made a filthy soup from Bovril and ration biscuit crumbled with a hammer they were so hard. Once he said, 'Bloody

Darby and Joan', and grinned at me in the lamplight. There was always a good deal of gunfire from the Caen direction. We didn't talk much. Listened.

I was late for D–Day. I landed on D + 4 or 5 . . . He took the office-truck across from Portsmouth. I told him that I'd packed all my gear in the truck and not to lose it in the sea. He promised. And didn't. I was late getting across because, to everyone's appalled horror, a day or so before the whole operation was to eventually start, it was discovered that the 21st Panzer Division had moved 'East of Caen'. That was a bit too near, and no one had any idea if the information was correct. It was part of my job to try and look through piles of earlier photographs of the area to see when these unexpected German tanks had arrived. Also to check for signs of the 88-millimetre guns they had and which terrified us, with good reason. This took days. By the time they had been traced, only a few days before the landings, and in scattered array − not in formation but bivouacked under trees and in barns in the area (resting you could say) − Chris and everyone else had taken off for war. The mess at Odiham, the airfield where I was working and from which I was waiting to be flown across to join them, was deserted. My bedroll was made down in a long, empty dormitory. Everyone in the world it seemed was airborne except me.

On the night of Monday the fifth, just after midnight, I heard the distant roar of a thousand thousand planes begin to fill the sky. I remember crawling out of bed in the dark, standing by the windows, rain pattering very lightly, the window frames rattling, the wooden floor starting to tremble, and the whole sky being suddenly darker than night with the enormity of the massed planes thundering, wave after wave after wave, unceasingly, towards France. The roaring continued and reached such a peak of sound that I remember being physically forced to my knees by the terror and magnitude of the noise above. Kneeling by my bed I started to pray unthinkingly, something that was *not* a part of my being. I don't even know what I was praying for. The men above? That certainly. For their safe landing? For the start of winning this long and dreadful war? I suppose that I prayed for that, but I have not the least idea why I *wept*. I only know that I did because I can recall the salt of my tears running into my mouth, thin, diluted salt, like blood. And still the floor shook and trembled, the windows rattled and clattered and the air was sucked out of the room, roared back in, burst my eardrums and sent me crouching, burrowing into my bedroll.

Four or five days later, after it was clear that we were there to stay in Normandy and the Engineers had laid the steel rolls for a landing-strip in the cornfields at Sommervieu for our recce planes, I was bundled, with all my photographs of the area, my handgrip, but without my cap which fell off as I raced across the tarmac, to clamber on to my first ever Dakota. I sat in hunched, amazed silence watching little puffs of smoke burst and drift away below us like dandelion clocks, and someone said over-cheerfully, 'Missed us! They haven't got our range. *Yet*.' I was absolutely convinced then that this form of transportation would *never* catch on. Over my left shoulder (I was on the port side) a great plume of black smoke drifted and meandered into the bruised-plum sky above Caen; below, on the heaving grey swell of the sea, there were a thousand ships – or so it seemed – scattered about like toys in dirty bathwater. An armada in dismay and disarray. It was not all neatly lined up as I somehow had thought it would be. Ships were at all angles, some even listing in the creamy-green-grey lacy waves. There was smoke loitering, and large clusters of scurrying men, the wreckage of houses and seaside villas spilled along the beaches, then we raced down across the debris-strewn sands and crashed, clattered, bounced and skidded along the metal landing-strip, battering at the standing corn, whipping past trucks and jeeps and scatters of hurrying ground crew.

Chris was standing over at the far edge of the strip; he'd waded through the high corn. As I jumped to the ground, still clutching yesterday's sortie photographs of the area, he waved slowly, calmly, a wooden stick in his hand above his head. I grabbed my hold-all from someone. The propellers were still turning, the draught whipping my hair. Chris yelled, as I got near him, 'No *cap*! Where's your cap! And take this.' He shoved the wooden thing, which I saw immediately was an entrenching tool and not just a stick. I tried to grasp it, but because I was loaded with gear, it fell and he had to pick it up. 'Bloody Laurel and Hardy we are. You aren't going to *like* it here, ducky,' he shouted. '*Very* noisy and nasty. You've got to dig yourself a hole. Come on, get cracking.' He turned and went back through the crushed corn. I followed him, stumbling across to an orchard on the edge of the field. I saw the office-truck covered in camouflage netting under some trees. 'There's a ditch over here,' said Chris. 'I've put up my tent by it. It's softer digging and under cover.'

I spent the next hour and a half digging myself a slit-trench. I was supposed to be able to crouch in it and keep my head down. It was a hell of a long job. I gradually realized, through running sweat, that all around me was noise. I'd become so used to it that when the naval guns, firing over our heads in great salvoes in the direction of Caen, which tragically had not yet fallen to us, stopped for a moment, I had a dreadful singing in my ears, like tinnitus. Chris said it was just the silence. Every minute, or so it seemed, a plane landed on the strip or took off. Some were our Canadian recce Mosquitoes, some the Dakotas bringing in supplies and taking back the wounded, masses of them, lying in the trampled corn on stretchers, waiting to be carried aboard. Some, rather a lot I thought, weren't wounded but dead. In neat piles, a label tied to a toe, fluttering in the draught from the Dakota propellers. They lay inert under bedraggled groundsheets, sometimes a helmet over a face. In a strange way they didn't seem to me like the dead. Rubbish, inoffensive stuff waiting for removal. There was no feeling of regret, no sadness, they were just a part of the 'set'. That evening, just after I got my tent rigged up on the edge of the sunken road, or what Chris had called earlier a ditch, we got badly strafed. The heavens opened with chattering gunfire, spurts of earth flew up, leaves swirled about, twigs spun. Anti-aircraft guns on the perimeter of the strip started blasting into the night. Gigantic flashes of instant, white light which burst the darkness so that for a flick, a split second of a second, every leaf, blade of grass, clump of plantain was vivid in detail – a Dürer etching. Then instant blackness and one fumbled and blundered against trees or the sagging walls of hidden tents. In one great roaring flash I saw Chris skittering about in his green, mauve and silver striped dressing gown like a crazed figure in a pantomime. He always slept in flannel striped pyjamas. He had two pairs, and pulled on this awful dressing gown before he ventured out, even to pee or clean his teeth or, on this occasion, to see if I was all right on my first night under fire. I yelled that I was. The explosions and roaring flashes unbalanced one so I had my arms round a tree. 'You *tell* them you were coming?' he shouted sarcastically. Even yelling, his voice held laughter, and in the astonishing light-and-dark he guided me across to the sunken road. We fell into it with a crowd of others: airmen, cooks from the mess, clerks, interpreters like ourselves, and various unknowns caught by surprise. 'Messerschmitts', yelled Chris. 'Make a dreadful mess if they hit you . . . shredded, you'll be!'

Apparently ever since the strip had been laid they had made constant and desperate efforts to blast it out of existence, and all the planes parked around. That night I think the only thing they hit was the roof of the mess tent, which fell in on itself, and a 15-hundredweight parked, unwisely, in the open. It blazed of course, and gave them target light. So we crouched in the lane, burrowing into the sandy sides like terrified rabbits. Which is exactly how I felt. After a bit they sheered off and swung out untouched over the orchards and roared eastward. My tent was sagging like an old potato sack, shrapnel had holed it badly. Chris got a couple of rents in his and told me not to touch anything I might find in the grass. It would still be blistering hot. 'Always wear your helmet over your privates. Okay?' I assume that I looked blank because he snapped, '*Cock*. Your cock! Staff of life. Get it?' I understood, nodded. '*Never* on your head. You lose your head you're dead. Lose your dick and you'll wish you *were*. Understood?'

I must have said that I had because I recall that he asked if I slept on my back because if I didn't his advice didn't count. I said I wasn't sure, probably on my side. He gleamed with laughter in the light of our torches, criss-crossed on the ammo box, said he was always *certain* I would sleep in the foetal position, thumb in mouth. So I could wear my helmet anywhere I bloody well liked. Cancel instructions. I didn't think it was worth answering him. I didn't absolutely know what foetal meant, and anyway, I was too occupied crushing up the ration biscuits, finger-thick and iron-hard, with the heel of my boot for Bovril soup. It was comforting after severe shock, which I had so recently experienced. I was always terrified that I would defecate under the noise and a near brush with instant, easy death. This time I had not done so, by dint of frantic buttock compression, but it had been a very near thing once or twice. Unless you have been through unimaginable terror and noise you cannot imagine how little control you have over your bladder and bowels – one of the things people always overlook when they consider the gut-destroying fear endured during the Blitz or in action, and, in a different, unimaginable world, in the plight of the thousands of people, not only the unhappy Jews, who were shoved into cattle-trucks and sent off to certain deaths in the camps. They were locked in the trucks for days on end, all sorts and conditions, not all of them farmers, workers or peasants. There were also the rich, the burgers, elegant and fastidious in their well-cut suits and costumes, some even with smart hats. Forced to lie in their own filth. The defecation of terror. A breakdown of human dignity beyond belief. I was to see this in due course after that first noisy night of fear and bewilderment in the orchard at Sommervieu. One moment the calm, the rules and regulations of Odiham airfield: meals in the mess, towels in the washrooms, a telephone for picking up, flowers on the tables, and sixty minutes later one was crouched in the sandy walls of a sunken road praying to live. You had to come to terms with life, and death, instantly. Otherwise you were lost.

I remember a perfectly odious captain (part of our lot) who bullied and swore and drank himself witless in England, but who, ten minutes after his landing, crawled into a slit trench from which he declined to budge. Wailing and weeping, shaking, sobbing, he even refused food and was only finally removed when a medic clambered down, gave him a shot of something, and he eventually got hauled off like a fallen steer, strapped to a stretcher covered in his own filth and set a little distance from the wounded. The braggart and bully felled: all six-foot-three of him. I suppose today that I'd feel a bit more understanding? It's probable. But then I was more shattered by his fall from civilized standards – the skin, so to speak, of 'behaviour' and 'control' was membrane thin. I think that shocked me more than anything I'd seen up to date. And I had a lot to see ahead. But it was a tough lesson learned. Never show your fear. If you do you are destroyed utterly. It was a lesson well learned.

But back to the biscuit bashing. Chris hugged his knees in his awful Meaker's dressing-gown, the firing had faded away, water boiled in my mess-tin. Chris said that on the Monday night, the night of the departure for the landings, Gertrude Lawrence (at that time entertaining the American troops) walked slowly up and down among the silent, dark, waiting ships in the dockyard at Portsmouth, a torch shining on her face so they could just see her, and sang unaccompanied, walking among the ships, jammed with apprehensive men as they began slowly to pull out and slide away to France. She sang popular songs, things they all knew. She started, he said, with 'This is a Lovely Way to Spend an Evening', which made them murmur, laugh and whistle and call out to her in low voices, and then she went on to things like 'All the Things You are' and 'Where or When' and the voices swelled softly as they all joined in, a whispering of fading song as they slipped away into the night. I thought that was pretty moving, and poured hot water on to the mashed-up biscuits and stirred in the Bovril.

All was calm outside now. They had managed to douse the blazing 15-hundredweight, which was a comfort. There had been a rough and ready roll-call and none of us seemed to be missing, so we both hunched up in the light of our torches and I spooned out our disgusting supper. I hadn't had time to get unpacked so I slept on my groundsheet on the trampled corn floor of Chris's tent, a bit less holed than mine. Well, it was a form of sleep. In the foetal position.

Some weeks later – I seem to remember it was after the eventual fall of Caen – Chris got very, very drunk indeed. It didn't happen often, and usually only after a tense or difficult run of work. He was really loaded. I got him to his bed and tried to haul him on to it. Quite suddenly he opened his eyes wide with horror, and started hitting out at me, screaming to get away, that I was covering him in my blood and guts. 'I'm covered in your guts! It'll never come off!' He was suddenly a complete stranger, raging in a harsh, gibbering voice I could never have imagined he could use. Others, alerted by his yells and my shouts for help, eventually arrived and we got him soothed and settled, weeping silently, snotty-nosed, apologizing. It had been a terrible nightmare. What it really was, it transpired *much* later, was a blinding memory of a fellow pilot, his best friend, who, returning from a successful sortie with him during the Malta siege, had unthinkingly removed his flying helmet, and in so doing, hadn't seen Chris's frantic signals and walked right into his own propeller. It was never spoken of, and only ever came to awful light when he had taken what he called a real skinful, and that only happened after extreme stress or when, sometimes, memory beckoned or was triggered off by something apparently trivial. That brutal experience, and the polio, were apparently the reasons he was seconded to APIS. However, this evening all was under control, more or less, and Bovril was no substitute for a skinful of Scotch.

And that was that, really. I mean there isn't anything much left to say about Chris and me. We went on with the war, not always comfortably, but intact. It ended, we separated, and returned only much later for the little Surbiton supper. After that, silence for years. We both picked up the ravelled sleeve of our lives and started knitting like fury. Then one evening, at home in France, an unexpected telephone call. I had just finished watering the terrace when I heard a remembered voice. 'Hi! Pip? It's *Chris* . . . Know what day it is?' It was the fortieth anniversary of the landings. Had I seen it on the television? Did we *have* televisions in France? And what about that insufferable Reagan woman being *hatless*! *Hatless* during a ceremony for the dead! It was Chris all right. He and Margaret had a family, he'd retired and moved down to the West Country to paint and potter and they ran a little gift shop. He sold his paintings, she made little figures and dressed them in cotton scraps. Life was easy. Life was good. He'd got my telephone number from my father and we exchanged our addresses, but we had no reason to speak again, and only a distant bond of a fading war to hold us together.

But one day, much later, he did call again. Margaret had died of cancer and he was utterly devastated. Would I talk to him? Could he call me whenever he had to speak to someone? We had known each other for so long. Did I think he could come out to France, find a little place there, do some painting, get away from the memories? Could I help find him somewhere? A room? A modest little hotel, somewhere that he could retire to now that he was alone? I promised him I would. He'd *try* to start up again. Well, of course he wouldn't. I knew that. He knew it . . . He was too old, it was too late, his grief too overwhelming. On a vicious winter's day, with the sea raging and a force nine gale battering the harbour, he was seen to stagger along the jetty carrying what appeared to be a package of books.

His body was washed up a day or two later, weighted down with heavy stones. Finding life intolerable without her, in his quiet, deliberate, determined way, I imagine he had gone to join his wife.

The first thing that I noticed about Hugh was his feet. Hardly surprising really, because they were almost ten inches from my face, sticking out of his mosquito net. White, bony, slim and sinewy as skate wings. They moved vaguely as I sat up and peered through my net up to the top of his charpoy, or bamboo bed, where his head was.

'Trying to get comfortable,' he murmured. He was affable and extremely polite.

'But you are *up* the wrong way, your head should be where your feet are. I mean, it's a bit much having a pair of feet just inches from one's nose.'

He half curled his extremely long body away, removing the feet from my immediate gaze. It was siesta time, or mid-afternoon, and the heat was blistering. 'I should have thought that to have a complete stranger's *face* shoved only inches from *your* face was perhaps worse? Not? heavy breathing? sleep-dribble just before your nose? Anyway, I've only just lain down; just arrived at this awful place. I do apologize. We are fearfully crammed here, have you been here long?'

I told him about a week, that the place, a holding barracks outside Singapore, was crammed indeed, but we were lucky as officers because the ORs were in much worse conditions, some in hammocks or on the floor, and he said he knew that because he'd been down to the other floors (we were gratefully on the top with a sort of open veranda all round, so there was a faint breath of air) and that he was a doctor, he was in the Medical Corps, and his name was Jolly. Hugh.

Memory has spun me back to Tanglin Barracks in 1946 and that hideously jammed, concrete-floored, mosquito-net-draped area on the top floor. And Hugh Jolly's white, bony feet. I had arrived, wretchedly because I had longed to stay on as a soldier, as the famous draft of one from Batavia (now Jakarta) in Java. As a draft of one you were literally that. On your own. You had no responsibilities. No soldiers in a platoon, company or modest group to fuss about and see to it that they obeyed orders, didn't smoke in bed (mosquito nets caught fire with exhausting regularity), had their VD dealt with, and got their mail sent off to Mum in Huddersfield. In short one lacked, sadly, the essential 'parenting' which went hand in hand with being a Good Infantry Officer. Except that I was a specialist (APIS) and had recently been ADC to the Military Governor of an island slightly larger than the British Isles, and far less friendly.

Anyway, here I was, stuck with Hugh Jolly's feet and, as it turned out, to my enormous delight, with Captain Hugh Jolly himself. He was, like his feet, amazingly long, like a very elegant crane. Even his nose looked like a probing beak. He had tumbled, sandy hair, a cliff of teeth, bright, clear, all-seeing eyes (he was a psychologist) and an enormous Adam's apple which rode up and down his throat like a lift when he laughed; and Hugh laughed a great deal of the time: big, roaring belly-laughs. We became friends. As with Chris, he was older than I, far brighter, and I often wondered, and still do after all these years, how we ever became the close friends we did. There was little which we had in common, but, in some strange way, we managed absolutely perfectly and stayed close until, years later, the pressures of our very different worlds eventually separated us. But even then we remained friends: the experience of a war, especially to men, is something that is not shared with strangers or forgotten by the survivors. You can always tell, even across a crowded bar, someone who was 'with you then'. Odd, it never quite goes away.

Hanging around Tanglin Barracks in monsoon heat, with bugger all to do and no area of privacy, was pretty bleak. All one waited for was the posting up on the noticeboard of what ship had arrived and which ship would be sailing, for where, when and with whom. All, at that time, anyone cared remotely about was when we would go home. Tragically the great majority thought that this had to be the best thing they could ever hope for. They had not the least idea that, in most ways, their useful life was over, that no one would really care about them much when they got back to cosy, comforting Blighty. Blighty, had they known it then, was a new, dismaying land. Pinched, ruined, bitter, impoverished beyond belief, bled dry by a war that, eventually, only American support had made it possible to win (and, therefore, pay for). But, of course, they didn't know that.

Some of us were extremely uneasy and there was a good deal of restless fretting and arguing going on below decks too: the *Daily Mirror* had penetrated to the Far East by now, not just with sexy Jane and her maddening dachshund, but with furious talk of 'reform' and 'workers' rights' and 'Vote Labour'. It was all just a bit too soon for men who had left the comforting steadiness of 'Olde England' and were now awaiting embarkation back to a completely altered state, a country writhing in discontent, sourness and acute poverty.

If you hadn't been told otherwise you'd have been convinced that we had lost the war. Which, of course, was more or less true. Others, here and there, had really won it for us, and we were now the handmaidens, and would be for years to come, but it took us a hell of a long time to be convinced. By then it was far too late. For some years men had struggled in what was called a 'tropical hell', fought a bestial and brutal enemy, and suffered grievous and fearful losses to defend the very last vestiges of what had been then the invincible British Empire. Now, the Empire lost in American bargaining and furious anti-Colonialism, plus British ineptitude and error, these same men, proud, unaware but anxious, were drifting about Tanglin Barracks waiting to return to what was no longer a welcoming blanket of security and love, but a threadbare sheet, much mended, and fraying at the edges.

Sprawled in the filigree shade of a frangipani tree, Hugh was shucking peanuts he'd got from somewhere. 'What are you going to do, Pip? I mean when you get back. You said you were an actor?' He spilled me a dribble of nuts.

'Was. Yes. But I don't want to go on with that. It was years ago now, and it's a pretty silly job for a man.'

He threw back his head and trickled nuts, one by one into his toothy mouth. 'So what then? Can you *do* anything else?'

And of course the hideous fact was that I couldn't. I hadn't been trained to do anything useful. Entirely my fault. I could paint, a bit, but not ever well enough to move away from what Chris had termed 'Commercial art, the arsehole of the painter's world'. So I'd probably be quite good at drawing toothbrushes or tins of Mansion polish, but not much else. I said, without conviction, that I'd most likely go off and become a schoolmaster. This almost made Hugh choke. He coughed a bit, cleared his throat and asked me what, if any, qualifications I thought I had. I said none, none at all, but that apparently I wouldn't need any where I was going: a modest Edwardian house near Windlesham which a brother officer and his wife were about to start up as a prep school for seven to elevens. I'd been offered a simple job: to supervise cricket (about which I knew nothing) and football (ditto) and ease them into geography and perhaps art – a little more hopeful. Generally the idea was to help get the school started and be a sort of male nanny to the little beasts. I'd have a room of my own, time off, three meals a day and a very modest salary. Enough to buy my cigarette ration really.

Hugh took all this in thoughtfully, said he didn't think I was really equipped for that kind of life, any more than I would be for becoming a priest or monk. He felt I was, and he used the word clearly, 'being *misapplied*'. I thought this was a pretty good phrase, one I could duck behind. Hugh was a psychologist, he said, so I assumed he'd know. However, after that we never referred to it again. A few days later, after a sweaty trip into a depressed and defeated Singapore and a cheap meal in a Chinese restaurant where we drank out of half-beer-bottles neatly filed along the edges so no one got slashed, we discovered our names stuck up on the notice-board, and a few days later, in high euphoria, we sailed for England, home and beauty, on the *Monarch of Bermuda*. The Liverpool *Evening Express* eight weeks later announced our arrival as 'the largest batch for "demob" in one ship. 2,600'. It was a tight squeeze.

I never made the school at Windlesham, as it happened, which was just as well for the school and countless trusting parents. Instead I made my way, almost by instinct like an elver, through rough pastures back to the river of the theatre. It was, after all, about the only thing I had managed to do before the war which brought me any hope. Not much, but just enough. I could say that it was my 'craft'. Hugh had been right, I would have been woefully 'misapplied' as a teacher. Even worse as a priest or monk. But those were his suggestions, not mine.

It was strange, awaiting disembarkation in Liverpool on a grey, winter morning, hanging over the rail and staring down at the cobbled dockside in a fine rain, to consider just what fate had in store for me. I minded leaving Java greatly. I had, idiotically, fallen very much in love with a radiant girl who had been my secretary-translator. But she, wiser than I by years of experience, knowing that she was Eurasian and that a life in the grey, cold UK would be unthinkable, chose not to join me on the *Monarch* (there were, I note in my 'clipping', '73 civilians on board'), and slipped discreetly away without fuss, to leave me to return alone. I don't think, for one moment, that she took me seriously at the time. I amused her, and I was, at twenty-six, quite attractive. I was also the ADC to the GOC . . . But there was not much more than that. I do know that she came back to Europe, married happily, and had a family. We never met again. But mutual friends, much later, kept me informed.

Leaning over the rail, cold, feeling fairly wretched instead of being tremendously excited, very alarmed at my lack of knowledge, my suitability to fit into civilian life, I wondered miserably what the hell I'd be doing on that exact day one year ahead? 'This time next year.' Pointless thought, for not even the wildest imagination could have furnished me with the truth. The truth being that exactly one year later I'd already have made two films, would be at work on my third, would have a car and a driver and own a very pleasant five-storey house in Chester Row. For ten quid a week, fully furnished. I'd also have a mistress, and a cat. What more, I ask you, could a demobbed officer, sunk into self-pity and apprehension, ask for? Who could have even remotely thought things would work out in that manner? I am still amazed today.

However, if I was, as Chris had said so long ago, cleared for take-off, then he was almost correct, except that things were not altogether serene and easy. The flight I would have to make was very, very bumpy indeed. Life, this exotic new life I would discover, was going to be brutally hard. I was absolutely unprepared for it, and had to learn it all by myself as I went along. No easy task at twenty-six.

Hugh was up at St Thomas's Hospital, or Charing Cross, I really forget which now, working with children. I, waiting for my Rank contract to be signed, had a two-room flat in Hasker Street, then an artisans' street, with outside privies and elderly ladies in pinafores sitting on kitchen chairs on the pavements, knitting in the evening sun.

I had given my ration book to a pleasant woman in the Express dairy, and lived on a diet of Kraft cheese, milk and Weetabix. I managed very well. Sometimes Hugh came down on his bike for tea. I was in a play at the time so free until the evening performance, except, of course, for matinée days.

'Are you going to keep this idiotic name, "Dirk", when you go into the flicks?' he said. It had been chosen by my manager, Forwood, and myself, over a salad lunch in the Peter Jones restaurant months before, already used twice in the *Radio Times*, and printed in all the papers. Hugh drained his teacup, smiled his curled smile. '*Far* too foreign. The English don't care for foreigners. Can't you be a "John" or a "Robert" or a "Michael", that would be far wiser. Familiar.'

I said that it was, after all, my name. I didn't want to change it, I'd removed the 'van' and the 'den' and the diphthong, and that was that.

Hugh sighed, poured himself another cup and assured me that with a name like that I'd never be taken seriously. But I was stubborn and it stayed. I shall always remember his amused eyes gleaming, grey, fixed on mine, over his teacup. Four years later, at the end of 1950, I had managed to survive nine major films with my 'foreign' name and was, as far as the cinema-goers (and Rank) were concerned, a 'pop star'. But Hugh always called me 'Pip' and grinned when we met, shaking his head in amused bewilderment.

He had a very pretty wife called Geraldine, and asked me to be godfather to his daughter, Carole. There was a christening in a little village church, lots of ladies in large hats, the priest, a font, flowers, and much laughter and sun.

Life, four years after demob, was not so bad. I was settling gingerly into my new life, pushing hard for success, cantering along, unfortunately without very much concern for those about me. By the time I had moved into the house in Chester Row with Nan Baildon to look after, and cherish, me, I was in danger of losing my way a little. Hugh did a bit of tactful counselling. 'Are you going to marry Nan? It occurs to me that you might have that in mind? Marriage?' His quizzical eye was flicking 'concern'. I said I wasn't sure yet. She wanted it, but didn't really care for the cinema world.

'You'll be doomed together, then,' he said cheerfully. 'And although you are a grown-up man now, in spite of some unfinished pieces here and there, *don't* do anything too rash. She's older than you, wiser. Don't, I beg of you, hurt her. Be gentle. She's devoted to you and simply doesn't fit into your life as it is now.'

And she didn't. It all came to pass that he was right, as usual, and Nan packed her bags after three years, and taking her cat moved out of my life. I felt wretched. For a while. And then 'dried my tears', unshed it must be confessed, and plunged on into what was fast becoming a hectic and exciting career.

Then a golden creature called Mai Zetterling, cascading blond hair, a body to kill for, eyes wide with allure and (apparent) innocence, asked me one day to join her in a play she was about to do by Jean Anouilh. This was intellectual stuff, far removed from most of the antiseptic, sweet pap which I had been absorbing as a daily diet in the cinema. It would be an enormous challenge to return to the stage. Even though I had done one or two short pieces in between films, I had not sustained a long and really demanding role in the 'serious' theatre. I accepted Mai's suggestions, and did my best to comply with her very first demand, made one evening when she came to my house to dine and 'discuss the script'.

'Don't let me fall in love with you,' she murmured. As she swore she had lost the way to my house and had walked for half an hour in torrential summer rain, arriving soaked to the skin in a pale blue chiffon dress and absolutely *nothing* else whatever, apart from a necklace of silver coffee-spoon bowls, this proved, sitting hunched together before a blazing log fire, to be a slight strain. For a time. But the play went on and we were all a triumph. At last, I felt, Hugh would see that, in spite of its 'foreignness', my name would not be detrimental to me. The serious papers were indeed taking me seriously.

Hugh grinned his grin and was there when, suddenly after a run of about four months, I realized that I was heading for trouble. Bad trouble. I had failed to remember that I had practically no theatrical technique at all. I was quite unable to 'save' myself at matinées, for example, and gave two all-out performances on Thursdays and Saturdays. In a tremendously emotional part, with a very professional actress 'saving' herself whenever she needed, I worked myself into a frenzy and, although it riveted the audience, it drained me so desperately that one evening, applying my make-up in the dressing room, I knew, without any doubt whatsoever, that the walls of my room had moved in and were doing so all the time that I was out on stage. I even went to the absurd length of placing pieces of paper on the floor against each wall, so that I would have proof of their inward progress. Each time I re-entered the room, of course, the papers *had* moved. Each time the door was opened a draught sent them scurrying. But I was convinced that I was losing my mind. In the second act I had to lie for hours, it seemed, on a bed without much to say, and this was when the demons really gathered. The stage grew dark, the figures of my fellow players became blurred and crimson, the bed itself began to sway and bounce like a dinghy in flood. I called in anguish for Hugh at his hospital and he cycled down to Shaftesbury Avenue and stood in the wings, solemn, arms folded, his bicycle clips still on. While he was there I was marginally better. We discussed it together. He suggested that I had perhaps gone further ahead than I could actually manage. That Nan leaving me had filled me with terrible guilt. That I had been a soldier only four years before 'without expectation' and that now I had lost the way. I pleaded with him to help me through the play at least; we were a sell-out and I knew that if I left it would close. He said he had a pill with him, wrapped in tinfoil, which he had secretly taken from the drug cupboard at the hospital. No one knew that he had done this, he had not signed the register, and he, therefore, could not possibly give it to me unless – and he made this clear and cold – it was *absolutely* essential. It might have very harmful side-effects. He was convinced that I *could* fight the demons without his pill and the danger of getting him into serious trouble if discovered. Each time, he said, that he returned from this evening visit to me he'd replace the pill and no one was any the wiser. I could have it *only* if I could not cope another moment. Not otherwise.

For a week, or ten days, the reassuring sight of Hugh slipping into the darkness of the wings and standing among the fire-buckets, arms folded calmly, gave me immense courage. It almost stopped the walls coming in and the bed behaving like a mad donkey. But, in the end, I had to beg him to let me have the stolen pill. Reluctantly, almost aggressively, I was given the thing, and swigged it down with water. He said it would give me quite some time of relief. It did. The next evening I didn't need one, and the next, and eventually Hugh, good, caring fellow, was able to cycle back to his hospital and his wards and deal with his *real* problems. The strain of suddenly becoming a 'pop idol', of crowds screaming and crowding the stage door, of police to help me to my car – all these idiotic things, and also Mai's clear irritation with my selfish behaviour, did, eventually, bring me down and after a year I had a very modest breakdown, a rest, and then a return to the theatre and a long tour. I managed. It was all right. Owing, I was certain, to Hugh's magic potion which I was far too afraid to ask him to obtain for me ever again. So I found my own way of dealing with the demons. Which, of course, was what he had intended all the time. He had cured me with the stolen pill, and forced me to come to terms with myself. Which, after a time, I did.

Years later, when he himself was a man of TV and radio, wrote for the papers, was lauded and admired widely, he and Geraldine came down to Pinewood to lunch with me, see round the studios, meet the 'stars' and watch a bit of the filming – the usual old trip. It amused them because it was on one of the 'Doctor' films and seemed altogether appropriate. As they were about to drive away, in the car park, after a very happy day together, I reminded Hugh of the desperate nights at the theatre, and how courageous he'd been to steal the drug for me.

'What did you steal?' said Geraldine laughing. 'Hugh! You never told me that.'

He grinned his grin, his eyes steady, holding mine. Tanglin Barracks flooded back. The troop ship. The years past. He started up his car. I remember leaning away from it to let him move off. 'It did the trick, didn't it?' he said.

'It *did*! Thank you.'

The car moved slowly away from me. I remember the evening sun flashing along the roof.

'It was an *aspirin*, Pip. Lovely day ... Thanks! See you.' They drove away through the gates.

Somehow we never did see each other again: life caught us both up in various ways and our paths separated. Nan died in New York from cancer; Hugh from a sudden heart attack; Geraldine, a few years later, in a car crash.

Carole, my god-daughter, and I, when we remember to, send each other Christmas cards.

No Laughing Matter

The flat in Hasker Street, my first 'home', you could say, since I left the family house in 1940 and started out on my travels, was in truth merely two bedrooms on the second floor of a very modest cottage. There was no attic; it was a flat-roofed artisan's cottage. The landlords (there were two) lived in gilded, Gothic splendour on the first floor and in the basement. They had started to prettify the house, put in a lavatory, that sort of thing. Running out of cash, I imagine, they decided to let off the second floor. Accommodation in London was difficult to get: I was grateful to the actor I had met at an audition who sublet the place to me. He was off on a six-month tour of the North and wanted someone to keep his seat warm. I took it on for a pound a week.

I moved in with a suitcase, some books and a couple of pictures. I was at last private, on my own, in my own space – even though my 'front door' opened on to a dim landing, below which I could hear my landlords having their customary rows, slapping each other and hissing furiously like snakes. Sometimes, if the noise level really rose worryingly, I felt impelled to start down the stairs in case of some brutal attack being made by one on the other, and then they would leap apart, stare up in mute hostility, toss balding heads, and, after a furtive search for the front-door key, hustle out into the street scowling and slamming the door. A mild distraction in the day, and one to which I quickly grew accustomed. No one was actually going to harm anyone. It was just their little way. So I settled for that and ignored the crumps, bangs and wails which often wafted up from below.

On my small landing there was a two-ring hot-plate, a plug for the kettle, a small saucepan and a tin tray. This was where I cooked. Well, boiled water and milk and made tea. Weetabix and Kraft were finger stuff: boring but easy and, I was assured by the information on the packaging, full of nourishment. I sometimes bought an apple. Apples were not on ration like oranges, which I detested and detest to this day. Tea reigned supreme for some reason. I don't know why. I never drink it now. But then it seemed to be the thing to do. I gave little tea parties. People brought biscuits or pieces of homemade cake. We sat about in a clutter of Woolworth cups and sorted out the whole of Europe, the past war, the present theatre, and let unfamiliar names roll about our tongues like wine at a 'tasting': Cocteau, Clair, Sartre, De Beauvoir, Aragon, Barrault, Greco, Anouilh, Montand. All French, none English. Were there any English writers or players who excited us? I can't remember. Osborne had not yet rattled his lids, and Fry and Eliot were on the way, but they were not names we used.

The longed-for new fifties were still a couple of years away, so we dragged much of our pre-war life and experience around with us like old tatty bedding. These exciting creative names had come from a recently occupied and glamorous unexplored France. After six years of war it was difficult to know quite how to cope with our new lives, so full of opportunities. When to jump and *where* to jump. It was rather a waiting time. Wait and see what will happen next. So the tea parties were the peak of the day, the time for serious discussion. In the evening I went off to do my play and forgot about it all, but I remember that we sprawled around smoking prodigiously and drinking endless cups of heavily watered tea. I replenished the pot constantly, until the water was the colour of baby's widdle, and hoped that lemon rings would conceal the lack of sustenance, and chattered, and argued. No one drank anything else but tea then. Not because we *didn't* drink, but because there was nothing *to* drink. None of us could afford a bottle of anything. A beer, perhaps; but a quart bottle of light ale didn't go far or lift the spirits. Tea was comforting and companionable. It seems bizarre today, but that is how it was. A clutch of young people all pretending to be Woolfs, Bells, Stracheys or Huxleys, which we were very, very far from being, just bewildered, bemused and bruised youth coming to terms with an uncertain future and a devastating past.

Then my future began to glimmer in the gloom of uncertainty. Rank signed me to a contract, and paid me a thirty-five pounds a week 'retainer' until I started work for them. Thirty-five pounds a week was an absolute fortune. I sat stunned, with a cheque book and my new, 'unserious' name printed on the cover. The young actor who owned the flat suddenly came back. His tour had folded (tours often do). He said that two of us couldn't possibly share two rooms, and I had absolutely no intention of doing so.

I went off to Willet's in Sloane Square and came out with the key to a perfectly enormous, five-floor Georgian house in Chester Row, ten pounds a week, fully furnished. It had a garden with two great lime trees at the far end, a huge bombsite on one side full of cracked cellar floors and hollyhocks, bramble, bracken and buddleia. It was lithe with wild cats: a Rousseau painting without a frame.

This was what you could call the next stage in my development, a daring attempt to establish myself as a civilian adult rather than a redundant, fully equipped soldier for whom there was no further need. The house was pretty shabby. The war years had been cruel to it: the bomb which flattened the houses next door had forced its yellow brick façade to bulge gently outwards rather like a famine victim, the steps were shattered by shrapnel, windows didn't shut and wouldn't open, and the inner walls had cracks through which it was almost possible to see into Sloane Square – there was nothing in the way and they had only just rebuilt the station after the terrible bombing of it one afternoon. The house, however, had been cared for once, and the furniture, while undistinguished, was elegant and good. But it was an odd feeling at last to rattle about in my five floors all alone.

So Nan Baildon was summoned to come and look after me. Which she did with almost unseemly alacrity. We had been close friends from the Calcutta days when she was a senior squadron leader (WAAF), and I was posted to her team for the Singapore planning operation, 'Zipper', which never happened because they dropped the Bomb instead. We spent a great deal of time together. She was older than me, but it hardly mattered. I wrote reams of awful poetry and a frightful play and she typed them for me. None, fortunately, now exists. I can hear the clickety-clack of ceiling fans high in the shadows of the Saturday Club where we went to dance, recall the scent of jasmine and the heavy odour of the daturas round our mess, remember the long trek we made together up to Tibet. I still have the frontier pass authorizing us to cross the frontier from Sikkim by the Jelap–Nathn route as far as Phori in Tibet. We never made it quite all the way eventually. We were woefully unprepared for the harshness of the journey, but we made a good stab at it and gave up very reluctantly. I still regret the chance missed. I knew I'd never get another try, and I didn't. But Nan settled herself into Chester Row easily and surely, and we started a new life together.

I bought a small round table at Peter Jones, my first piece of real furniture, a symbol of permanence, and we used it as a sort of coffee table. I still have it; it has survived better than much of the rest of that time. The house was demolished after I left and entirely rebuilt. It is now a perfect replica of what it originally was, without the cracks and bulges, and stands at a comfortable million-plus on the estate agents' books. When it's on them. The bombsite is three new houses, and they have all been renumbered. It's as if we'd never existed there. Wiped clean away.

As soon as the contract money – some amazing £3,500 per year – was in the bank, I bought a gramophone in a second-hand shop, a huge cabinet thing in satinwood, with doors which regulated sound, and the house was filled with *Oklahoma!* and *Annie Get Your Gun* and other records which friends sent from America. The amazing new long-plays. A different, more confident life started with Nan. We had drinks parties. I had the money now for gin and Pimms. The only trouble was that I didn't know that Pimms was alcoholic, so I sloshed in the gin generously and we gave the best parties ever held in Chester Row. People came from miles around, the news spread like an oil spillage. I was always vaguely surprised when I stumbled over some of last night's guests prone on the sitting-room floor as I blindly made my way with a splitting headache down to the car en route to Pinewood in the mornings. Nan said she was sure I'd made a terrible mistake, and that it was all getting a bit out of hand. These drinks parties were costing a small fortune, and gin, and Pimms for that matter, were still hard to get. She said she would check it out. After a month or two she did, and the parties lost their glow and appeal rather; but *were* less hectic. It was a far cry from the sprawled tea parties in Hasker Street, although the conversation was much the same, but the booze and music gave the whole business a great deal more punch. We played all the French music we could lay our hands on, and grew sentimental and tearful at 'La Vie en rose' or 'Clopin-Clopant', and 'Ménilmontant', and when the Pimms–gin efforts were at their peak, people would crowd round the huge gramophone sobbing uncontrollably to Khachaturian's *Sabre Dance* or the frightful strumming of balalaikas, and the volume was turned up so high that bits of the cracked ceiling fell in flurries of plaster all over the tearful singing (la-la-la stuff) of the happy revellers. All a very different state of affairs. That's what a bit of money does.

But the bud which had burst forth on my barren, timid twig in Hasker Street, the tiny bud of resurgence and adulthood, delayed by six years, started to grow and put forth tiny leaves. The twig was going to become a bush or a tree, if I was very careful, and didn't, so to speak, spike the Pimms. To be sure, some of the leaves got frost-bitten, there were little caterpillars among the tentative shoots, it was not altogether a flourishing business; rather, it was a desperate effort to grow up far too quickly and rather too late. I didn't manage it awfully well. When I got drunk, which I frequently did, not violently you understand, just maudlin – probably more objectionable – I would witter on about My War. Except about Belsen – that, never. I was furious, and tearful, that no one, absolutely no one, not even Nan, wanted to hear me. I learned in time to shut up and sat tearfully sullen and loathsome. Inevitable, I suppose? Something had to give sometime.

There was a splendid party for New Year's Eve, 1949/50. We all longed to be shed of the forties and get on with a clean slate. Television had already started again, sweets were now off ration, things gradually appeared to be getting slightly better generally – but not, alas, in Chester Row. Amidst the aftermath and carnage of that New Year's Eve party, at some moment in the morning of the New Year, a tremendous row broke between us and Nan fled the wreckage in tears. I can't, today, remember what on earth transpired; I remember only the anger, sadness and shame. It got patched up and we struggled on together for another year. But the words had been said, the frustrations made apparent, the resentments made clear. We carried on in a desperate 'for the sake of the children' state. And that was the main problem. There *were* no children, and, as far as I was concerned, there never would be.

Looking back to that wretched time I know that it was the

'wrecker'. I wanted nothing to stand in my way. Success was starting for me, I was determined to take my share of it. Children, at my age, simply didn't figure in my plan. For Nan, a little older, time was running close. One evening in the bar of the Grosvenor Hotel, Victoria, sitting uneasily with my father and a double gin, the whole business was brought to a head. I placed all my miseries, uncertainties, lack of confidence and bewilderment in his lap. He picked them all over quietly, like shelled peas, biting the side of his cheek — always a dangerous sign from my childhood days — and then he quietly said, 'I imagine that you are telling me that you can't carry corn? That it? It's taken you by surprise, all this sudden success; can't handle it? Correct?'

I agreed miserably, reminded him that four years ago, or about that, my main effort had been directed to picking bombing targets: factories, villages with crossroads, troop concentrations, harbour or railway installations. I'd actually been permitted to kill hundreds (if not thousands) of people by remote control: a yellow chinagraph pencilled circle on a photograph. Now, in my new suits from Aquascutum, my Pimms and gin parties, my film work — three films a year, the constant interviews I had to give, the opening of swimming-baths, cinemas, and judging beauty queens — my five-floor house and live-in mistress, everything had gone over the top. I was swimming out of my depth and wanted his help. I was drowning.

He looked at his watch, took a sip of his drink, set the glass on the little round table. I can see it now; this very moment. 'And Nan?' he said mildly. 'What about Nan in all this?'

I remember taking my time before I said that I wanted to marry her. How did he feel about it? 'She would be good for me, Pa.' She, I was sure, could arrest the dismaying tumble I seemed about to take into disaster. I suppose that I expected a sympathetic pat on the knee from my father. I didn't get one. Instead he said, looking down at his glass and in the same gentle voice of reason, 'Are you in love with Nan?'

I wriggled a bit. 'Well, no. Not *in* love. I do *love* her. We are tremendously close, been together for ages, she knows all my moods, understands me perfectly . . . I think we could make it work.'

My father raised his glass without looking at me, drained it, set it down, took his watch out of his pocket, flipped open the lid, slid it away again. 'Well, don't expect my blessing. Think hard. Think of yourselves in, say, ten years' time . . . you'll be thirty-six or so. Nan? Older, in her mid-forties. The age difference won't be easy to overcome. You are in a very demanding, tempting profession. She's a decent woman and I can see that she is devoted to you, but in time that devotion will suffocate you, if I know you at all. You can't just marry her as a sort of . . .' – he looked helplessly round the dingy, ornate bar – '. . . a sort of bath-plug to contain your excesses. That's not fair. Tell her. Make a clean break, don't use her. Go your way and let her go her way, it's only right and honourable. It is what a gentleman does. Cut her free.'

I, of course, can't recall this absolutely verbatim but it is, in essence, exactly what he said and I have never, completely, forgotten. I sat silent, he got up, patted pockets, smiled pleasantly for the first time. 'You'll have to come to terms with life by yourself. I had to, after my war. It wasn't easy, but I did it. I must say you have picked a pretty awful profession, full of pitfalls and temptations. Never mind. Now, I really must get my train. Your mother gets so furious if she has to put my supper in the oven. Says it's ruined. You've got a lot of work to do; *do* be aware of self-pity, *very* unattractive.'

We walked together down the steps to his platform gate, a guard looking at his watch, whistle in his mouth, flag furled in his hand. I watched Pa hurry down to third class, and then I walked slowly from Victoria to Chester Row. In due course, not at all brutally, it was agreed between us, Nan and me, that we should go our different ways. We'd had notice to quit from Willet's, because the house was to be demolished; we'd be homeless anyway. So, as I have told you, Nan left with all her bits and pieces, and the cat, and also took away with her the last vestiges of 'Pip', or 'Pippin', as she, wincingly, called me. I was never to be called 'Pip' again.

A slender, sleek new gramophone. I learned to call it a 'record-player' in time, with new music to match the new house and the times. We had dumped the forties and now were all out for the glory and excitement of the fifties. A brand-new, glistening, untouched-by-war decade was upon us and we raced joyfully to embrace it. *Call Me Madam* and *South Pacific* were all the rage, and the music, as well as that of Mozart, Schubert and Elgar – a catholic choice, I agree – blasted through the beamed rooms of my new, rented abode.

The Forwood family house, or Home Farm, quite empty, unfurnished, cobwebbed, was mine should I want it for ten pounds a week. It was an historic, ancient place, in a cherry orchard thirty-five miles from town. There were a big duck pond, acres of lawn, herbaceous borders needing immediate attention, and a giant 300-year-old pear tree. There was also a ghost who had clanked about for years with a sword and white·shirt, a relic of the Wars of the Roses. He had been executed and buried in the barnyard. It was, apart from the house itself, which the family now rented out to anyone who would maintain the fabric, a proper working farm, with cows and pigs and a scatter of hens. Home Farm was long, low, a tumble and jumble of rooms, a tilt of roofs, twists of chimneys, plus a bit of timbered Edwardian excess stuck on at one end to the pink Tudor bricks. There were latticed windows which let in every known wind from every possible quarter, no central heating, a kitchen a half-hour walk from the dining-room, and a vast fireplace in the drawing-room, called, for blindingly obvious reasons, the 'Oak Room', *in* which you either sat and roasted or sat *before* and froze in an overcoat. There was absolutely no alternative, however many cherry tree logs were piled against the huge iron fireback.

I rented it, with the three-acre garden, and was more than content with my lot. The Forwoods very generously adopted me as part of their large family and I have, gratefully, been a part of them ever since. I had no proper 'ancestral family' of my own. There were the evasive people in the château in Courtelle on my father's side, and on my mother's side a fairly dour group up in Scotland. But we hardly ever met, after a disastrous attempt at getting me educated there, and I thankfully returned back to England and to my parents and the brother and sister who finally constituted the English family. The Forwoods, a bustling, energetic, welcoming lot, were a distinct bonus in my life. But their family house, ancient and 'picturesque' and ten quid a week, contained at that time nothing more than dust, cobwebs and a scatter of fly-spotted electric lamp bulbs hanging around.

To start anew was my aim. The local papers were of intense interest. I combed them all assiduously. I was frantically alerted by the word 'auction'. If there was an auction within fifty miles of Home Farm you could bet your bottom dollar I'd be there with my little catalogue, my pen and my cheque book. Amersham, Wendover, Tring and High Wycombe, and every other town in Buckinghamshire, were pillaged by my eager hand-wagging. I bid for practically everything on display in village halls, seedy estate agent's and rotting Edwardian villas up weedy drives from north to south. Of course, as you might imagine, I desperately needed advice. It was all very well to be keen and alert, something quite else to be hysterical. I was often that. Sometimes, to my acute bewilderment,

I'd find myself the reluctant, indeed *unknowing*, owner of, let us say, 'a picnic hamper, plus contents', only to discover that it contained one rolling-pin, a bedpan, bicycle pump, tin of patches (various), bundle of flat-wear, aluminium, various, assorted mustard spoons and one plastic canary bath, cracked. I had absolutely no idea how this had become my property, but paid up, chastened and alarmed. Hysteria had driven me to foolish excess; what secret sign could I possibly have given the auctioneer to have earned such extraordinary booty? I once took possession of a life-size figure of Diana and a large wall-safe with no keys. They were, thank God, returned.

However, I learned. Sometimes Forwood, always alert to my erratic behaviour and my capacity for wild excess, came with me on occasions and once managed to secure 'One boardroom carpet, 45 x 20 with floral border'. He got this for nothing because, at that time, everyone in the area appeared to be living in prefabs and caravans. We lugged the giant roll back to Home Farm by tractor and, cut into pieces, it close-carpeted a number of the rooms. Later, emboldened and alerted to the fact that people now only wanted doll's house furniture and new at that, I bid for Victorian arm-chairs, and grandfather clocks, enormous, buttoned settees, pot-cupboards and sets of horsehair dining chairs. For peanuts. In a very short time, with old curtains, and sundry pieces from my parental home, too large for the tiny cottage in which they now lodged, Home Farm was practically furnished. Empty of luxury, I agree, but there were a bed and a chair in each room, and the rooms were curtained and carpeted. Someone gave me a set of assorted glasses. I got at auction in Aylesbury a sixty-piece dinner service (some breakages) because no one wanted such a monstrosity. It was actually early Lowestoft, but the plates were too large for the post-war families who apparently lived on frugal rations in garden sheds, so in time we ate off china and drank from glass. Amazingly, at the same time, petrol came 'off the ration' and life seemed, at last, to be gathering pace. It was a very pleasant feeling indeed. I almost forgot that not so long ago there had been a bloody war. Well, almost forgot. Never entirely: that set of memories has remained with me all my life. But my work flourished; amazingly I was suddenly a 'teenage idol'. The new decade seemed to be kind to me. Rank picked up my contract every July – they had the right to dump me if I failed to make a profit for them, or reach their modest expectations. I overtook those, to both our surprise. My money increased slightly every year. All signals were set, it would appear, at 'Go', I was working my backside off.

However, Forwood faced a certain despair. He had finally been forced, very reluctantly, to agree to a divorce from his pretty, volatile actress wife. A victim, like many others, of the peace, he had returned to find his marriage a ruin. Hard to hold a marriage together when you are young and abroad and depend on airmail letters for protestations or signs of affection. So, divorce was reluctantly agreed, he conceded defeat after bitter protests and arguments, and gave up the custody of his small son. There had been no adultery, but adultery *had* to be proved. This was one of the barbaric little delights of post-war Britain. A relic of past times held to with firm belief. Absolute nonsense, and bitterly humiliating. One's freedom, anyway in this case, depended on being discovered *in flagrante delicto*. Just before Nan and I went our separate ways we were able to provide Forwood with the perfect setting for 'sin': our top-floor double bedroom, with two single beds and a seedy atmosphere. We had never used it. An attractive young actress (naturally enough, workless) accepted the role of the 'guilty' party for fifty quid and one evening came to Chester Row for supper with us all in the basement kitchen. Nan got some pasta, there was cheap wine and a salad, it wasn't too wretched. After we'd listened to records and done the washing-up Angela (not her name, but her son is rather important today and would buckle at the knees if he knew how helpful Mummy had been years ago) went up to her bed. Forwood got a blanket and bedded down in the drawing-room, Nan and I went our ways. The morning was to be early, like an execution at dawn. They really chucked it at you.

With the dawn Forwood, rumpled and more or less sleepless, slid, fully dressed, into the bed next to Angela, who apparently just moaned faintly and grumpily asked the time. On cue the bell rang and the detective from whatever agency was on the doorstep. Nan took him upstairs and threw open the bedroom door with a flourish, disclosing the 'adulterous' pair wrapped to their chins in blankets in separate beds. The *farce* of it all. I paid close attention to the detective simply because I didn't really think anyone could really look as absurd as he did, a film version of a private eye: bowler hat, a stiff collar, sagging buff raincoat, round tin glasses and a Hitler moustache. He made short notes in a small book with the jaded demeanour of someone who did this kind of thing too often and disapproved bitterly on principle. Angela and Forwood lay prone. Nan and I stood like gaolers just outside the door, as he had requested us to do. Presumably so that he was not attacked, or that his prey did not try to elude him. As the householder I identified the pair, he sighed wearily, snapped an elastic band round his notebook, stuck his pen in his weskit pocket and we went downstairs, where he put on his cycle-clips, tipped his bowler to Nan, and loped off to his bike, which was leaning against the kerb. It was now fully light. The milkman arrived.

At a fairly subdued breakfast we all sat glumly round the table and no one spoke. We felt slightly soiled.

Forwood, at that time, lived alone in a small house in Chesham Mews and tried to cope with my increasing workload from there, which was impossible. No one else had made quite such an impact with the fans as I had. Everyone was taken by surprise. I was 'hot'.

There were a lot of empty rooms in Home Farm, it had been Forwood's old home, it was felt reasonable now that he chuck up his job with Al Parker (the agent) to take me over completely. He had, after all, thought I had 'a quality' long before, in 1939. Now I was proving him right. So this he did. I shall never quite know now if he had regrets, but he had complained about having to get jobs, at very good money, for crowds of really dreary actors whom he despised, so I assumed he came willingly. But then I *would* assume. I never really ever found out how he felt.

I had Home Farm now as my base, but no one to run the place. I left it at six-thirty each morning and returned about seven in the evening, unless we shot late. I decided I'd need a traditional cook-housekeeper whom I had found advertised in *The Lady*. Mrs Walters had grey hair kept in place with two Kirby grips, wore button-strapped shoes and survived three full years at Home Farm, overcoming her initial surprise at seeing '*all these famous people! Well I never!*' lying about the lawns in summer and the settees and chairs in the winter.

One who came to stay was Kay Kendall, not yet as famous as she was to become. She liked the house, wondered what on earth I'd do with so many rooms and begged one of them for her own use at weekends. This was quite acceptable to all. She stayed for five years. So something must have been right. Friday nights, after the slog of the week, were best. Sitting beside a log fire in the small study, Kate in her glasses (she was as blind as a bat really) knitting something, and Bruno Walter conducting something on the wireless, the dogs snoring in the golden heat, and the scent of Mrs Walters's not *altogether* awful dinner cooking, was very agreeable indeed. And with a couple of large whiskies or so, it was almost possible to believe that there had never been a war or a Hasker Street or Chester Row. I'd simply always lived contentedly in this ancient house. But that, of course, was utter nonsense. All it was

was a remission. There was a host of 'alarums and excursions', bangs and terrible collisions ahead for me. I'd not escape them.

Aunt Gwen was, perhaps, the most loved member of the Forwood family. She was very tall, heavily built, not at all pretty, patrician and rather fastidious. She wore pince-nez, her hair was a sort of loaf, or perhaps bird's nest, of grey, bound with ribbon. I only ever remember seeing her wear what was known then as a lady's two-piece costume: jacket, with two buttons, skirt to the ankles, neat lace-up shoes, high-necked blouse with a cameo brooch. Sometimes a vague kind of hat was skewered on to the bird's nest, and, sometimes, in summer she wore a discreet floral print with a number of bows and a belt at the waist. She was married to a Mr Carlyn Weller, and lived, very comfortably, in a large house on the cliffs at Branksome, near Bournemouth. Her very English-country-woman appearance belied her astonishing achievements as a child. She had found notoriety and fame on both sides of the Atlantic through two books which she had written, and illustrated, for children. 'Miss Gwendolyn Forwood' was famous when she was only twelve. The books are hideously romantic by today's standards: lots of fairy princesses, wicked witches, golden-haired knights in glittering armour on galloping white horses, turreted castles and a fantastic mass of exuberant blossoms, roses, cherries, bluebells, daffodils – the usual stuff, bluebirds and robins everywhere, the whole swamped by countless dwarfs, pixies, goblins, the skies swooping with flying, winged fairies, or radiant angels leaping all over the place with wands and stars. Anyway, it was that sort of awfulness and sold then prodigiously. It was, however, extremely well written.

Aunt Gwen was a 'notable' from Chicago and New York to London and Edinburgh, but I suppose, really, her greatest claim to fame was that she had become Forwood's surrogate mother in 1915, days after he was born. His own mother found him frankly tedious as a baby and his father was on the Western Front. Gwen was childless and craved one, so it suited everyone in the family that she should bring up her nephew much as if he was her own child and set him on course. And this she did diligently, passionately, until his proper parents suddenly, cruelly, reclaimed him, some years after the war. The usual wretched sadness. However, Aunt Gwen became part of *my* adopted family and epitomized every aunt that there ever was. Having none of my own, apart from those distant people up in Scotland, and the evasive people in Courtelle, I had need of her. She was calming, soothing, comforting, and I loved her. One felt that in her house all would be well, one would heal, nothing would be ever distressing or ugly. Wrong, of course. The house itself, in a pine wood among trim lawns and great hydrangeas and camellia bushes, was a riot, inside, of porcelain angels, cherubs and dreadful little girls simpering in lace bonnets. It all sounds awful, but in truth it really wasn't, because that was the way she wanted it, and that is the way she lived, in prettiness and innocence. You just willingly put up with it for her. We used to drive down to Aunt Gwennie's, a whole crowd of us, on Saturday nights after the show, to bathe, if there was a moon up, from their private beach, or to dance to the wireless or record-player, and eat, even though so late, enormous cold suppers of lobster or crab, which she ordered from Poole down the coast. I think she enjoyed these dotty evenings as much as anything she had ever had. She adored the young, loved, above all things, life, gaiety and music. And here it was all about her. The fag-end of the forties and the very early, uncertain years of the new fifties were huge fun at Branksome.

In those days we really didn't expect very much. After six years of war, before which most of us had been adolescents, we were perfectly happy to settle for what was offered. Travel abroad was almost impossible – the currency allowance was ludicrous, about

£25. The roads in Europe were torn to shreds, the food still difficult, and it was altogether better, just at first, to stay at home. Aunt Gwen therefore, with a private beach and unlimited access to seafood, ran a modest 'hotel' for her family and their friends. We all ignored the British weather and just relished being cosseted and, after being abroad for so long, at home.

It's all gone now, that setting of tranquillity and, I suppose, a certain privilege. Everything has been wiped away and hundreds are now spread where the golden few once played. Gone is the house, torn down and carted away in trucks, the pine wood was bulldozed, the camellia and hydrangea bushes ripped out, the pebble paths obliterated, the beach concreted, the little owl who used to call wistfully from the oldest pine long since fled. A huge tower block of flats and garages stands where once we all lay about in the dappled shade, among the pine needles, the sea murmuring in the quiet afternoon, while we did the crosswords, read books, and waited for tea to arrive on wooden trays, a tea-cosy on the pot, a big tin of biscuits and a Victoria sponge (if Aunt Gwen had managed to get some eggs) and, sometimes, a large glass dish of little brown shrimps fresh from the sea.

Fortunately she didn't live to see the brutal destruction of her pretty, cherub-scattered villa in the pines. She got cancer, quite suddenly, was felled, and died abysmally, baying like a mad dog. So one pays. When it was diagnosed at first she was valiant and calm, as one would expect, and worried only for her husband, isolated by deafness and lost in his silent world. How would he manage? Then, when it was deemed to be terminal, she asked me only if she could return to Home Farm to die in her parents' big bedroom above the Oak Room. We galvanized the house for illness. Mrs Walters, with the dreadful relish of her kind, was willing and able, we had two disagreeable Irish nurses from whom I instinctively knew we could expect no mercy, and the house was busy with countless friends who brought gifts and flowers, and also the large Forwood family who so adored her. Finally it all became too much, and no one in the end was permitted except her deaf, bewildered husband, and as she had no strength to shout at him, and could only lie helplessly and watch him talking to himself, even *his* visits had to be curtailed. He made no complaint. I rather feel he was relieved. Being a silent witness to stealthy death is not at all amusing. Finally only Forwood, myself and the nurses were left in the pleasant airy room looking down across the lawns and rose gardens to the great pear tree. The very worst thing – well, almost, but not quite – which I have seen, was the gradual, irreversible, brutal destruction of a creature who had existed only ever for beauty, gentleness, sweetness and elegance. Swiftly she slid away, down the road to vicious agonizing death. Why, I wondered in my shocked bewilderment, why *this* way for *this* woman? One of the Irish nurses, with a tight little smile, said that her 'pain was being offered to Jesus, to compensate Him for the suffering He endured on the Cross.' I thought about that for a second and bit my lip. It would have pleased her had I argued. I just sat in a little buttoned armchair in a corner of the room listening to the harsh breathing. Forwood and I kept a sort of watch, to ascertain when the morphine was starting to wear off, but when it did we still couldn't persuade the nurses to help us. 'It's not the time. She's got another hour to go before the next dose. Doctor's orders, he says every four hours and every four hours it is.' Implacable, but then so was death. All one longed to do was ease the pain. But as it was a 'gift to Jesus' there was little, at that time, that could be done. Aunt Gwen was just allowed to scream and plead, until the appointed time of her next injection. We sat holding her hands.

I was not, you will realize, unaware of death. I had come across it fairly early on in my army career. That first huddle of ground-sheeted bodies lying at the edge of the airstrip at Sommervieu, near

Saint-Sulpice, a label fluttering from one big toe, had of course alerted me. But it was a kind of 'concealed' death. I saw nothing that day closely. They were just 'the dead', and one expected dead people in a war, I supposed. After all, that is what war is about. Killing each other. Simple.

It was later, walking through a summer meadow far from the beach-head that I almost stumbled across a kilted figure lying in the cow parsley and campion, a bloodied sheet of the *Daily Mirror* tactfully stuck over his face. He was my first real 'dead in action' man. On his back, arms wide, fingers gently curled. The flies had already started to gather. I didn't like it; it didn't make me feel uncomfortable, didn't actually frighten me, but there was unease. I did not, that morning, consciously think, 'that could be you' or 'you'll be next', but the image stayed on my mind, almost burned on my retina, until very gradually other worse sights and sounds obliterated it, and it faded. Faded enough to be remembered now, however, and set down in a book. After all, I had not *seen* it happen, I was not physically involved. It was an old death, judging by the flies and the hard-crusted rim of blood on the paper. But the next death was one which did involve me.

Driving in a sensitive area in the jeep, Ernie Ball sitting beside me, one foot up on the metal side, the sun high, distant crumps of mortar fire, which didn't trouble me, I was more concerned with whatever information I had to impart to the Brigade Intelligence Officer at our next destination. We were in a small convoy. In sensitive areas, that is to say where it was not absolutely certain that we had cleared out the Germans entirely, we drove together. It was considered safer and wiser. Then suddenly there was an almighty roar and the jeep ahead blew up sending shards, a wheel, and smoke, flame and dust into a ball of confusion, and we, moving too fast, or not thinking fast enough to stop, crashed into the turmoil. I remember Ernie shouting, someone yelling, '*Mines!*', and falling in an uncontrolled sprawl over a bank into a field. I was face down in the yellow corn, blood all over my hands, running down my face. Beside me, heaving, lunging, a bloody trunk. Just one arm searching the sky, a head but no face, the remaining fingers were claws. It was saying something. A gurgling sound came from the ravaged head. I remember a single white tooth. 'Kill!' it bubbled. 'Kill!' Stupidly, panic-stricken, revolted, I reached for the pouch on my webbing belt above my holster. For some idiotic reason we were forbidden to go about with a 'bullet up the spout' unless we were engaged in actual fighting. I struggled with the pouch press-stud, pulled and tugged and spilled the bullets which scattered into the corn. I couldn't see for my own blood running into my eyes, but I must have made some futile effort to ram a bullet into the chamber when I heard a shot and someone else had done what I had been asked to do. I was dragged to my feet, shaking with shock, Ernie was lying by the side of the jeep, which had tilted over, petrol was pouring, someone (who?) was wiping my face roughly and saying it was only a cut and could I move everything? I don't remember much more than hanging on to the man and blubbing. I wasn't brave at all. I didn't hurt anywhere, apart from my head which was grazed and cut, but I was unable to stand alone. I'd caught my knee somewhere. Ernie was being got to his feet, shaking his head; he was alive, and surprised. He'd been thrown clear, as indeed had I, but I had gone down the ditch with the driver (it transpired) of the first jeep. My blubbing ceased almost as soon as it had started. I held on shaking and bloody, and Ernie Ball lurched over to me to see if I was all right, and to test himself and see if *he* had broken anything. He hadn't, but the three in the first jeep were gonners. I knew that (about one of them) for myself. That was my first confrontation with unspeakable death. It would only be a baptism, I'd see others, but I will never fully erase that one from my mind. All others have, mercifully, dimmed with the years. I see them clearly only if I sit and consider, or if an odour (it is usually an odour – death has a sickening scent) jogs memory. But the engulfing pain and distress are, after fifty years, muted. Only that bloody trunk on the road near Villers-Bocage remains sharp in my mind, and, in truth, only that when I take the trouble to bring the memory into the forefront of my mind, as now. And if, by mischance, I do, I say, aloud, 'Don't! Not that!' And it'll fade slowly away. It is otherwise set at the far back of memory, only to spring instantly to the front if I should see a car crash on a motorway, or someone struck down in a street. Then I am forced to look away. The blubbing, I was assured, was fright and sheer shock. We had no counselling in those days, and no one claimed compensation. You expected this to happen in battle.

Equally I know that it was the fact that I had failed to honour the terrible request which had been made. Someone else had to finish him off, I failed him in my clumsiness and youth. And for that very reason I am now an active member today of Voluntary Euthanasia. I have to pay that debt, *and* Aunt Gwen's. Fortunately – and consider that word carefully – fortunately, there were other men braver than I who helped a number of hideously wounded men to die swiftly and easily, men so grievously hurt that they would never have been got back to the casualty clearing stations or even have got medical help in the field. Our war was a swift, mobile affair. One didn't wait.

Aunt Gwen, a tough woman, hung on in spite of unbelievable pain, for a long, agonizing two weeks. Finally we used to play the radio and record-player downstairs together and at full volume when she started screaming, and it still didn't blur the sound. Mrs Walters walked about white-faced, hands to her ears, muttering, 'Oh! Poor lady! Poor creature.' And indeed that is what she had become: a poor creature. I sat with her one evening, just as the light was failing; she was asleep after her 'fix' of morphine. I knew it wouldn't last long, and wondered, as I had wondered so often before, why it was considered by Jesus (or whoever it was) that she had not yet paid her dues for His suffering. She had led a gentle, loving, caring, considerate life; now, paying so brutally seemed excessive. Her face was writhen, lips dragged back from toothless gums, eyes sunk into black hollows, arms as bony as those of the witches which once she had drawn in her fairy tales. But there were no remissions for Gwen. Eventually the family doctor overrode the Irish in the kitchen and gradually she was eased away. I think that we were all so grateful that she was at last at peace that we had no time for grieving. The undertakers had a difficult job with her coffin, carting it down the winding, wooden staircase. I was in the town shopping, preferring not to be present, Mrs Walters mounted guard and saw it all through with relish, and when I got back and started to unpack the shopping bags in the kitchen she came pattering through, a handkerchief to her lips, shaking her head. My heart sank, I'd done enough comforting, I had no reserves left.

'Mrs Walters! Don't cry . . . it's all done now, Mrs Weller is at peace . . .'

She gave a hiccup of wan laughter. 'It's not *tears*! I'm laughing. Oh dear! *Poor* Mrs Weller. What with you wrestling with her over her wedding ring' – her husband had insisted that he wanted her wedding ring. As rigor mortis was setting in this was a tricky operation, and I succeeded only with brute force and a jar of Vaseline – 'and the undertakers with her on the stairs! Oh my Lord! They got it stuck, the coffin! Chipped a big piece out of the wall. Just on that bend there. I shouldn't say this really, but they had to stand poor Mrs Weller on her head! Couldn't budge it otherwise. On her head! What *would* she have thought, such a sweet lady. But you have to laugh, don't you? No good crying, is it?'

None at all.

OHMS

Wandering down my personal corridor (I can no longer stride as once I did) to the final and inevitable door at the far end, I am constantly made aware of just now naïve and stupid I have often been. At the same time I am jolted into the realization that without so many really good friends, like Chris, Hugh, Forwood and even poor, cast-aside Nan, I'd probably never have made the journey.

Naïve I was, naïve I remain. It astonishes me that I have survived. Was it because of the casual, trusting manner in which I was brought up? The free, wilderness years at the cottage with our nanny, Lally? Was it the caring, but almost casual loving which I received from my parents? Were we, my sister and I, shielded, perhaps too much, from the vulgarities and uncertainties of the world? I really don't think so.

We were born immediately after a hideous war, which was supposedly to be the war to end all wars, and I assume that we accepted the innate trust that all would be well from two very young parents. The fact that it was soon to be shattered, and not so long into the halcyon peace, seemed not to trouble me at all. Blithely I leaped and danced, so to speak, in the daisy fields, brimming with affection for everyone, trusting everyone, and certain that they all felt *exactly* the same way about me. Affectionate and loving. Error number one. It took a hell of a long time to discover that this was not necessarily the norm, that cruelty, poverty, hopelessness, dislike, jealousy, wickedness and treachery even lay scattered among the daisies, like little mantraps.

It seems to me, looking back from this far distance, that up until

I was about sixteen I faced no serious problems nor asked any serious questions. You'd imagine, of course, that I would be curious about where we came from. Who made the babies and where did *they* come from? Well, I wasn't because I knew anyway. I'd been told, in a pretty casual manner, exactly how all that happened ages ago, and white mice and rabbits – even cats – helped to point the way. My sister knew too and was perfectly at ease with cockerels, hens, horses, foals – and stallions. It was no great deal to us. We both kept animals, so we both had to know, our parents insisted, how they reproduced, and it was a very short step indeed to the realization that something along the same lines took place between them, the holy pair. But we set that aside tidily. It was not ignored. We just didn't dwell on it. No necessity at all to muddy the waters with all kinds of biological problems. It was enough merely to be aware.

You could also be forgiven if you thought I might be curious about money. How to get it? What to use it for, and how much I owned? Up to a point I was. I knew when I needed it for, say, glass for my vivarium, or a wire front for a cage, planks for a shed I'd be building, for a model theatre from Pollock's shop in Hoxton, for an ice-lolly from the Walls Stop-Me-And-Buy-One tricycle, or even, and this hardly at all for I was not at all proud, for a new coat, pair of shoes, hat, gloves or some other item of clothing. But apart from knowing that I'd have to work to earn these things, washing and polishing the car, cleaning out a shed, trundling garden rubbish to the bonfire, weeding the vegetables or just, much easier, asking my wretched father outright, I had not the least interest in where it came from or what *he* might have to earn in order to give it me. It was just 'there'. Money. And I really had little need for it, apart from those odd items, plus humbugs, gobstoppers or wine gums. In moderation. I never knew how much my poor father actually *earned* at *The Times*. (It was a pittance, as it turned out. But I didn't know this until he was well into retirement and Forwood absolutely forced the truth from his tightly reluctant lips – and got a terrific increase for him only a few years before he died.) The fact was that when Pa joined the paper in 1910 or 1911 it was considered that only gentlemen worked there and had private means anyway. So they needed no payment. Simple. I rather remember, now, that Pa did make a mild murmur about being an orphan (my grandfather *had* frolicked off to South America and left his wife and child practically penniless) and a very modest sum *was* made available to him, by Northcliffe, but it really was *never* discussed, because to discuss money was considered exceptionally vulgar and was simply just never done. This irritated my mother a good deal when she felt in need of a fur coat she coveted, or a particularly pretty gown from Patou which she, sadly, never got. She did end up with a moleskin a number of years after. But it wasn't the same as mink or sable. But she bore the cruelty and made do with a series of outlandish, but hugely fashionable, outfits which she made herself with the aid of the Singer sewing machine and a patient, kneeling Lally to pin up the hems and sew the button holes. She managed brilliantly.

Clearly this Della Robbia innocence of mine could not go on for very long. I was bound to come a cropper in the real world, which I, with sublime selfishness, chose not to enter. Instead it came to me and rattled at the closed door of my complacency. First the 'lost' grandfather was rediscovered living in filth in a hideous house in Kemp Town, Brighton, near the Palace Pier. I, with my usual belief in all things fascinating and desirable, found this really selfish, abominable old man entrancing. I only had one other grandfather, and he was banished to sit out his days in the large kitchen of my grandmother's house in Glasgow (he'd done something fearful, kidnapping my mother at the age of ten and carting her around Great Britain on a touring series of epic plays), so I hardly saw him.

I associated Scotland, and all Scots, with despair, meanness, unbeliev-able greed and sanctimonious Bible-reading every Sunday with the blinds drawn.

This new, accented old Flemish mischief-maker was my delight and joy. I doted on him, and completely neglected my Scots grandfather. My loyalty to Grandfather Aimé was never in doubt. The fact that he drained my unhappy father of every penny (with his keep), denying both my sister and myself a 'serious' education so that his rent and food and god-knows-what were paid for, leaving us all impoverished after an absence of more than thirty years, never remotely occurred to me. I don't suppose that I'd have paid it much attention had I known. I detested school and found the hugely embroidered stories told by my Flemish grandfather enormously beguiling. Naïve as a newt.

The next thing which came along to unsettle my smugness was the shock of suddenly being hurled, quite correctly, up to Scotland (of all dreaded places) and a 'tough education'. I was thirteen. I'd idled my years away. Now came the cracks in the wretched bit of Della Robbia which I aspired to resemble. Sweetness, gentleness, kindness, all those deeply unfashionable and untenable things, to-gether with a singular lack of awareness and responsibility, were abruptly brought to a halt. I had to learn the rules of life in a 'foreign' land with very foreign people, even if they did happen to be blood relations. I discovered that blood didn't matter a fig either. But it took a little time. I still trusted.

Let me make it quite clear, here and now, that no one was actually chucking me to the wolves. I was *not* being punished for having been so idle, for thirteen years. It was simply that a new mouth – well, *two* new mouths, in fact – had to be filled and it was deemed wise and sensible to move me to relations in the greyness of Scotland. First my Flemish grandfather arrived and then there was the very surprising, not to say vexing, arrival, after eleven years, of my brother. My mother couldn't just roll over, like a sow, and squash the thing. Of course he was owed a life and a life he got. He's now just eased past sixty and I love him, and more than that, respect him greatly as a man: however, in July 1934 I wished him dead. So selfish was I when I saw this puling mass of regurgitated milk lying cosseted in the arms of my sister (who *had* been my very best friend for years) that I'd eagerly have strangled the creature. I didn't know how else to do it: a knife would be too bloody and poison too difficult. (I might make an error and take it myself.)

So school and therefore smouldering loathing for my 'sweet little brother' was what it had to be, and it was there that I started to learn, as one of my schoolteachers had commented in a school report (in red ink, too) that 'life was not all satin cushions and barley sugar twists'. I hadn't the least idea what she meant by that.

My father, I fear, did however. School was bloody. Lonely, isolated by my 'posh' accent and therefore punished weekly by having my head shoved down the lav and the plug pulled (amazingly the Nazis were some years away, but their brutality was already surging away in the fourteen-year-olds of Glasgow), I was considered quite incomprehensible by my 'loving' aunt and uncle. I didn't play football, or show any interest in the results on the wireless every dreadful Saturday evening, or in cricket, or badminton, nor yet bridge or whist, and the efforts one had to make at tennis very nearly killed me. So they did their best to educate me by visits to the Orpheus Choir, D'Oyly Carte, and a good many glum concerts which seemed, to me at any rate, to consist of oboes, cellos and fiddlers. And nothing else whatever.

Their lives, you may imagine, were sad, unfulfilled affairs. They were childless and, after six months or so of my presence, doubtless knelt at their bedside nightly to thank their beloved God for making them barren. We also had church every Sunday. A four-mile walk there and back. But that's another part of the story. So it is possible to realize, at this vast distance, how awful my punishment for being so smug and uncaring before now was. I was bruised, lonely and bewildered. I got picked up once by a strange man in a cinema. I really did think that his offer to buy me an ice-cream tub in the interval and his hot hand on my thigh were just friendship and kindness. Later, in his flat, he assaulted me. I was constantly amazed, and I was, in this singular and ugly adventure, humbled.

But I was never, thank the Lord, crushed. Rather like the shell-shattered trees in Flanders: however stark and ruined they looked in winter, come the spring they sent out buds and little green shoots. So did I. Four years later, cantering back to my hectically busy family, I was off to art school, but even there, among my fellow students and kindly teachers, I discovered treachery. I was viciously raped by a long-haired young woman in her crummy flat in the Kings Road. I was not at all prepared for the shamefulness of what followed, lying, flat on my back, drunk on a quart of pale ale and roasted by the plopping gas-fire at my head. The indignity was absolute, the energy required minimal, she heaved up and down on top of me rather like a huge porpoise, leaving me absolutely no room to manoeuvre, so that just my sad little arms flailed about helplessly. As far as I remember, she opened a tin of pilchards afterwards and offered me the use of her comb. But all this was learning to grow up, to become wise, to learn the pros from the cons. I didn't really. I just chalked every rotten experience up to Experience, and hoped that, like impure water in a filter, it would all drip slowly into my consciousness, purified of all horrors, and prove to be refreshing, nourishing and thoroughly satisfying. Of course, life isn't like that at all.

When the war slammed final iron doors on my childhood, I still refused to believe that it was really happening to me. This was some terrible aberration, it would all come right in the end, and meanwhile I would endeavour to remain comfortable, unfrightened and good at my job. I was well aware that to fail in my military work would lead to instant disaster, death even. So I worked myself silly, and survived because I considered myself 'indispensable', if not 'notable'. Or so I chose to believe.

I think that perhaps those awful evenings spent sitting with my aunt and uncle up in Glasgow must have had some brain-washing effect. Although fortunately I was quite unaware of it at the time. We'd sit, after high tea (gigantic), before the rather industrial-looking fire which heated the water and glowed a silent satanic red, my aunt quietly doing her lazy-daisy stitch on some piece of beige linen, my uncle dozing with the *Sunday Express* over his face, his breath riffling the edges faintly, proving that he, at least, was alive, and there was always Paul Robeson singing 'Ol' Man River' on the gramophone, a modest little Decca machine. (I still can't hear that song without a cloud of horror descending.)

I sat and played solitaire, or drew homesick pictures of a long-lost land I once had known called Sussex. It was my job to change the record when Paul Robeson breathed his last groan of praise to the Mississippi, and the other side, I seem to remember, was 'Only Makebelieve'. Which is *exactly* what I spent my time doing. I wasn't in this beige room with the framed *Nash's Magazine* covers on the walls, the clock ticking and the anthracite settling in the fire, the coke-hod on a piece of lino at its side. I was miles away, snug in the kitchen of the cottage, watching Minnehaha (our cat) washing himself, the paraffin lamp-light glowing on the bumpy white-washed walls, the corncrake calling down in the Great Meadow, and the complete feeling of surrounding love and security almost smothering me. By being somewhere else while yet in a wretched situation, or in a just unstimulating place, I'd rid myself of the panic attacks which would so easily arrive, and find calm and security. This facility has remained a hugely useful component of my existence. I have never evaded a difficult situation, but if I am ever caught up in one I employ the same mental isolation that I did in the best parlour with the lazy-daisy stitching and Paul Robeson filling the stifling room with melancholy. I switch off entirely and go on a voyage of mental recovery, recalling, when I can, all the pleasures so that I might stifle and subdue the pain. But of course, being this absent-minded, and that is what it amounts to really, has found me in extremely curious predicaments, from which I have usually emerged bruised and astonished, but otherwise intact. I like to think.

However it was not absent-mindedness which got me into my biggest adventure of the war. One lesson which my father drummed into us as children stuck with me and took effect: 'Observe, notice, compare and keep silent.' It paid dividends. I observed so hard, became so fascinated by detail, that it enabled me to get a job in Intelligence (think of that when you despair) and ended my war in Java as the ADC to the GOC (after General Christensen retired) of the island. General Hawthorn apparently impressed by my work of decorating our mess, by my unafraid frankness, and possibly because I spoke reasonably well and could, as he put it, 'sit a table', took me on. I thought at first that he had asked if I could 'sit *at* table', which rather surprised me, so I replied in the affirmative with tremendous confidence. And then had to learn just how to 'sit' a bloody table for twenty or so visiting officers, generals and brigadiers later on. I managed.

But one day, some months after we had liberated the civilian camps, got rid of the bestial Japs, and settled down to 'holding the ring' during the revolution, I opened the Old Man's mail. Normally Madame XY, his secretary, did this, but she was often late in the mornings, so I would do it before he arrived in his office. I set aside a couple of tiresome invitations. One was to a Brigade mess miles down the coast and completely surrounded by hostile Indonesians, the other to a fancy dress party at the Curaçao Club to celebrate the liberation. It was to be a masked ball and the General was implored to spend a few moments of his 'precious' time judging the costumes. It was an evening I knew he'd refuse out of hand – he hated all that kind of nonsense – but his secretary, when she arrived, said she was certain he'd adore it. It would be 'colourful, amusing, and make a break for him'.

Madame XY was a beady-eyed, middle-aged Belgian milliner who had got herself caught up in Java just before the war. She opened a fashionable shop, was arrested by the Japs, interned, and survived. When we arrived on the island we were in dire need of translators: we could neither speak, write nor comprehend Dutch or Indonesian. You try, 'Did penetration take place' in Dutch, to a distraught woman recently attacked by one of our Indian soldiers. It's hard enough to do in English. Anyway, translators were required. We put notices in the camps and circulated our requests urgently among all the refugee women. There was a reasonable salary, food allowance and so on for anyone who could help us.

A number of women who still had husbands somewhere in camps which we had not managed to liberate were happy to stay around in spite of being called 'collaborators' by the others. They would be protected by the Army, fed, and would stand a better hope of tracing their families, collecting up their cruelly scattered lives again: boys over thirteen, as well as their fathers, had been carted off by the Japanese to camps miles away. Also, a good number of Eurasian women, fearful of moving to Holland, or Europe, and knowing only their beautiful island, stayed on. It was from among them that I found *my* secretary (who skipped ship and left me) and from the main camp we got Madame XY for the General. She was extremely jolly, spoke five languages fluently, and knew exactly how to run a house. As the General now had a vast palace, built for an absent Chinese merchant who had scarpered the moment Singapore fell, we needed someone to manage the place.

As GOC of the island he had a great number of social duties as well as merely military ones. However, I was certain that he'd refuse the masked ball, and he did. *I* was ordered to go and represent him, with a note of apology and a case of whisky. I was not at all pleased about this. The whole place was seething with unrest as the Indonesians tried desperately to shove the Colonial Dutch 'into the sea' and proclaim an independent state. The word *merdeka* was written large on every wall and heard on every lip. Dealing with hand-grenades chucked into one's jeep was normal. Having the wretched things dropped into the lavatory, rolled towards you in the markets, or just thrown, in wide arcs, into a crowd, was not at all amusing. We called them 'terrorists', or more usually 'extremists', and because we were forbidden by the rules prevailing for a police force (which was, after all, all we were supposed to be) we could not ever fire back in self-defence, so we tended not to care deeply for them. And they loathed us because they were certain that we were helping the hated Dutch to hold power. It was, in fact, a question at all times of extreme hatred and mistrust. The island seethed with barely suppressed violence. From landing in Java in September 1945 until the end of October 1946, we lost 1,377 men in my Division, and this was supposed to be peacetime. So it was right to be slightly alert during a jeep journey through the night, even within the perimeter, to judge a bloody masked ball. I had no choice but to go: orders are orders, and my General was a tough nut. He suggested that I could take a 'mate' to provide 'covering fire' if need be. I decided on Bruce Barker, a pleasant, good-looking, valiant youth who worked in the office next to mine. He was as thick as I was, so saw no problems, just a jolly drive out to a club where there might be some 'popsies', as he called them. And some free booze.

With my Gurkha batman, Kim, in the back seat, we set off for the Curaçao Club. It was quite a way out of town but within the perimeter, so I felt fairly secure, and it had been the 'in' place for army and navy personnel (officers, of course) before the war and tonight was about to celebrate the wonder of 'freedom'. One presumed that they would all be Dutch. The 'extremists' could hardly be expected to be celebrating *merdeka* before they got it.

A long, low building up a dirt track lined with palms and frangipani trees. Music blaring down through the croaking of frogs and the rasp and rattle of palm fronds in the soft evening breeze. Lights gleaming through the trees. I remember there was a record of 'The Peanut Vendor' playing at full blast through a tannoy system. Everyone was milling about in fancy dress, great shouts of laughter and singing over the music. We swung round in the forecourt and stopped. I told Kim to turn the jeep so that it faced the way we had come in. This was normal practice, and I said we'd not be long. A hurrying crowd of oddly dressed people, harlequins, bullfighters, devils and so on, came tearing down the steps of the Club, arms waving, cheers ringing. They were all in extraordinarily beautiful and complex masks. A tall man, apparently our host, dressed in flowing robes of red and gold shimmering in the night, shook us mightily by the hands, and asked where the General was. I explained, offered the wrapped case of whisky and the note. If there was a change in the man's expression it was impossible to see because he was masked as some Indonesian god or something. There was a plump woman beside him; she wore a crinoline and a powdered wig with a mask of the grinning Buddha.

In a hasty scatter of speech which I could not hear the crowd around us were informed. No General had come. I told our host that I had been delegated to choose the winners by the man himself. It was all there, beautifully typed on Divisional HQ letter paper. The moment, and it was no more than that, passed, we were clasped to bosoms, clapped and applauded by the vast masked crowd in the huge ballroom, filled with streamers and flickering green and red lights. Our host suggested that we come with him to a private room out of the house for a drink while the 'marshalls' got everyone in line to start the parade. It would take a minute or two he said, so what would we care to drink?

The room was next to the main ballroom. The music raged away. This time it was a tango, 'Jealousy', I knew it very well. I removed my cap, and we settled down into the bamboo chairs while our kindly, masked host offered up three full bottles of gin, whisky, brandy and asked us to help ourselves. Plenty there, he'd get some ice and water. Be a few seconds, do sit down. It was a small room, apparently on the ground floor, empty except for the two bamboo chairs and a little marble-topped table with a fluted jar of hibiscus in its centre. The three bottles were ranged on a shelf on one wall like skittles. There was a window in another, a faded group photograph of some pre-war shooting party on the third.

Bruce gave me a large Scotch and poured one for himself. Through the closed door the music roared even louder. It seemed to make the air in the room tremble. Bruce shouted out that the speakers must be just above the door, and raised his glass in a mock toast. I looked at my watch, we'd been there about eight minutes and it was getting roastingly hot. I tried the windows, to open them for air. They were locked. The shutters beyond, I could see, were bolted.

'Locked tight!' I yelled.

'Why?' said Bruce. 'In *this* heat?' He set down his glass, turned and went to open the door. It also was locked. He gave a nervous, disbelieving laugh, spied through the keyhole. 'Key's still in the lock . . . what's going on?'

I suddenly got a sweep of fear. A panic attack. 'Let's get out,' I said.

We did, by Bruce chucking the little marble-topped table through the window, then I unbolted the shutters. We clambered out and spilled, gently, into a spiky bush, stood for a moment while our eyes grew accustomed to the dark. We saw the gleam of lights from the front of the Club (we were obviously at the back) and without a word ran like bats out of hell for the car park and the jeep. As we crashed into it, Kim instantly alert with his Sten gun, I just remember shouting, 'Drive! Drive quick!', as a tumble of people came racing down the steps of the Club shouting and waving their arms. Someone fired a shot. It was a crimson Very light which arced gracefully above us and crashed into the trees. We raced and bounced down the drive, shrieked left on to the mortar-pocked main road. I'd seen a few cars parked up at the top in the shadows, so we didn't bother to hang around. After about ten minutes, with no one apparently following us, we breathed again.

'Why on earth would they lock us in the room? Have we been *daft*?' asked Bruce.

But I was certain we hadn't been daft. Why lock windows and doors and turn up the music to full pitch and wear concealing masks? It was then, as we got to the lights of the town, dim, but at least safer than the dark behind us, I realized that once again I'd lost my cap. Left on the marble-topped table. It didn't much matter, apart from my Queen's Royal cap badge which I had had since I was commissioned. That made me rather miserable.

We dropped a worried Bruce off at 'A' mess down the road, and turned into the General's heavily guarded palace. He was sitting at his desk, a mass of papers before him and a large glass of hot water, in which he was steeping his senna pods. What really bugged me was that he didn't appear at all surprised. Just told me to sit down and calm myself. Which irritated me because I was calm. I thought.

But losing my cap, for the second time in this war, *had* brassed me off.

Patiently he explained that it was all probably a set-up job to kidnap him. Hold him to ransom. The GOC of the island would be a useful bargaining point. He said that it had been vaguely rumoured in Intelligence for a month, and he rather suspected the masked ball from the start because the Curaçao Club had a very shady reputation for arms dealing (the Japs had surrendered but given all their ammunition and arms to the 'extremists') among a number of other black-market commodities like penicillin, vitamin B and things of that sort. I asked him why he thought that they had locked Barker and me in the room. Looking through his papers, he just said that we were probably better than nothing, and that they would try to bargain something through us. He said, with lightly veiled amusement, that no one in the Division would have been unduly worried. He didn't think that we'd have 'been for the chop', because that wouldn't really help the Cause. To kill two young captains who had come as guests to their party and brought gifts? It would not go down very well internationally. He took the trouble to remind me of the behaviour of the Stern gang in Palestine and just how little good blowing up the St David's Hotel had done them.

I got to my feet, a bit ruffled at being compared to an hotel and at the fact that no one would have, apparently, taken much notice of our predicament. He pointed out, as I got to the door of his over-decorated room (in the Chinese style), that I was fighting for my country and that it would remember my valiant efforts in this unusual peacekeeping force. Anyway, as a couple of little captains, we *were* expendable. We *all* were, in fact. That's what being in the army meant, you gave up your life and security the day you 'took the King's shilling'! He said this with such gusto that I could have hit him. Instead I came to attention and was told to prepare a full, detailed report on the incident by eight the next morning. He supposed that I *had* noted the accents? Who spoke English? The colour of their skins? Black, coffee, beige, white? I reminded him they were all masked and in fancy dress, and he said that was no excuse. *What about their hands, eh?*

Rather like my father. Observe, notice – only this time, tell all.

I had just typed a row of asterisks, to signify the end of my report for the General, when Madame XY suddenly stood at the open door of my little office.

'My goodness! My goodness! So early in the morning!'

'So are you,' I said as pointedly as I could without being thoroughly rude; but she nodded, smiling, swung a palm-leaf basket in her hand.

'I know. I know. But you recall we have the Ambassador next week: *so* much work, things to remember, the invitations and the food. So much . . .' She was smiling brightly. I knew, of old, that she adored all the fuss and fiddle with visiting VIPs, arranging the flowers for the tables and so on. She practically had a seizure when Mountbatten arrived. Suddenly she said, 'Have we doubled the guard? The place is like a fortress this morning. A very officious Subedar tried to stop me from coming in! Imagine! Rudeness I do *not* tolerate.' She fished about in the palm-leaf basket, found a piece of paper. 'Subedar Naranjan Singh. I have his full name and number. Most officious and rude. I have to make a row with the General. What is all happening? Has there been an attack? A bomb?'

I said not, the General was merely stepping up defences, probably because the Ambassador would be coming shortly. That seemed to be acceptable, but she was still huffy.

'So rude! Pointing a rifle at me, making me to show my papers as if I had never been here before! *Mon Dieu* . . . and this . . .' – she

84

rummaged in the bag again and chucked my cap on to the desk –
'. . . this, I think, belongs to you?' As I looked at it in mute surprise,
she went out into the corridor. 'Don't be so absent-minded! What a
silly boy! Naïve! Remember, an eye is kept on you all the time.
You might have lost it!' And looking at her watch she cried, with a
false sense of alarm, 'My goodness! Already it is past eight o'clock. I
must get to work!', and with a little wave and a deliberate nod of
her head, she went down the corridor to her office. I heard
the door open, a burst of light song, 'One day my prince will
come . . .' and then the door closed and cut her off.

And I just stared at my slightly battered cap. What the hell did
this mean? Had she been at the Club? *Were* we being 'daft', as
Barker had said? Was I really so thick that I didn't recognize
treachery when I found it? Should I alert the General? Or just stay
silent? I stayed silent. I was completely out of my depth here.
Almost thirty years later I would be in exactly the same position,
only then it would be myself who was under suspicion, completely
unaware. Naïve, daft, ready to be shaken down. I was.

The British Consul's voice from Nice was rather crisp, sharp, brisk.
All those words. This vaguely surprised me because he had been,
when we had met on one or two social occasions, a slow, plumpish,
weary-sounding fellow, his regimental tie hanging like limp rope
round his neck. His office was pretty dreary (which might have
accounted for his demeanour), stuffy, green-distempered, stuck
about with photographs of racing motor-torpedo boats in skimpy
passe-partout frames. Today he was fussed: it showed in his voice.

'Just be kind enough to *be* here. Two-thirty sharp. He's got three
others to see locally, and wants to get the evening flight back. So *be
here*. Right?' He rang off, which left me no chance of whining that
I had people coming to the house with four large cypress trees,
booked ages ago, now to be postponed. I was pretty fed up. It was,

I felt certain, something to do with some kind of 'gong'. Medal. Why else would a 'chap from the Foreign Office' be coming out to Nice to see *me* and three others? I didn't want a medal. Forwood thought it pretty unlikely, but warned me not to accept the BEM, if offered, because it was usually awarded to traffic wardens and midwives, and although they did sterling and loyal work, I had been in my job for many years and helped entertain a great many people, throughout the world. I felt a little mollified by that thought, but wondered about such an abrupt assignment with the gentleman from the FO. Was it perhaps something to do with tax? If so I was as pure as a mountain stream, clean as spring air. I'd paid up in the UK and only ever earned my money now on the Continent. There were no back taxes to delve into: I'd emigrated and was absolutely clear.

I felt certain that, if it was *not* for the BEM or whatever, then someone had made a mistake. That made me more irritated, when I thought of the non-delivery of my trees. Now they'd have to wait another month or so before I could get them to come back again from the nursery in Cannes. I fumed in the heat of the journey into Nice. The British Consulate, then, was in a shabby modern block three floors up in a very small lift, just off the Promenade in a side street near the Old Town. Opposite its doors was a large bar-tabac, and when we pulled up, exactly at two-twenty-five, Forwood said he'd wait there for me. It would be cooler under the fans which clacked about on the ceiling. He also suggested that I stop scowling, because it was unattractive and rude. So I tried to look reasonably agreeable and in the humid heat crossed the street and took the lift to the third floor. Over the perfectly ordinary door of a very ordinary flat there was a modest Royal insignia, and beside the bell-push a smeary brass plate with 'HM British Consul. Please ring.' Or words to that effect. It could have been 'Dentist' for all I cared. I was still irritated.

The Consul sat hunched at his desk in a rumpled blue suit. A plain woman was typing briskly at a desk beside him. She looked up briefly when I walked in, and the Consul put down some papers, looked at his watch and noted I was on time (which I knew). Shuffling slightly, wiping his brow, he accompanied me to the adjoining room, where the chap from the Foreign Office was waiting. At the door the Consul poked his head into the room, said my name and ushered me in, abandoning me to the FO man. There was an electric fan swinging slowly from right to left in a corner. It fluttered some papers but only moved the hot air around the dingy room. Briefly we shook hands. He briskly indicated a bentwood chair at the side of a desk behind which he sat. There was no other furnishing, apart from a stack of cardboard boxes with HM GOV. NICE. AM stamped on their sides.

I sat, the chair creaked, the man from the FO had a fixed smile as he sorted some papers, sucking a fragment of some old tune through his teeth. Through the wide-open window I could see the flat roof of the apartment block next door. A spiky oleander in a large rusted tin, a sagging clothes line, and beyond, in the haze of the afternoon, the smudgy hills beyond the town. Suddenly the man from the FO, to whom I had never been introduced and who did not now offer me a name, said with a burst of boyish enthusiasm how much both he and his wife had enjoyed *Death in Venice*. An *amazing* experience, and in fact his wife had seen it twice, she was so taken with it; he himself thought it a marvellous performance. Vague images of the BEM or even an OBE, even a CBE, started to waver again before my eyes and I only drifted back to normal life when I heard the word 'questions' hitting my consciousness like a sharp little stone thrown at a window.

'Questions?' I looked at him for the first time clearly. Shortish, youngish, shirt sleeves with the cuffs turned back, cufflinks dangling. His jacket, I noted, hung on a wire hanger behind the door.

'Just a few questions,' he repeated easily, and would I please remember that *he* was there to ask them? *I* was there to answer them? Not to ask. All right?

I suppose that I nodded, because he continued cheerfully while all visions of medals slid out of my mind rapidly. This was something else altogether.

He suddenly produced a thin file from the papers before him, from the file a bunch of small, passport-sized photographs. These he laid out on the desk like a game of patience, except that each photograph was separate and did not overlap as in the card game. 'Now! Who do you recognize here? Go through them.' His voice was impersonal suddenly.

The photographs were mug-shots of a selection of Slavs, all taken with a fixed, and presumably hidden, camera, because each gorilla was caught just as he began to straighten up from getting out of a car. There was always the same bit of right-angled iron pipe, or railing, in each picture; it never varied, only the faces did. Marginally. The Foreign Office had an apparently inexhaustible supply. He kept snapping the things down on the desk-top in my stupefied silence, dealing them out like a conjuror at a children's party, only this didn't have the feeling of a party about it at all.

'Well? Recognize anyone?'

I sat mute with shock. Something was being implied here which I didn't understand and didn't care for. I had not set eyes on any of these high-cheeked thugs in my life. At last he snapped a final picture down. Looked up.

'*No* one? Recognize *no one*?' he said impatiently.

I heard myself mumble that I had never seen any of them. Why? He flicked a look of irritation at me, started to gather up his ugly hand of cards. A woman in a blue turban and a floral pinafore came out on to the flat roof next door, slung a rug over the line, started to whack it with a bamboo beater. I had a wild desire to leap through the window and join her.

'Look,' I said, 'I don't know any of those people, I don't understand why I am here.'

He raised a hand, in the other he held a paper. '*I* ask the questions. Not *you*. Now, I am going to read you a list of names. You will tell me when you hear one which you *instantly* recognize.'

I could see the printing through the paper, as the sunlight filtered through it. I read the name of a film in which I had played. I thought I'd just let him know. 'Excuse me, but I honestly don't know what this is all about . . . I can see the title of the film there . . .'

He looked tight, and cross. '*You* may not know what this is all about but others do. Pay close attention to this list. A name which you *instantly* recognize.'

Well, what he read out was, as I had seen, a production sheet of an old film. That is to say the complete list of names of an entire production from the stars to the dolly-pusher, even the caterer. I knew everyone listed. I sat silent, dry-mouthed. The woman across the roof turned her rug, started swacking the other side. Little puffs of dust drifted up into the still afternoon. I watched in misery, listening to his dead voice droning familiar, if sometimes half-forgotten, names.

'Now then,' he said triumphantly as he finished. 'Recognize anyone there?'

I felt compelled to reply as *I* wished, not as he perhaps would wish. 'Look, excuse me, but *I* was in that film. My name is the first on the list. I know the title, know where we made it, almost know what it cost and know everyone who was on it, so why do you have to read it all to me? What am I supposed to do?'

He looked pretty angry. 'I ask the questions here, not you. Understand? Is there any *particular* name that you recognize? One which sticks out? Reminds you? Jogs your memory?' I said no. I didn't, anyway, know everyone's surname. We never did in the studio. He looked blank for a moment. 'What *did* you know them as then?'

I cleared my now dry throat. 'Well people were, for example, Bobby Wardrobe, Florrie Make-Up, Agnes Hair, I don't think in all the years that I knew more than a handful of surnames, it was just Dave Chippie, Bert Sparks –'

He was quickly irritated, waved his hand. 'So there is no one on this list that you recognize better than any other?'

I told him that I didn't actually spend a great deal of time with anyone on the set socially. We all did our jobs and got on with the work. I didn't remember any *single* name particularly and no one had an idiosyncrasy that I could recall. The woman on the roof opposite dragged her rug off the line and carted it away. There was a brief silence before he said, 'No one in particular?' I shook my head.

He stretched an elastic band round his now closed file, looked at his watch. 'Very well. I see. Now, just because you have left us in the UK don't, for one moment, think that we still don't keep a . . . friendly . . . eye on you. We still look after you. We are concerned for your well-being *at all times*.' He had a small watery smile now. I felt suffocated with futile anger. 'I would suggest that if you are put in the position, through your work for example, of going across to the East that you inform us immediately. Don't ever make *any* move in that direction without informing us in the UK. All right?' His smile was as thin as cellophane.

'Why? Why? May I ask why I can't go East to work? Would it be harmful if I did?'

He got up and went to collect his jacket. 'I ask the questions, not you. Remember? They are very old-fashioned in the East. They still use the old blackmail trick. You might be invited to some jolly

party, right? They'd set it all up, take some compromising photographs . . . and then, well . . .' – he started to shrug himself into his
jacket – '. . . then you could find it difficult to refuse to do
something that they wanted you to do. You are at risk over there,
so be careful. Just a warning.'

He pulled a shirt cuff from inside his jacket sleeve, fixed his
cufflink. I felt sick. The implication was clear. I was not absolutely
trusted by my own country. Obviously they thought that I could
be compromised, that I was vulnerable and therefore a risk. For a
moment or two I really did think that I was in the wrong place.
This was all an awful error, someone else should have been sitting
wretchedly on the bentwood chair, while the bloody man from the
FO, who had so enjoyed *Death in Venice*, fumbled for his other
cufflink.

I got up. 'Can I go now?'

He looked up quickly. 'Of course. Remember though, won't
you? Even though you *have* left us we still do have your safety and
concern at heart. We keep an eye on you. *All the time.*' He almost
attempted a comforting smile, but I imagine that my stunned
expression prevented it from really breaking into anything more
than a cold grimace. I wondered, for a moment, what age he was?
A little older than I had been when Chris and I nicked the German
coffee pot? When Hugh and I had read our names on the board for
repatriation? When, all awry, I confronted my general and his
senna pods?

Time had galloped: I thought that I had forgotten Madame XY
and the Curaçao Club. *Was* she the plump woman in the crinoline
and powdered wig masked in a smiling Buddha? Suddenly they all
surged back again. Things like that, it seems, are never completely
forgotten. The mind sets them aside in its attic, ready for retrieval
when the appropriate time comes, like Christmas tree baubles. I left
the beastly room with a brief nod, walked through the Consul's

green–distempered room. He looked up apprehensively. I nodded at him too, and went out.

The journey home was not a lot of fun. Forwood was almost as horrified as I was. I had prided myself on being a perfect ambassador to every country I'd ever had to work in from the US to Greece and India. The FO, it would seem, were as out of date as the Russians with whom they were so concerned. I who had believed, almost to the point of idiocy, in correct behaviour and good manners was now, one gathered, suspect. Unreliable, vulnerable, someone to 'keep an eye on'. It was intolerable.

Forwood said calmly, after we'd gone a few miles and I had simmered down a bit, 'They are clearly on to someone, not you. They were checking through you. Maybe someone you knew? Worked with? An actor? Someone on the floor? They have a line, that's clear. And remember, you are unmarried, over fifty, suspect to their little minds. I expect they think you probably chat up the boys on the Port and breed Angora cats. That's how they think. *Death in Venice* didn't help much either. You are an actor, you have left the UK, live up a hill with your manager, hermit crab! *Ergo* – suspect. Try and forget it.'

His advice, as always, was wise and balanced, but it has taken me years to set that day behind me. I was told, while the little fellow was putting in his cufflinks, never to speak of this affair. He didn't say I couldn't write it down, and he didn't ask me to sign anything to say that meeting had never taken place. So now I have. I never wanted to return to the UK after that: but you can never be certain that fate won't take a hand. And it did.

Travelling

There were two kinds of 'travelling' when I was very young, and only two places to which one travelled. It was, in any case, a heady, near hysterical experience. One was when we had to pack our suitcases for the exciting journey to Victoria Coach Station and there catch the Greenline coach to Brighton, Pool Valley. Only we'd change at Lewes for the bus to Seaford, then meander slowly over the Downs to Alfriston, our final destination, apart, that is, from our cottage high up on the hill. That was the first journey which I can easily recall, even today. The lino-and-rexine smell of the bus across to Alfriston, the scent of the downland air when we stepped off into Market Square, of thyme, chalk and sheep, the caress and tickle of long summer grasses against bare legs as we humped the suitcases up the hill and searched our pockets and handbags for the big front-door key.

I remember that all far more clearly than I remember last Wednesday or even yesterday. But 'then', for me, is set in crystal. So is the second bit of my 'travelling': the tremendously adventurous voyage by boat over to France. This was not a frequent event. It took place about once every two years . . . about . . . we could never be quite sure. It depended greatly on the parents and what *they* had planned to do. A holiday with the children? Or a glorious holiday without them? If the latter, we, at least, went to the cottage with Lally and, frankly, that was best. But the journey to the boat, the wheel and scream of gulls, the smell of wet seaweed and salt, the creak and groan of decks, the hiss of smoke and steam from the red and black funnel, the rasp of sisal rope and the stickiness of tar:

these were engraved for ever upon one's senses. And then France! Oh joy! The scent of coffee, roses, shrimps, damp sand, hot croissants, and the comforting smell of the little tablets of solidified methylated spirit which Lally burned under her portable kettle.

All these were to remain with me for life. An enormous comfort. It never, at that time, ever occurred to me that I might 'travel' anywhere else. I had no boyish longings to go to tropical islands or climb mountains or explore the Antarctic. Although I read avidly, I was never made restless by *Treasure Island*, *The Swiss Family Robinson* or *With Scott to the Pole*. I was perfectly content to stay where I was.

But of course life seldom runs on an easy course, and there are a great many outside hazards which, unexpected, unknown even, eventually intrude. They did with me. I suppose my very first bit of 'travelling' entirely on my own was to the detested school in Glasgow. Tearful faces at the carriage window, admonishments to eat my sandwiches, whispered instructions as to where the lav was, 'just down at the end of the carriage. It says "vacant" or "occupied" on a little circle on the door', whistles, smoke, steam hissing again, but in a metallic, oily way, and then the jig-jog-jerk of starting away from Euston and the settled rumble of the train getting into its stride, taking me away from my beloved family and home.

My unshed tears (one never blubbed in public, and the compartment was usually full) were always compounded by a huge cut-out hoarding somewhere along the line just after we had left the huddle of back-to-back houses which marked the rim of London: a treacherously laughing, jolly young woman in a mob-cap offering one a giant jar of Ovaltine, a basket of eggs under her arm, wheat sheaves all around. I detested this apparition beside the line somewhere near – where was it? – Watford? Hemel Hempstead? Leighton Buzzard? Misery had always so swamped me that I never did find out, or care. It simply lied to me with its jolly laugh and the cruel implication that Ovaltine would make everything better.

So 'going up north' and passing this wretched female marked misery and the inevitable fact that I was on my way back to the school, my aunt and uncle and the appalling little town where we lived. Or rather, where I stayed. I would not ever admit to 'living' in the bleak place, with its tramlines gleaming, in a permanent drizzle, running like sabres through the cobbles, and the square concrete and asbestos-roofed houses which ringed it.

My uncle had lost his fortune recently in the Depression. I didn't know what it meant but detested what it had done. Going south, for the longed-for holiday, Christmas or the summer (longed for, I am certain, by my unfortunate, childless relatives no less than by myself), then of course this treacherous woman in her bonnet with the gleaming smile promised joy and delight! I ached and ached to see her (wherever she was placed) offering her preposterous jar of vitamins, gaiety, and her basket of improbable eggs. She was simply signalling now that, within half an hour, I'd be arriving at Euston station where certainly an adoring Lally and my loving mother, perhaps even my sister Elizabeth, would be waving joyously on the platform. Then, and then only, did I feel kindly towards the woman from Ovaltine. She promised delight and joy at this Southern end. Sadness and hopelessness at the Northern end. Two things with which I had become wretchedly familiar (and you can add solitude to the list) but with which I learned to deal exceptionally well. I just never let anything show. Training, you could say? And I am eternally grateful that they were forced into my education: I know very well that without the experience of them I would never have endured the years, indeed the life, which lay ahead.

My parents had thought that they were being wise in giving me a good, solid, Scots education. I was resisting, of course, but, all by myself, I learned every lesson needed to get through adult life, from courage to control, to determination and deceit. I never learned despair, however. I refused to have that on my curriculum and ducked it, fortunately. Anger, of course, misery and the increasing value of elliptical speech, but despair, never.

All these things – I suppose that you could call them 'advantages'? – were to stand me in good stead when I really had to travel out on my own later in life. From the age of thirteen, when I went off to Scotland for the first time alone, I had never made a longer journey than London, Euston, to Glasgow Central. The heartache of crossing the wretched river after Carlisle, the boundary between the two countries, was not easily set aside. But this next enormous journey, at the staggering age of twenty-three (you will note the ten-year break?) was again across a childhood familiar: the Channel. But not (after a decade in the wilderness of schooling) with Lally or Elizabeth as before, and not indeed on a ship, but in that Dakota flying over a seething foam-flecked sea the colour of washing-up water, on my way, with the photographs required, to meet Chris, four or five days after D-Day. I had never flown before and fervently prayed that I would never have to ever again. Crammed we were: probably fifty of us, sitting yellow with fright along the fuselage, the centre of the aircraft stacked high with huge boxes of ammunition, Red Cross goods, and bundles of neatly lashed ominous brown canvas stretchers.

The man on my right shouted, above the roaring of the engine, that if we *should* be hit by stray flak we'd just go up like a box of Roman candles on Guy Fawkes Night. He half grinned when he said it, but his fists were clenched so tightly on his thighs that I knew he was as apprehensive as I was. He represented, for me, the ghastly Ovaltine woman on the way up to Scotland who promised only wretchedness ahead.

However, we did get down, as you know, and Chris was there

awaiting me, with his entrenching tool waving in his hand, above his head, and me with no cap. Coming in over the coast, in a mist of smoke and those drifting fires and little puffs from the ack-ack guns around Caen, it might easily have been a devastated Wimereux below us, where we had always spent our French holidays. It was Arromanches. But the confusion and destruction, the bouncing and bobbing of the plane and the sudden swerve we made to land on the strip of metal in a cornfield was not conducive to intense thought. I do remember that I was almost wryly amused to recall arriving on this coast only ten years before, clutching buckets and spades and the wicker hamper with the tea things. From then on, after landing in the corn, I stayed where the war was. We trundled through the Normandy countryside into Belgium and Holland and, in the end, through Germany.

So, travelling had suddenly become a part of my life and I must confess I really rather enjoyed it. There was, as a matter of fact, to be one other Channel crossing by *boat* to remind me, very vaguely indeed, of the ones we had made in childhood. After my first forty-eight-hour leave in 1944 and a miserable (because of the cold and damp) night spent in Dover Castle, I boarded a ship for Calais along with perhaps a thousand others. Numbly, filled with our own private thoughts, we watched the dingy grey cliffs of Dover drift away behind us in a streamer of flying, wind-whipped steam. For many of us it *would* be the last sight of 'home'. For all of us we thought that it *could* be. So no one was actually jigging about and singing. In heavy silence, that grey day, we swayed about packed together on the top deck like a huddle of doomed cattle. No one relished this, no one really knew why, exactly, we had been stuck with this war. Something to do with fighting for democracy? But you'd be hard put to find anyone who could have told you, or spelled the word even. It was merely a politician's word. We didn't believe it anyway, but as our smug, brave, battered island faded away behind us into the sea spume and the wheeling gulls, I think we did believe that if we weren't going to wherever it was, to *stop* them, the Germans would swarm across and that would be our lot. Not just ours, crammed on that sliding deck, but everyone's Mum or Dad, or Mary and Flo, or the small newborn child some of us had held in our arms on that leave for the first time. We did not, I think, share one patriotic feeling among us. We thought only, and quite properly, of ourselves and our families. The 'talking and discussions' could and did come from all the 'clever dicks' we'd left behind. Standing in the lee, leaning really, against the edge of a companionway, bracing my legs against the leap and swell, I accepted a cigarette from a tall, angular officer beside me. We crouched low to try to get a light, and dragged in the comforting smoke. We knew, from each other's badges, where we belonged, and he asked did I know where 'our lot' had got to? I said I'd left them somewhere near Liège and hoped the Military Police at Calais would tell me. I asked him if he'd had a pleasant leave and he said no, not really. It was a forty-eight-hour compassionate job because his parents had been killed by a V2 in Fulham. He'd done what little he could, which was not much, because there wasn't much left around that he was able to deal with. And then we stood in silence, swaying about, the fine rain misting around us, getting sharper as the wind gusted. We swung to starboard and readied up for the harbour.

I remembered then, as I remember now, the huge excitement of those earlier childhood landings. The hustle and bustle, the grabbing of bags and suitcases, the thudding of hurrying feet along the decks, the rattle and slither of ropes being thrown, the clatter of enamel basins where the bad travellers had vomited, and the laughter and shouts of the French dockers, all mixed up with the blasts of the siren, the running-up of the flags, the fuss of Lally, counting our luggage and telling us to stay close and hold on tight when the gangplank swung up. None of that today. Just a weary, wet huddle of silent, anxious men with another trip ahead in an uncomfortable troop train, waiting for us just across the railway tracks. In my ID card, tucked into its talc-cover, I still have a pressed daisy which I picked that morning on my way down to the station from the lawns at Dover Castle. Even though I destroyed all my personal papers when I left home in Provence, this one piece has escaped the bonfire. It had been stuck into the back of my passport. Odd.

Of course I didn't need a passport for all the travelling I had to now face. The Army and the situation of war saw to that. I just went where I was sent. After Europe came the first giant step I had ever taken, as far as travelling abroad and alone (draft of one) was concerned. I was sent on embarkation leave. A boring business really. My parents were heavily occupied: Pa exhausted, at his office at *The Times*, Ma radiantly beautiful, floating about doing good works for the better-looking officers of the American forces. She felt, she said, that they 'needed comforting' because they were so far away from home, and missed their wives and mothers quite dreadfully, and she made them happy and amused them with her 'funny stories' and endless cups of tea. Later they would supply the beer, gin and whisky which they much preferred, but as she pointed out, sitting about being entertained in a 'real English house' with a log fire and bowls of flowers, Mozart and kindness spilling all around, could only, surely, make the best of impressions and serve as a very positive 'thank you' for their timely presence? She was as aware as anyone else at the time in England that without them we'd have been lost. So she set to and got in a constant ration of happiness for radiating. She did it all very well indeed.

My sister Elizabeth was in the Wrens and loving it. I think all *she* really did was make constant cups of cocoa and flirt madly, but she looked splendid in her blue uniform, and I never really got to see her. My brother was now a shy, wide-eyed child of eleven, dumped unwanted at boarding school. I saw him only once there, and not again until I returned from the Far East. It's a long gap from five to thirteen.

So embarkation leave was a bit dreary. There were no friends left, that I knew of, in London, and Vida Hope, my constant companion before the war, was producing plays and acting and there never seemed enough time to meet. So I just slouched about the Downs on my own, went into pubs for a beer (if they had any), listened to my father's rather heavy collection of records – Bach, Brahms and Bartók – and left home, some days later, almost gratefully, for Wentworth Woodhouse, which had been requisitioned and was now an officers' holding base. From there we got sent off to our ships for further duty.

The war, of course, was over in Europe, but all signals were GO for the war against Japan. It seemed to me that I had rather forgotten that; in my usual not-quite-together way I had thought that as soon as we'd bumped and clattered into the smoking rubble of Berlin that really would be *that*. We would have reached the WIN square on the board. Instead of which I landed on a snake's head, which, in my parlance, meant BACK TO START. But, by this time, I seemed to have found my place in the Army, the least obvious of recruits in the whole world. I really loved my work, I liked being a draft of one, I very much liked being looked after, which the Army did supremely well, so long as one could breathe or move or show signs of life. And apparently I did.

My last night in England for a very long time was spent in the splendour of Wentworth Woodhouse. I slept up in the night nursery full of slightly chipped white-painted furniture, a Landseer print on one wall, and a stuffed squirrel in a glass case on top of a wardrobe. The next day off to Liverpool, and the camouflaged bulk of the *Carthage*, bound for Bombay. She had been finished just as the war broke out and had never sailed as a passenger ship.

So she was instantly turned into a troop ship into which hundreds and hundreds of us were forced like dates in a box, side by side, and just as sticky. As an officer, I was assigned a double cabin with seven others. I have not the remotest idea now how eight men managed to exist for eight weeks in a square cell (at least with one outside porthole), but we did somehow. I had one modest kitbag, a small green canvas suitcase from the Army and Navy Stores and a shoulder-bag. That was my lot. And to survive with it for two months took a great deal of manoeuvring, which is why, today, I am maddeningly tidy.

The Bay of Biscay proved not to be a whole lot of fun, with everyone in sight chucking up and spewing astonishing amounts of what appeared to be carrot soup everywhere. In a very short time our jammed cabin reeked of the sour stench of vomit and sweat, which lingered there long after the Suez Canal, the Red Sea and, eventually, Bombay, which at least, as we drew in late one morning, had a very vague smell of cloves and sewage. Pleasanter by far than the cabin. And at least I had seen the Canal, and the strange Egyptian gentlemen who ran alongside screaming for baksheesh, lifting their djellabas to shock us with their dusky genitals: that was amusing if odd, but I think that we all recognized the fact that there were some pretty odd things to which we would rapidly have to become accustomed on our journey – this was no longer Clapham, Sidmouth or Leeds – flying fish in the Red Sea; the unbelievable heat at nights, lying naked on the deck (forbidden but we stole out until caught); watching the stars burning ice-white in the clear, black night, the rigging raking gently among them, the ropes shuddering, the planks of the deck hot.

Because I was responsible only for myself on the voyage I was, at first, coolly resented by my fellow officers in the cabin. Then, when I offered to do some of their duties to relieve them, I was accepted and found, to my intense satisfaction, that I was very often able to do what they had done, only better. I could, as it was called, 'handle the men'. This amounted to little else than going down into the steaming hell of the lower decks where, ranged in swinging hammocks, in almost constant darkness, the ORs, or other ranks, were forced to spend their time. The smell there was dreadful, of unwashed bodies and feet, of farts and vomit. There was nothing for anyone to do, apart from a few daily duties and PT or lectures to keep them on the alert, but the rest periods were agonizingly painful, lonely and long. There were, of course, a good number of louts among the hundreds, but equally there were others, the softer, gentler, bewildered men, caught up willy-nilly in the trawl which dragged everyone panicking into a world beyond all comprehension.

There were, of course, always endless games of poker. There were also mouth organs, and they made up intense games of Bingo. Some did read – not many, because books weighed and were bulky in kitbags, although I think there was a Red Cross library somewhere on board. There were also visits (not fearfully frequent, it appeared) by the padres, the Catholic and the C. of E. I don't remember a Rabbi. Perhaps because we had no Jews aboard or because I missed him when I was down assisting some of those who found it difficult to write letters home? I was quite good at this. I had done it in the first months of my service up at Catterick Camp for, to my mild astonishment, there were a number of men who could neither read nor write. So I'd go below decks with a notepad and pencil, some envelopes from the NAAFI, and we'd set to and then let it all pour out. At first some men were shy, anxious, perhaps ashamed, certainly inhibited. But gradually we made a bridge of trust between each other and, apart from the blight of continual censorship, we got off some jolly good letters to ladies in Kennington, Halifax and Wolverhampton, etc. I sometimes found crafty ways of concealing, in a pattern of apparently simple words, things which had a deeper significance for the receiver, although I have often wondered what transpired when some bewildered wife, lover, mother, mistress, tried to make her way through my labyrinth of unfamiliar words. Not a lot, I expect.

The same must have gone for the censors. They were mainly ordinary young officers, and a lot of us were really not over-bright in literature – great with a cricket score, a football or rugby match, or the report from a boxing ring, but a bit lost when something a little deeper was required. I sometimes agreed to be the censor officer myself: it was a repellent, inquisitive, saddening job. I think I was generous, obliterating only anything which might, however innocently, betray a position, a town or place, a battle, a ship or a quantity which could be dangerous: the number of men, of officers, regimental names, of rounds fired or ships in convoy, that sort of thing. Some officers, I know, used to read out the more intimate and yearning parts of a man's letter and hold them up to scorn and laughter. I never knew how they could do that and then very possibly meet the writer the next day on parade or doing duty. But they did. Human nature, I suppose? But because I was not attached to anyone down on C, D or E decks, because I was happily a loner, I was vaguely trusted, and they were never betrayed.

Writing letters (not *that* many to be sure but enough to keep me busy) and checking on feet (always a problem) or boils (ditto) or teeth and crabs so that the MOs were informed and the man comforted, as far as possible, kept me occupied on the long journey out and gave me something to fill in my time and also something to think about. Travel, they always said, broadens the mind. Well, this was proof that it did. It was far more interesting, and far less hurtful, than London, Euston/Glasgow Central. I did not attempt to think of what might lie ahead.

There was Bombay one morning. It appeared quite suddenly, melting through the early mists from a sea like a sheet of rippled tin. Vultures wheeled above in the lapis sky and we watched wistfully as ships, crammed with waving men on their way back on repat to the UK, steamed out into the white glare of the day. All I saw of Bombay was the Gateway to India, a huge arch rather like a giant Marble Arch, railway lines, docks, cranes and millions of half-naked people swarming, a stick stuck in the ant-hill. The stench was heavy: oil, bodies, dirt; somewhere, faintly, spices. There were one or two people lying in tumbled heaps alongside the tracks. At first I thought they were sleeping, but the flies invading their haggard faces and sightless eyes set me right.

Then the troop train and five days and nights (an extra-slow journey because the line was up owing to an earlier accident) across the vastness of this new astonishing continent. Mile upon weary mile of scrub and desert. Here and there huddles of villages, thorn trees, men ploughing with gaunt oxen, women wandering from wells, brass pots balanced on their heads, children like flocks of dirty sparrows scattering and racing alongside the train. Vultures again. Kites high in the immensity of the bleached sky stretching to infinity with nothing interrupting its distance. The isolation, the poverty, dust, the fragility, were not at all what I had imagined. No verdant jungles here, no prowling tigers under lush trees, no leaping monkeys, no stealthy leopards. The India I saw, from that terrible train, was sere, desolate. It was a fearful let-down the first time around. I had expected story-book splendour. Instead we trailed for days across stony, beige desert.

Looking back now, I wonder what on earth we did all through that journey? There were six of us to each compartment. Slatted wooden seats. We slept, I suppose? There were card games of course. Scores were kept, screwed up and thrown away into the hot glare beyond the window. We had books – a few – a catholic collection: *Barchester Towers* to *No Orchids for Miss Blandish*. We shared them. I know that we stopped at deserted little stations and filed, stiff-legged, into whitewashed waiting-rooms set about with wooden tables. Fans clacked under motionless geckoes flat on the ceilings. Sometimes there was a punka-wallah, a skinny barefoot child sitting by a damp sheet stretched on a square of thin bamboo cane, waving the thing listlessly about with calloused feet, flies at his eyes so familiar that he no longer bothered to brush them away.

Trestle tables were neatly laid: a knife, a fork, a spoon. What did we eat? Some kind of gruel: soup, I imagine. A bit of grey meat with tinned peas. Pineapple chunks from America. Everything pretty well inedible, a thumb-print on the edge of each plate, warm lemonade in sticky glass bottles. Unlovely. Then a cigarette, time for a pee, and back on to the awful train, hissing and steaming wearily, waiting across the track, a dying dragon. We rumbled through the afternoon, into the dusk, then sudden night. I suppose we must have stopped again for an evening meal? I don't really remember, the days melted into each other like sodden warm Kleenex. I do recall that there was a thunderbox shoved into a cupboard at the end of each one of the carriages. These got emptied during the lunch-stop. It was obviously wise not to have diarrhoea on this journey. Tough luck on the untouchables who had to clear up. Once I sprang away in shock when a large black rat shot out as I clattered open the door. Not a happy trip.

What must follow now is a sort of zig-zag of impressions, a kaleidoscope. Twist the tube, change the patterns. Everything was speeded up; bewilderment, fatigue, made your head light. I remember Sealdah station, Calcutta – a vast arena of girders, iron pillars, seething crowds – and throwing open the carriage door the moment we stopped, sending some wretched man, yoked to two giant terracotta pots, crashing into a turmoil of scrawny legs and arms, broken pot, and millions and millions of tiny leaping fish. In an agony of shock I stopped to help him to his feet. He was naked except for a scrap of filthy cloth round his loins. Shaking with despair at my unthinking action and the spilling of his catch, I tried to pull him to his feet, to be roughly assaulted by a fat, ginger-haired, moustached, red-faced, stocky little major from Transport. Screaming. Thrashing at the cringing Indian with his swagger cane, sending him sprawling once again into the shards of his pots and the enormous tumble of glittering little fish. 'You! Get along! Get your gear together. The trucks are waiting. You don't bloody apologize to these bastards. *Animals*, all of them, bloody *animals*! Shouldn't have been on the platform. Come on, get out of it, you black bastard! Out! Out! God! I loathe their guts, loathe 'em all. *You'll* find out, *you'll* learn to loathe them too!'

My first sight and sound of the British Raj at work. I was pretty shocked but I did as he had told me, grabbed my gear and lumbered off with the others to the trucks in the station yard. Cars, gharries, milling hundreds, smoke drifting, the smell of horse shit, kerosene, cooking. Hawkers bawling, a child of about six waving a bamboo cage of terrified fluttering birds: '*Sahib! Sahib!* You buy! Ten rupee? You buy?' The white dhotis, ambling cows with curled horns, bare legs, the scent again of cooking oil and ordure.

There followed in the truck a sort of race through a rush-hour in hell, which proved only to be Chowringhee, the main thoroughfare, and then Green's Hotel: tatty Edwardian; in the dim bar, crowded with khaki bodies, great beakers of fresh lime juice: no ice on account of dysentery. After the train and its thunderboxes I knew I didn't want it. We all got sorted out in what, I suppose, had been the ballroom, and despatched to regiments, brigades, sections, whatever. Bewildered, eyes red with fatigue, we got bunged into trucks and dumped at our destinations. I hung out of the back of my truck amazed and overwhelmed by the hurrying crowds, the lumbering holy cows (someone told me), the bamboo, palms, the scarlet flame-of-the-forest trees, the frangipani scattering purple blossom like the cheapest confetti, ox carts, rolled matting, sleeping (dying?) people on the pavements, buses covered with brilliant advertising in incomprehensible scripts. I had never seen so much exhausted but vibrant life, and above, in the lapis sky, bolstered now with enormous plumped-up pillows of cloud, shaded by dark brush-strokes of rain, the wheeling vultures and the ubiquitous kites scavenging for the filth spilling from the great rubbish bins along the road. A different world, all right. I was travelling and how. But in spite of the seething, surging masses, the monsoon rains, the clattering gaudy buses, I still had, burned into the retina of my eye, the shameful image of that cowering man, hands writhen as tree roots, protecting his thin bald head, sprawling in the cascade of tiny wriggling fish. It was as if I had stared into the sun. He remained, and remains still, an image of shock.

India hit me hard that very first morning. I know, very well, that it always does. However, in time one grew accustomed to the filth, the stench, the dire poverty, the seething millions, the wob-bling cycles, the wheeling vultures, the lepers with their bells, with running sores, the dead babies lying in their own excreta, blue-hazed with flies. To do anything else was disastrous. One adjusted because all sense raged against what one saw, but equally all sense reasoned, calmly, that there was nothing whatever to be done about it. It had been this way for thousands of years and no amount of my suburban fussing was going to alter anything. Survive. Or else. One lived surrounded by despair and disease, unless one came against good, cleansing death. However, I can still see that wretched figure at Sealdah Station. Even now, fifty years later, the image is dimmed but there with a strange kind of clarity. Unlike the unthinkable horror of that small place in Germany among the heath and pines which the mind still absolutely rejects and obliter-ates the split-second-of-a-second when it tries to intrude (during thunderstorms is bad, strangely), the cowering, humbled body beaten by a furious cane remains. The earliest manifestation I ever had of physical persecution? Surely not. After all, the heath and pines . . . and there, at that point, even now, I stop.

It was, I suppose, my introduction to a new world. Travelling was after all how you got there. And the travelling was not about to stop: I was shoved again on to another truck and driven some miles out of the city. To be sure, the road was clearer, less crowded if pot-holed; great palms, telegraph poles, oxen pulling creaking carts. I reached my posting and clambered out, luggage chucked down into the road, meagre instructions given: 'Turn left after the Dunlop Bridge, can't miss it, up the track and you'll find the palace.' A sort of dirty-cream fretwork of crumbling plaster, lizards, a long pool overgrown with lilies and rushes, canna lilies spearing from rusty petrol cans, a tousle of ugly zinnias. A veranda with scattered planter's chairs. Empty. Stubby, dusty palms scratching battered fronds against the peeling whitewash. Behind all this (there was no sign of any life) I found a scatter of thatched huts; shirts and underpants hanging over the bushes. A tall, turbaned, toothless man suddenly hurried down a dirt path, hands clasped in greeting. The Sahib has order? Hi? This was the officers' compound. I was led to my empty hut: beams, concrete floor, thatch, a louvred door, no glass in the windows. Here I was to sleep. Separate huts, a bearer to each; mine was also toothless, and I can't even remember his name, but I remember the smell of garlic on my pillow when he smoothed it during the making of my bed. He unpacked my voyage-battered luggage, spread it on the bushes to air, in the sun bursts between the monsoon rains: blistering hot for ten moments, steam rising from the drenched earth, then black sky once more and the torrential rains, drops as big as florins, frogs ambling slowly across in the mud, the sweet fresh smell of rain. This was where I was to live, until the assault on Malaya and Singapore.

The mess, in the palace, had a bamboo-fronted bar; jars of

gladioli; scattered Lloyd loom chairs; glass-topped little tables with old *Lilliput*s and *Men Only* here and there; fans; a sisal rug; a Signals radio on the bar; tall bar-stools nudging beside it, calves at the cow; a poster pinned to the wall, of Windsor Castle. I bought myself a gin sling and a squadron leader, who suddenly arrived with a cheery smile and gappy teeth, asked if I was just out from the UK. I must have looked as obvious and uncomfortable as a new pair of shoes. He laughed kindly about my arrival in the middle of the monsoon. No flying now, no photographs, no work. Good Lord, no! Jolly bad arrangements, what? 'Hang about,' he said finishing his Tiger beer, 'someone will tell you what to do.' No one did. No one expected a draft of one or cared that it had arrived. I was as welcome as a hair-louse.

But that evening, Tilly lamps spluttering (there was a power cut), shadows leaping, the bar full of tobacco smoke and busy, someone bought me a drink and suggested I have a dekko at the office, the photographs and maps. Go through all the info files? Plenty to catch up on, they'd been working on the Op for ages. Malaya, he said, raising his glass, next stop!

Then a heavy scent of some perfume I might have recognized: civilized, elegant, from another time and place. And there was Nan: flowing white chiffon, a jade cigarette-holder, hair falling to her waist, caught up at each side by a tortoiseshell comb; heavy-breasted, red nails; trim, very female, smiling, scented; my senior in age and rank. She slid gracefully on to a stool at the bar and asked me, easily and casually, to buy her a gin and quinine. She arrived in my life just like that. Suddenly, unexpectedly, there she was and I strangely felt secure. Someone had found a tin of chocolate biscuits up in Delhi and had sent them down to her. She offered them round and asked a bearer to put on some records. 'Music! Music!' she called. She was alive, confident, laughing.

The next day we went together into the almost deserted offices and looked through the maps and photographs: big blow-ups of beach areas, mangrove, nothing which was familiar to me. She said it would take time. I should spend a week or two checking out all the stuff that they had been working on for so long, catch up. I said I would and I did. There was nothing much else to do, and it was a great relief after the train.

I began, slowly, to learn the new names – Kuala Lumpur, Batu Pahat, Ipoh – started to differentiate between fine sand, hard sand, mud and rock, pebble and mangrove, marsh and paddy. There were no defensive areas, no trenches, fox-holes. This was a different enemy: he moved swiftly, under cover, furtively, unseen until he shot you. He left no signs, and in any case, the vegetation cover was incredibly dense.

After a couple of weeks I was permitted to look at the Top Secret files. These gave me absolutely no delight, but frightened me out of my wits. It was clear, from these reports, that the Japanese were subhuman creatures who mutilated and beat their prisoners to death. I read everything with mounting horror. Nan assured me, in a quiet voice, that everything was true. They had very different standards, a different religion, had not fully come into the twentieth century. I was appalled by the excruciating accounts of horrific atrocities. One thing was clear in all the later reports. At the end of the summer, this *very* summer, every single prisoner – soldier, civilian, male, female or child – was to be systematically slaughtered. Food had run low, petrol also, lines of communication were overstretched, the guards and troops servicing the prisoner-of-war camps were needed for more urgent duties. All this at the end of the monsoon.

One evening at the bar in the mess a tall, rather genial officer in the Medical Corps down to us on an inspection visit offered me a little round box with a red band round the sides and a black cross on the lid; inside, nestling in a wad of cotton wool, a dirty pearl. A small capsule. I asked him what it was. Should I know? And he said no, not unless I had already got one. It was cyanide. If I was going into action I really ought to have one handy, in case I was taken prisoner. He took it from my inert hand, closed it, pocketed it, named a price, which angered me as much as it astonished me. 'Japs are heathens. They'll cut off your eyelids, leave you staring at a naked electric bulb while they interrogate. You are in a specialist job, so they'll get everything out of you. No sleep. Well, you can't, can you? Without eyelids? I'd think about it, old chum.' He told me to speak to no one about the capsule. I didn't. Not even Nan.

Crushed against her on her wide charpoy, the mosquito net like a much-mended wedding veil, I was pretty well preoccupied one afternoon and not performing very well. This alerted her instantly. 'Oh! Pippin! Floating off into your dream world? Thinking of one of your plots? Nothing *wrong* is there?' I shook my head and she said that I really had to give up smoking in bed. Look at the net, full of darns. She'd practically used up all her white thread. 'Do put that out, sweet one. You'll burn us alive one day.' I stubbed it out on the tiled floor. Had to clean it up after, because of her bearer finding it.

We had to be extremely careful about this coupling. It was only ever possible during the long siesta or when her co-officer, Alison, had gone into town to have her hair done, or to see *her* friend, an officer in a Gurkha Regiment. Afterwards we'd slide stickily apart, the heavy scent of our sweaty bodies and her stale 'Je Reviens' sour in the wet heat. Sometimes, when I remembered, I'd make a wide loop at the back of her hut and pad to the showers across the cropped grass of the compound, a towel and my clothes under my arm. I was quite pleased with this silly deception, far from my own hut, but no one was deceived. We were too often together, and

Nan was almost aggressively possessive. Of course everyone guessed, but it really didn't matter much: the monsoon was possibly coming to an end, a feeling of relief was drifting in the air, we might all, quite soon, get back to work again. We never did.

One evening, during a raging storm, above the monsoon rain lashing and ripping the big plantains and tearing at the oleander bushes round the open door of the mess, we heard, on the Signals radio-set, that the Americans had dropped the Bomb.

Enola Gay had laid her egg.

For a few moments we sat, or stood, in stunned shock. It had been uneasily expected, but the real fact was shattering. We knew, in our silence, broken only by the rattling rain, that life now had been for ever altered. They dropped another bomb two days later on Nagasaki, and a couple of days after that the Japanese surrendered and that was that. Thousands of Japanese had perished, but far more allied prisoners and civilians had been saved. Another war had ended for me just as the other, European, one had done. Suddenly. Abruptly. The war machine stopped. The talc-covered maps, the thousands and thousands of photographs, the detailed models and charts, all these were suddenly rendered useless. We were unemployed and unemployable. Gradually, after joyful but cautious celebrations, we began to sort out our thoughts and dare to consider repatriation and home. I wondered if the medical officer had managed to flog his capsule, before it too became unwanted. We started to make plans for an uncertain future. We were still stuck in India after all.

Nan suggested one evening, 'Let's go up to Tibet! I *long* to! And we'll never be able to afford to in peacetime. It's such an opportunity, Pippin! Let's!' So we did. Absurdly. We got all the passes, the maps for the trip, permits, food, compo rations, stout boots, injections, fuel, backpacks and so on and set off, initially, for Darjeeling in the hills from where we decided to start the trek. We were utterly unprepared, on the verge of madness brought about by the euphoria of sudden peace.

It was total and complete disaster. We didn't last long. Ill-prepared for the walk, for the ugly mule we hired, for the sullen guide who overcharged us and who then melted into the night after three days, without a proper knowledge of the language, unaware that the only fuel we could possibly burn would be cow- or mule-dung in dried patties, and ignorant that we'd freeze after sundown and roast at noon. Unaware, too, that the sight of a 'man', in uniform but with full breasts and hair plaited round its head would throw unsuspecting mountain people into a state of silent shock and confusion. I didn't realize that we would be regarded with suspicion and fear. They watched us from a distance, ranged round us in half-circles like terrified dogs watching a cobra. The women pulled up their rags and hid their faces, peering with wide eyes over the filthy cloth; the children, usually a pest with pleading and pulling, now hung back, awkward, uncertain, giggling.

We trudged on upwards, living on a diet of rice, army biscuits, tinned American bacon, and packets of dried apple rings. We ran out of glucose tablets almost the day after we left Gantok, which is really almost as Golders Green is to Wandsworth: pretty near civilization. Sometimes we did manage to get an egg or two, juggling coins in our hands as an inducement, and once I stole a stray scrawny hen and wrung its neck, while Nan pretended not to look and whistled unevenly.

After we left the near-civilized areas we were definitely out on our own. Water we got from streams (an awful lot of streams in the hills) and we started to lose our tempers pretty early on. Sleeping in our 'fleabags' or sleeping-bags was not comfortable: rocks bit into hip bones, creatures slid in for warmth. We lost our maps, bickered, cut fingers on a cheap tin-opener, spilled matches down a gulley, set fire to half an acre of bamboo and bush, and generally behaved like the idiots we were. But we did see dawn rise on Everest, out of the darkness of pre-dawn, watched the glory of the white, pristine, untouched peak soar into the clear blue sky of a new day just before great veils of drifting, slow-writhing, mists began to rise from the valleys to smother it in white cloud. At least we'd seen that, *and* the sunset on Kanchenjunga. And got suppurating blisters on feet unaccustomed to heavy boots.

We walked doggedly upwards in sullen silence. Walking along slowly I began to brood. Was the broderie anglaise of her mosquito net merely a sign of her power over me? Were all the little cigarette burns, so neatly darned and spotted about, were they really only the signals for each 'joining' we had made? Were they, in fact, her sort of 'scalps'? Victory signs? *Was* I being trapped? Taken prisoner, used, *possessed*?

Plodding on, twisting ankles on sharp rock, I worried and ruminated constantly and started to panic. I didn't frankly give a tinker's gob about seeing Tibet. The war was over. I had no reason, not even Nan (especially suddenly *not* Nan), to stay here. I wanted out. We had seen all we really needed to see. She had made the suggestion, to troll off and find Tibet. Tibet had never been high on any agenda I had in mind. I saw little pleasure in this dreadful hike and I knew that she did not either. We had got it all wrong, had not planned it, had danced off like a couple of schoolchildren playing at explorers. I was sick of tinned bacon, sick of trying to light wispy fires with brushwood and diminishing matches, of hobbling the reluctant, evil-minded mule to graze, of being whimpered to about the cold, blisters, and wouldn't I come into her sleeping-bag to 'warm her up'? I was also, though I tried not to admit it even to myself, sick to death of her suppressed, noble tears. Of *course* it wasn't fun! Why had she expected that a climb over vicious rocks up winding tracks for miles through the hills of Sikkim down towards the Brahmaputra and, eventually, Tibet was going to be the equivalent of a happy hike from Basingstoke to Yeovil?

Well of course, she hadn't. Hadn't at all. But that was the way that my sanity and patience started to crumble under duress. Seeing her miserable, sitting on a large boulder, bare feet bloody, hair now tumbled, tears spilling on to the map on her lap, did not induce pity, as it should, only anger and impatience, in me. This, I reasoned furiously, would *never* have happened with Chris! We'd *never* have got into this mess. It would never have become a personal affair, even if we had got lost, finished the matches, run out of rice and found ourselves unable to converse (in sign language) with the mountain people, who regarded us now with grave misgivings. And they wouldn't have been scared witless by the sight of him. I didn't know quite *how* we'd have managed, he and I, but far better than this. And I'd *never* have been asked to share his sleeping-bag, or warm his feet, or have his hands thrust into my battledress jacket to bring 'back the circulation'. To be absolutely fair to Nan I was often on the brink of tears myself. We seemed to be climbing to the top of the world (at least 8,000 feet), and breathless, wet, starving, our packs dragging us ever downward, straps chafing, boots lacerating, bleeding and pussy feet, with no possible hope of a decent meal or anything resembling a nice cup of tea ahead (I had long since finished the bottle of brandy we'd packed), all hope faded like the good air in a sealed-off coal mine. The canary died.

We finally gave in. Standing one morning, unshaven, unslept, the mule struggling while I tried to un-hobble it, I said, 'Fuck it. Let's go back! Chuck it. This is madness, we've done enough,' and Nan, I remember, said very bravely, '*Pippin!* That's giving in. Those mountains far ahead. The gold on the edge, all pink in the sun? That's *Tibet!*' and I remember saying, 'Sod bloody Tibet,' and silently, together, we started to lace up boots, clear up sleeping-bags, and then turned to embark on the backward track. Honestly I didn't feel good about giving in. Neither, I know, did she, but we had reached the end of our pathetic civilian endurance. So we went home.

Today, of course, I suppose the road we attempted fifty years ago is now too well trodden by hippies or New Age people, drop-outs from all nations, and various people intent on finding 'them-selves', their 'souls' or 'freedom'. Or something idiotic. The tracks are probably stuck about with scattered Kodak cartons, candy wrappers, syringes, discarded tins and burned spoons. Apparently they are about to install portable lavatories at the foot of Everest *when* they have collected up all the tourist garbage. But at least we saw it before desecration, and I bet the hill-people fairly flourish today selling their tatty bits of silver and packets of grass. But fifty years ago the very sight of Nan in her trousers confused them utterly and threw them into bemusement.

Anyhow, to resume, we stumbled and slid, and about a week or so later reached Gantok once more, knowing that civilization, in the shape of Darjeeling, the Himalayan Cheltenham, with its Everest Hotel, was not very far. The Everest Hotel, then, was a huge Edwardian pile looking absurdly like some faux timbered manor house near Crowborough. Set up a drive frothing with massed rhododendrons, it had been the epitome of the hill station hotel for senior officers and their wives and families, but no longer: the war had swept a great deal of the past away. The smoking rooms, the ballroom, and the various other 'rooms' were jammed with American officers on leave in their 'pinks' and trim jackets, with their Eurasian ladies, something which would not have been even remotely countenanced five years before. There were a number of British officers around as well, but not 'regular ones'. These were disparagingly known as 'civilian officers' and might well have been civil servants, bank clerks or school teachers before they had

been chucked into Aldershot or Camberley: 'Not at *all* our class.'
Things were changing, and the Everest Hotel was almost the first
to see it. Glen Miller and 'In the Mood' instead of Palm Court and
Rose Marie.

I didn't personally give a fig, apart from the fact that Nan and I
looked as if we had recently escaped from a POW camp, and
were therefore refused entry into the tea-lounge or ballroom (with
our feet that would have been a sick joke). We bathed and generally
cleaned up. Nan had her blisters dealt with, and life gradually
began to ebb back after a few drinks and days, so that I was able,
without a lot of grace I know, to apologize for my behaviour and
having cocked up, as I had, the initial arrangements. Nan sweetly
dismissed my stumbling, grudging even, sentences with casual
waves of her cigarette-holder, smiled kindly and 'understandingly'.
It was no one's *particular* fault. We had been overwhelmed by the
suddenness of the end of hostilities and, after all, it *was* her idea
in the first place. I knew alas that she would have forgiven me
child-rape or patricide at that time. I was, now that we were
warm, comfortable and civilized, once more adorable in her
eyes.

One morning I swung about on my heels uneasily, by the
windows. I had something to tell her, but was funking it. I had,
earlier, put a call through to HQ in Calcutta to assure them of our
safety. They had told me that there was a signal for me, three days
old, to get down to the docks and report to some Captain on an
LST which would take me to my next posting: Batavia, in
Indonesia. My informant was very jolly. 'Fearful mess down there.
Got a sodding civil war on their hands. Chopping up all the Dutch
civilians. Be quick, old dear!'

I thought perhaps I'd better tell Nan right away, but then let it
stew about, and decided to say nothing, except that I was going
down to the bar to order a very large John Collins. To prepare

myself for the journey down to Calcutta and, later on, Batavia. Wherever that was. It didn't take me long to find out.

The voyage from Calcutta to Batavia was far longer than I had thought, and very slow on a landing ship tank which seemed to inch across the flat sea. And there I was, once more, as a draft of one going down to open up an office in 23rd Indian Division all for myself. I'd be the one and only interpreter. No one had the least idea if there were any planes to fly sorties, or *if* there were, any photographs for me to interpret. But nevertheless I was on my way. My telephone information was correct. There *was* a civil war banging about down there, a pretty vicious one too. The Indonesians were obsessed with colonial rule and its destruction. Which meant death to all the Dutch who had ruled them for some hundreds of years. The Dutch were presently all interned still, by the Japs, in POW camps, where, according to the Indonesians, they must stay until they were destroyed.

The Japanese had indeed surrendered, or most of them who had got the message of the bombs had, but they had very thoughtfully laid down their weapons into the waiting, lusting arms of the Indonesians who were now more or less in control of the island (almost as large as Great Britain). Our job, I gathered, was to help release the civilian internees and get them flown out to Europe. Or somewhere. I could do my interpreting *when* there were planes free to fly and take the needed photographs. Easy. No problem. This was exactly where I had always come in in a war: the original bugger's muddle.

But the slow, gentle days at sea gave me plenty of time for thinking. We were only carrying trucks and ammunition and various stores. There were two or three other army officers, apart from navy personnel, on board. I relished the solitude. I'd had quite enough of India, quite enough of the gentle web of love and affection which was surreptitiously being woven about me by Nan. A proverbial moth in the web of love, rolled into the tidy chrysalis of 'togetherness'. Which I knew I didn't want. The thought of a 'nice little flat', or worse, 'a cottage near town', a fire and my supper ready ('I'll have to fatten you up, Pippin – nourishing stuff! You're like a rake, darling!'), perhaps a dog or a cat at my feet, happy chatter about neighbours or family filled me with utter dread. I was twenty-five, and having a great deal of fun 'travelling'. I did not want that to stop, and I was now, on board my LST, determined that I would remain independent to do just as I wished, whenever I wished. I had had no adolescence really, a limited adulthood. I wanted to catch up, to fill in the gaps. Distances once had been dictated by the Greenline bus to Seaford or the Flying Scot to Glasgow. Now much more was on offer. My horizons had widened. No one was going to limit them. No one ever has.

One night, during the thousandth game of Monopoly in the tiny wardroom, someone beckoned me out on deck and told me to watch as we crossed the Equator. I'd see the line. A *real* line marking the hemispheres. Whether I did or not, I *believed* that I did. And, anyway, the water in my basin *did* run round the other way down the plughole. I had never at that moment felt so amazingly far away. Above, like a chunk of cheap costume jewellery, the Southern Cross hung (a little tilted) in an immensity of white diamonds, with only the little ruby portlight, the emerald light of the starboard side, winking in the taut rigging. Far away to port, low like the shadow of a crouching beast, lay Borneo, one tiny light blinking from a lighthouse, and, behind us, in the long, rippling wake, gold with phosphorescence, spilled the Java Sea, and I thought I could see the zig-zag of the line in the tremulous gold and ink-black of the waters. I was tapped on the shoulder and reminded that I wasn't wearing a life-jacket or my Mae West, and that even if the war *was* over, some Japs didn't recognize the fact, or didn't even know. I said that they did in Borneo, there's the lighthouse, and my companion just said that there were submarines in the area bent on suicide rather than on surrender. I got a stab of fear remembering the cyanide pill in its little round box. 'Come on, let's get down.' We walked towards the blacked-out companionway, just the little ruby and emerald lights rocking gently against the stars, the Southern Cross a blaze of brilliance. The wardroom was fugged with smoke and gin. The Lieutenant-Commander looked up as we clambered down. 'Leaving in the bloody *middle* of a game! Christ!' I apologized and said I'd been to see the Equator, and he half smiled and asked if I'd seen it? And I said I thought I had, and he grinned and said, 'Good show! My throw, remember? All ready? Correct and ship shape? Here we go . . .' He rattled the dice and spilled them across the Monopoly board. 'Five! Super! . . . Three . . . four . . . five! There! The Angel, Islington! Absolutely wizard!'

I thought I had never been so happy. *This* was my life. Good company in a wardroom, just crossing the Equator, playing Monopoly. What could be better? And independent.

Two Ingrids

She said that her name was Minouschkin, and was this my first time in Cyprus? I said, 'Good Evening', and yes, my first time. Did it show? And she laughed and tapped her cigarette into an ashtray.

We were standing jammed up against a very long bar of My Blue Heaven, a 'typical', I had been assured, noisy, real nightclub in Nicosia which my hosts, Ellen and Alexi, had insisted that I should see before the evening finished. They had taken me to a fairly agonizingly dull dinner at the Ledra Palace Hotel, and this generous gesture was to round off the jolly event.

Ellen smiled bravely. 'You will hear real Cypriot music here, music of the people, of the island, you will get a "feel" of the place. The "atmosphere".' She patted my hand happily. This was before we entered the place. Once inside all she could have done was yell at me above the noise. I had gone up to the bar to replenish our drinks, Scotch for Alexi and me, orangeade, predictably, for Ellen.

Alexi was a true Cypriot: a huge moustache, a big gut, both of which he carried before him with pride, indications of wealth, like the rings on his fingers. Ellen, on the other hand, was almost demure, soft-spoken, red hair flecked with grey, and from Ayrshire. They had been happily married for years. I found her 'real music' utterly deafening and, frankly, not terribly addictive. One bouzouki is, after all, pretty much like another; six of them all going off at the same time were as near to hell as I could imagine, plus the roars and laughs, the huge bellowing shouts, and nervously having to dodge the flying plates which appeared to be shattering all around in slithering, leaping shards.

'A wedding!' shouted Alexi happily. It all felt more conducive to burst eardrums than folklore. But I was their guest and they had taken enormous trouble to make my evening memorable, so it was incumbent on me to show delight and joy. I gave a fairly good impression, mainly for Ellen, whom I liked, but I could see that she had reached the wilting stage as well. It really wasn't her scene. Alexi had removed his jacket and was marvellously at home the moment he sat down.

He and Ellen ran a chic, prosperous theatrical/literary restaurant just off St Martin's Lane. I had become a regular patron. It was near all the major theatres, calm, discreet, unwelcoming to the press, with excellent food, and, once they got to know you, you were cherished – over-cherished really, because Alexi insisted on joining your table, if you were a favourite, with his little squat bottle of 'special' ouzo, the instant that he reckoned you had finished your coffee. No matter with whom you were dining, a group or simply one, he'd drag up a chair and sit down always with exactly the right amount of little glasses gathered up in his ringed fingers. Truthfully it became rather boring, and was one reason why I began to phase the restaurant out of my plans. It was not always tactful or even agreeable or convenient to have Alexi present, eyes twinkling with kindness, rings glittering, the cork popped from its bottle.

However, I was on his territory, I was always polite, and tonight I was on his territory even more than ever. I was filming on the island. Alexi and Ellen were staying at their retirement villa, on holiday, up in the hills behind Kyrenia. I had been 'caught' and promised to contact them when I arrived. This I had done, and Nicosia and a wild night of 'Real Cyprus' was the result. I was promised it would not be any 'tourist rubbish!' There weren't many tourists anyway at that time in Cyprus: the sterling allowance for 'abroad' was frozen hard in 1952, the Beatles hadn't even plucked a guitar string, and we were, anyway in the UK, all more or less reverting to the beige-bottle-green-and-navy of before the war. We hadn't started to emerge, even cautiously, into the new decade. The few tourists that there were were aged Britons, mournful and faded, retired from India and Egypt, who, unable to face the rigours and taxes of England, had all settled into the Dome Hotel in Kyrenia, or various boarding-houses, well wrapped up against what they called a 'cutting March wind'. From where I sat I longed for a breath of that, to me, dulcet, warm wind, because I was finding the 'real Cyprus' and its music fairly grim. I had thought it might be authentic and fun – grave error, it was quite awful. However, I behaved well, showing delight and amazement, for Ellen, who sat bolt upright as if nailed to her chair: stiff in black jersey, from Marshall and Snelgrove, a rope of faux pearls and a brave, weary smile.

Alexi, of course, was adoring it all, especially the music, but it was quite evident that Ellen's idea of rapture in that direction was Victor Sylvester.

'You get the *feeling*, Dirk?' Alexi yelled. 'The happiness! Everyone is happy and we show it.' He was shouting over the sound of smashing, splintering china. 'We are free here, to *show* our feelings, not like you British! *We* live!'

Ellen smiled, sighed and waved clouds of rank smoke from about her head. I mean, if you *liked* flashing lights, six belting bouzoukis, jammed tables, flying crockery coming in at you from every angle, plus a clutch of violently gyrating Egyptian belly dancers ('All completely real! From Alexandria!' roared Alexi as if he personally introduced the breed with its wagging tassels and undulating bottoms draped in tired, shiny, beaded satin) – if you actually *liked* all this, then My Blue Heaven was your dream-place.

Added to the absurdity of its name, the décor was bizarrely that of Crete, not Cyprus. It was a mock-up version of Knossos, with a giant plaster Minotaur slung on chains over the bar, eyes flashing red and green like traffic lights. A good number of the clientele resembled, with quite striking accuracy, the Leaping Boy Dancers of legend: heavy make-up, corkscrew curls, gold necklaces and almost nothing else. Ellen's lips were taut with Scots disapproval. 'Degenerates! How do they let them into a respectable place!'

I felt she had succumbed to Cyprus pretty heavily if she considered this place at all respectable. Alexi thumped the table with jewelled, hairy fist and, apart from sending the drinks flying and a bowl of olives scattering, he shouted that it was Life! We must be tolerant! Life is for living! Enjoy! And it was at that moment that I rose and wound myself through the screams and laughs of the wedding party under the flickering mirror-light high in the dome and reached the bar.

The barman (owner I would discover) was watchful, genial, pushed my drinks across to me, held out his hand for payment. Fumbling with my wallet – I was unused yet to the local pounds – I noticed him flick his fingers above my head and a slight, boyish creature, dark hair cut very short, a simple black dress, wide eyes, was suddenly at my side. She said that her name was Minouschkin, was this my first time in Cyprus? And you know the rest. That's how we met.

'Cyprus money is not so difficult, I show.' She plucked some notes like feathers from my wallet, said I was crazy to walk about with so much money showing, paid the bill, speaking more-or-less French, and raised a flute towards me with a happy grin. It just seemed to 'arrive'. She thanked me, and sipped at what looked to me very like ginger-ale.

'Did I buy that? I seem to have very little change left . . .'

She nodded happily. 'Mikki is good man. He is barman and the boss, he see I am so hot, so thirsty, so he make me this and you pay. Thank you!' I nodded. 'I like very much *champagne*,' she said.

'So I can see.'

'He very good man. He big boss. I work here, he know. You like here?'

'Very much. Yes. I absolutely *love* here. It's just a bit expensive . . . twelve quid for that!'

She quickly put a hand, fragile as cobweb, on my sleeve. 'Ah! You now shout to me! You are angry?'

I began to collect up my three glasses. 'No, no! I mean, you do rather *have* to shout here, don't you? It's hardly like a church.'

Mikki, or whoever he was, slid a plastic tray towards me, and I set the glasses on it, with a grateful nod. He shrugged and started picking his teeth with a matchstick. The bouzouki music was rising, the thudding growing, the sweat starting to bead on my brow, slither down my throat.

'You drink whisky in Cyprus! Is crazy! Is why you are hot. I get you champagne! Mikki.' She flicked her fingers at him (it seemed to be a house signal) but thankfully he had turned away to serve a paunchy American sailor.

'Yes. I've been drinking Scotch all night. It is fatal to mix spirits with wine! Lethal!'

Her eyes were round as an owl's. 'What means "lethal"?'

'You will be very ill. You could die.'

'Eyeee! You hate champagne? I love –' I began to move back towards my table, she beside me. 'I not understand you. You speak too quick. But you are funny. Yes! I think you are funny. I do. Maybe you are with the movie people here? Is possible?' She turned away but, out of the corner of my eye, negotiating an hysterical table of laughing people with my plastic tray, I saw her flick her wretched little fingers again. Mikki waved and I hastily moved past a line of singing policemen – they might have been soldiers, they were uniformed – and, looking back, saw that Mikki handed her something and she came elbowing along behind me.

Alexi beamed away. 'Bravo!' he cried, and poor Ellen, who refused, sweetly, her orangeade, pushed her wristwatch higher up her plump and freckled arm and was squinting at the time in the flickering light.

'Alexi! It's terribly late,' she said. 'When you have taken that we really must all be going. We have to drop Dirk off at the Ledra Palace, he has an early "call" for "wardrobe" in the morning, and they're "shooting" over at Kithryia. Have I got that right, Dirk?'

I nodded cheerfully. 'Absolutely right. You've got the film jargon off perfectly.'

Just as I sat down, Minouschkin was at my side.

'I sit down, yes, please? You find chair for Minouschkin?'

There was a sudden frozen silence at the table. Not a breath was drawn. From Ellen's face it was clear that someone must have defecated before her. Alexi was agonized.

'No. Sorry. No. I'm with friends, old friends from London. We would like to be on our own, thank you.' I was quite firm.

Minouschkin set her glass deliberately down on the table, dragged an empty chair from the next table, and sat down. 'So! Now I sitting down. How are you, friends-from-London? Well, I hope? Do you like here? Is amusing, no? I like very much here, is very typical.'

I leant across to her. 'Will you please leave the table? I want to be alone.'

'Is like missis Garbo, this boy. But look! Is not so! You do not like to be alone.' She held up a small pink plastic disc swinging on a bit of elastic. It had No. 7 engraved on it in blue. She laughed merrily. I looked blank, Alexi was ashen, Ellen had turned to stone. 'You see? I am No. 7. Only for you. So now you will not be alone.'

Ellen quietly reached for her stole draped behind her chair, started to arrange it casually round her shoulders. 'Alexi! Come away, dear, leave the children on their own. Dirk will easily get himself a taxi, there's a rank opposite. *What* a happy evening!' She had risen majestically, her tapestry evening bag swinging on a gilt chain. I started to rise, but she waved me back. 'Don't budge! Alexi? Come along.' She pushed herself away from the table, a large tug moving out of harbour, nudging lightly at the jetty. I sat down in torture. I had no idea what had exactly happened. Minouschkin was combing her hair roughly with her fingers, staring blankly into the distance.

Alexi turned to get his jacket from the back of his chair. 'You have got into a terrible mess! Terrible! Know what you have done?' He was hissing at me. I bridled furiously. 'No! I bloody well don't know what I have done! What *have* I done, for God's sake?'

He started to thrust his arms blindly into his sleeves, his face was very close, arms waving about like an octopus, I could smell the Scotch and garlic on his breath. 'You've bought yourself a whore! That's what you have done! And you do not invite a whore to my wife's table! You do not bring a whore to *my* table!'

Minouschkin, perfectly well aware of the conversation, suddenly said, 'You give Minouschkin money, please? I will buy some cigarettes.'

I watched her elegant, tiny, trim little body in her neat black dress push her way through the crowd. Alexi had risen, was buttoning his dinner jacket. 'Maybe I should have warned you about this place. The "other" attractions?'

I stood up to face him. 'You bloody well should. How was I to know? I only touched down on your ruddy island a couple of days ago.' Alexi shrugged sadly. 'Well, how could I have *bought* the girl? I said ten words to her, at the bar.'

Alexi now looked as sad as a Basset hound. 'My fault. I will explain to Ellen for you. No insult? Eh?'

I was boiling. 'Of course no insult! God no . . .'

Wearily he reached across the table for his unfinished Scotch, drained the glass, wiped his lips. 'You'll have to get yourself out of this. It'll cost you. But I know Mikki Popadopolous, he's a toughie. We live here, I don't want trouble. Here comes your bargain . . .' He turned and stumbled away as Minouschkin arrived, a real glass of champagne in her hand now, a packet of Marlborough in the other. She sat down in Ellen's chair. 'They have gone away? They were very rude to you, you know?'

'Minouschkin, do I get any change from the money for the cigarettes?'

She had ripped off the cellophane, was tapping a cigarette into her hand. 'Oh no! Is expensive. Champagne! And cigarettes. Thank you. You are kind boy. If you are with the movie people you can afford. No? Are rich in Hollywood, it's true?'

I gave in dejectedly. 'It's true. It is true about you? What my friend said?'

She blew a feather of smoke into the air, picked a piece of tobacco from her lip. 'I am *dancer*! I dancer very good. I do speciality here, at midnight. I am with "Mordeci's Pretty Misses", MPM. We go everywhere – Beirut, Alexandria, Cairo. We are very popular, you see. I am specialist. I do "Ingrid Bergman", all blond.'

'I see. And where do you live? Here in Nicosia?'

'No, no! I am from Beirut. Is in Lebanon. Is very beautiful, you know this place?' She sipped her drink as elegantly and modestly as a sparrow.

I leant across to her, forcing her to look directly at me. 'Then why do you do this job here? Why do you work this place? For Mikki?'

She looked away swiftly, then started her story. It was like a wind-up gramophone, the patter was so easy for her. She had told her 'story' so many times.

Granny was dying of cancer in Beirut. Right? Cancer was expensive, doctors, bills, hospitals, so she had taken up dancing. Well. And from dancing one thing leads to another. Especially in the Lebanon. She had to work to pay for granny's illness.

I had made a few dire scripts for Rank, and this measured up to some of them. 'I'd like another Scotch, as you have your champagne. Can you do that flicking-finger business again? Get me a drink?' She was looking slightly bewildered. I picked up the little pink disc with No. 7 on it. 'Another Scotch? Okay?'

She nodded and flicked her fingers across to Mikki far away at the bar. 'He will bring. Is done. You speak funny to me . . . My grandmama was from Paris, you know? So we all speak French. Everyone in Beirut speaks French. But *her* mother was from Russia!'

'Was she a princess? Or a duchess?'

Minouschkin looked rather vague. 'A princess! *Of course!* A princess. From St Petersburg. Was in Paris for her honeymoon when was the Revolution! Was most fortunate.'

I agreed warmly; most fortunate. She looked so vulnerable, so anxious that her impossible story had not been accepted that I dare not suggest to her that she probably came from Upper Norwood, had had a couple of months' training in 'dance and movement', or whatever, at some kind of Alvilda-Bancroft's-School-of-Dancing in Cricklewood, and that her real name was probably Doreen Seal. But I simply funked it. That was, anyway, my idea of the script. Not hers.

And then Mikki, himself, was at the table with a large and very strong Scotch. I gave Minouschkin my wallet: she riffled through it like a Rhesus monkey looking for fleas: 'You pay for me, okay?' I said. 'But remember I have to pay for No. 7. You'll know how much.'

Mikki was standing pretending he was not waiting. Scratching his bottom. 'Have plenty! Plenty money, quite plenty.' She gave money over to Mikki who pointedly looked at his watch, then at her, and went away.

She raised her glass to me. '*Probablement, c'est le vrai champagne? Eh? Il est* très *gentil, Mikki . . .*' She nodded her head wisely.

'It should be real,' I said. 'You've landed your fish; that's your reward.'

She scowled, set the glass down. 'You speak ugly things to me.' I shrugged, choked on my first gulp of Scotch which was as brown as mahogany varnish, and tasted the same. 'We go to No. 7? But no kinky. I not do kinky. You want to kinky you ask Patricia, Sheila, they very good.'

The thought of 'doing kinky' with either a Sheila or a Patricia was so awful that my expression of horror made her laugh.

'You funny! You *really* sweet. I make lovely for you. Okay? You will see.'

Perhaps she *didn't* come from Upper Norwood . . .

She ruffled my hair, kissed my nose, slid off the nasty little bumpy bed and took a washbag over to the enamel bidet behind a tatty floral screen in the corner. I lay prone for a moment, looked at my watch, stared up at the ceiling: cracks, and damp rings where a bath above had overflowed once. Or something.

'That took twenty-five minutes! Do you realize that? Minouschkin? *Twenty-five* sodding little minutes!'

She was sloshing about with water. 'What is wrong? I will be *late*, I am speciality, I tell you!'

I got up and pulled on my socks. 'I know, you told me. Twenty-five minutes!'

She suddenly called out that if I wanted to make pee-pee the lavatory was down the corridor, otherwise to use the basin. It was in a corner, a damp towel hanging by it, a dead spider and an old bottle of TCP, half full, on the side. There were two taps, one hot, one cold, they were both Shanks Ltd. They lied. There was no hot. A trickle of rusty cold. There was a clatter as she shoved the floral screen apart and came into the room, absurdly covering her sex with the squashed washbag.

'Twenty-five minutes, I mean, you *do* realize that?'

She rubbed her shoulders dry with a grubby vest. 'You are angry with Minouschkin? I not like that. To be angry. Why?'

I ran more water into the basin, gathered up my crushed trousers and shirt. 'Not angry. Just pissed off, that's all. Two minutes with a tuppenny tin of Vaseline would have amounted to the same thing. But cheaper. You cheated me.'

She took no notice, was pulling about in a tumble of old clothes hanging on a sagging wire. 'You *are* angry! I do not understand this "Vaseline". I must be ready soon, I tell you.'

We were both, by this time, dressing. She had slipped on a green spangled G-string, then a number of off-white petticoats, fitted herself into a pink- and gold-sequined bra, pushing her tiny breasts (the size and splendour of a pair of press studs) into the wired cups, then white socks, black patent ankle-straps, and on top of this muddle a blue and white gingham dress with a thousand buttons down the front and a dainty white collar, rather like the ones Hollywood stars wore to play 'plain secretary' parts. Crowning this she pulled on a blond wig with a side parting. She asked me to help her with the buttons. There were so many. I had never had to button a speciality into her costume before, but I was learning, feverishly, that there was a first time for everything. She combed the wig. I pulled on my shirt, rolled my tie into a ball and pocketed it.

She then took a sort of Homburg hat with a broad black ribbon round the crown, set it carefully on the wig, and holding out a drab raincoat she asked me to help her into it while she pulled on a pair of cotton gloves. She nodded her thanks, said how pretty I looked in my blazer and I'd forgotten my shoes. Which I had. She tipped the hat to an angle, examined herself in the bit of mirror at the end of the bed, tied the belt of her raincoat and asked me if I thought she looked like Ingrid Bergman. I said no. Not remotely. She looked crestfallen, asked if I had actually seen *Casablanca*. I said I had and that she still didn't look like Ingrid Bergman. She shrugged and said, oh well! everyone else did, and anyway she had a prettier nose, and giving me a swift peck of a kiss, she left the room, the pink disc left dangling from the keyhole, and we walked down tiled stairs to the bar-room. On a tiny stage, set beside the bar proper, a 'Patricia' and probably 'Sheila' were finishing off their routine dressed only in mortar boards, thigh boots, and various strategic tassels, wagging whips, to huge applause and a rumpty-tumpty piano reprise of 'Tea for Two' (for some reason), then they pranced off cracking the air suggestively.

I leant up against the far wall by the door, under a photograph of a cleric in a chimneypot hat (he would shortly become the President, but not quite yet). The piano, and now some light drums, started in with 'As Time Goes By' and I stiffened with shock. In a rumble of masculine approval, scattered applause, and a pink follow-spot, Minouschkin, my own paid-for-Minouschkin from Beirut via Upper Norwood, came slinking on to the stage, all five foot two of her, hands thrust into her pockets. Then, very slowly, she began to remove the gloves, finger by finger, dropping the tatty cotton to the stage. She milked it, then the hat was removed, discarded with elegant disdain, the belt of the raincoat, then the coat itself. The patent leather shoes were unstrapped after a good deal of effort, entailing a wild flurry and display of the white petticoats (there were three I recall) and as each item hit the stage the drum beat: 'You must remember this . . .' *Bong*. 'A kiss is just a kiss . . .' *Bong!* And so on. And then she stood quite still, bent to yank off her socks, more flurry, threw them to a gaggle of youths, and was alone, simple, peasanty, in her gingham dress. Then came all the buttons. These took ages to undo and drove the crowd to an uneasy anxiety. The bra was flung into their midst, the petticoats slipped off one by one, and finally she stood just as I had last seen her up in room No. 7, only with a green G-string sparkling. She slid her fingers under the strings, waggled her hips, spun and winked wantonly. It was about as stimulating as watching tin rust.

I turned and walked out into the street and the sharp March air, hailed a sleeping taxi-driver from the rank. I reckoned wryly that Ellen and Alexi had unwittingly given me a real sight of the un-touristy 'old Cyprus'. Then I vaguely thought about the bottle of TCP on the washbasin. Too late now. I opened my wallet, flicked through it. The driver asked if I needed the light on? But I said no, thanks, I can see all I need to see.

She had left me exactly, and precisely, enough for my fare. With a bit over for a tip.

The front door was suddenly flung wide open with the most fearful crash, rattling all the panes of glass in its not over-substantial frame and sending the corgis, who had both been dozing comfort-ably at my feet, into an explosion of hysteria. They raced out into the Big Hall, colliding together down at the door with furious snarls, leaving me to follow them.

At the far end, by the now wide-open door, the late May sunlight streaking across the red tiles, stood my house guest, as I expected. Furious, in a fluster of rage-almost-contained, she chucked her bag, her coat, a bundle of papers, letters, a script in a blue cover and a bunch of wilting spring flowers on to the long pine console table and glared up at me.

'My dear! I am in a rage! Uncle, dear, a *rage*! Get me a Scotch!' Her fair hair was flying about her head like Medusa's, the sun glancing through the silent cloud, eyes blazing, standing tall, glowing, powerful, furious: a veritable Valkyrie ready to take on allcomers and demolish the whole crowd in Valhalla.

Here, in all her splendour and glory, was the *real* Ingrid Bergman. I went down the steps into Lower Hall while the dogs, swift to recognize a furious friend rather than a vicious killer, skittered out into the yard and chased, uselessly, after the receding taxi, now easing down the long drive, scattering gravel.

'We have a problem, Tante?' I began to gather up her scattered goods.

'We *have* a problem! And you better be very strong tonight. *We have a problem*. Put those damn flowers in water, they'll die ... some fan ...' She began to take off her coral pink jacket. 'You know? He's a fool, that man. He's certifiable. Redgrave! He was so unutterably rude to me, you can't imagine!'

I took the coral jacket. 'Michael was? To you? Surely not, Tante ...'

She ran fingers through her windblown hair. '*To me*. Before the *entire* cast, Fay [Compton], Daniel [Massey], Max [Adrian], the technicians and so on. It was humiliating! I nearly struck him, Uncle. Very nearly, and I'm a big girl.' And then she saw my faint glint of concern and laughed her huge laugh which always illuminated everything near her, her eyes glowing with joy. 'Don't look so worried! *Of course* I didn't. I said *nearly*. My Scotch ...' She followed me up the hall to the Yellow Study (yellow because of its carpet, curtains and ancient pine panelling).

'So it's been another bad rehearsal?'

She crashed down into the low Regency sofa. 'Bad! It was awful, awful. I am expiring with fury. My drink, don't forget my drink!'

I gave her a large glass of J&B. My own glass was already charged, beside my chair. The dogs came wandering back, breathless, tongues lolling, sniffed around, settled down on their bellies with their legs in the shot-rabbit position, and dozed. Ingrid had a good swig.

'So what happened? Why so awful?'

She leant forward, cradling her glass in both hands. 'He said, my dear, in front of the *entire* cast, that I didn't know my words after three weeks' rehearsals! And that he would have to postpone the opening for a week! Until I *did* know them!' She was so beautiful, so radiant in her outrage, that I longed to kiss her.

Instead, I said, 'And *do* you know your words?'

She poked about in the ice cubes in her glass with a long finger, sucked it. 'No,' she said shortly.

I sat down in my chair. 'Well, perhaps he had a point? He might be right, Tante?' (She was 'Tante' because she called me 'Uncle'.) 'It's his show. He is producing, directing, playing. His production. And you are curtain up in less than a week. Point?'

She pulled a foot out of one loafer. 'Before the *entire* cast! As if I was an extra! Bloody Michael Redgrave! I was so furious. *His* show indeed. Hah! Maybe it is. But *I* am his star! They'll come to see me. *Me!* He's mad today! Completely mad! Shaking. To say all that before the entire cast, the technicians. He is not professional, not at all! It has never happened to me in all my career. All my years in Hollywood, no one has ever behaved like that to me. Selznick, Curtiz, Fleming. Never. And I came over here to do his silly play as a favour! Because he was opening a new theatre! Ouf!'

I began to try and ease her down from her peak of fury to a plateau of reason. You *could*, actually, reason with Ingrid. If you were very patient. 'Dearest Tante, if he is right, and you admit that you do not know your words –'

But she held up her glass like the Liberty torch. 'I don't know *all* my words. I am not word-perfect. Okay. That's *very* different. How I work. I will be, I will be. I always am finally. But I like to feel easy with my words, free. I do not like to be in the straitjacket of exactness! Exactly what the author wrote? I like to make the lines *mine*! He is a classical actor – Shakespeare, Chekhov, all that stuff, reverence for the sacred words. Well. I'm a movie actress, and he'll have to put up with it. He should never have asked me. Got that Claire Bloom, or someone, Edith Evans! I don't know, one of those intellectual women who play classics. I have been a movie actress for most of my life, I have made many movies, nearly all crap, but I make them good! They know that. That's why he asked me here! For his box office, not Turgenev!'

I shifted in my chair. She sat back, pulling at a long piece of her hair.

'Tante, dear. This is *right*. It *is* Turgenev: *A Month in the Country*, a classic of classic theatre. It is not something from the Hollywood sludge-pile. It's real and important.'

She pulled off the other loafer, threw it to the floor. 'Well, it's a bore! A bore! Pompous idiot! *"We'll have to postpone if you don't know your responsibilities to the theatre!"* My God! I really could have killed him!'

At that exact moment, with a light tap on the door, Fred, my parlourman, stuck a worried little head into the room. 'Will you be three for dinner, sir? Or is Mr Gareth back from town?' I said three, and he pointed out with exquisite politeness that the front door was wide open, perhaps he should close it? The evenings got chilly?

Ingrid said, in a gentle voice used only for calming frightened horses, 'I am guilty, Fred dear. I left it open, I am *so* sorry. I quite lost my temper.'

Fred bobbed his head. 'Very good, Madam,' he said and hurried away.

It was Fred who, two years earlier, on a dark November evening, had burst breathless into the room half-dressed, braces flying, appalled at having to interrupt, but did I know that 'they' had killed the President? He'd just heard it on the television while he was changing for dinner. I told him to tell the kitchen, and switched on my set. That was a very bad evening indeed. This evening was easy stuff. Only a mental assassination and that wasn't *very* serious.

Ingrid said, 'Poor Fred! I make extra work for them all, they are so sweet to me. But that idiot Michael Redgrave! Did you see him in that film about some schoolmaster? Something to do with Browning. A book?' I said that I had. '*That's* who he is! Cold, cruel. Maybe, sometimes, he *can* be quite sweet. But, *sure*, I *know* my *responsibilities*, so this evening after dinner, even before, we'll go into the drawing-room, you and I, no dogs, no Scotch, no interruptions, and you will take me through bloody Turgenev until I am absolutely word perfect. Right?'

I said right, and then she asked, with a quick worried smile, if I had an early call in the morning at the studios. I replied no, I was presently going down to the vegetable garden 'to pick some mint for dinner', and she roared with laughter. 'Picking mint' had become our euphemism for being out of work. We 'picked mint' instead. Simply because, every evening when I was not on a film, I'd go down to the garden and pick a bunch for cook. So, that evening, we beat the hell out of Turgenev instead. And the next day she was practically word-perfect and best-girl-in-the-school. Thank God.

I had been asked, some months earlier, to contribute, in some way, to the brave new theatre building presently in Guildford. I'd agreed to read the Prologue by Christopher Fry, written especially for the occasion, and then later it was found that there were no suitable hotels in the area, at that time, to accommodate the demands of a great Hollywood star. Could I *possibly* help out? So I made the guest room and bathroom over to Miss Bergman, installed a new telephone line (she was *never* off it) and gave her my parlourmaid, Hilda, as her personal maid. Which was fine by Hilda. She didn't have to wait at table, only looked after Ingrid – her washing, ironing and her rooms – and walked about in a wreath of golden light so happy was she. (Her salary, of course, was increased comfortably.) Ingrid was pretty demanding in a careless way.

So we all settled down to a new kind of routine, Forwood, his son Gareth and I. It was a glorious spring and a radiant summer. It was perhaps the happiest time I can ever remember at Nore, and Nore was crammed with happy memories, anyway for me.

Nore stood, still stands, on the side of a hill high above the Sussex weald. It's been there since the thirteenth century, when John Atte Nore farmed it, and perhaps even longer because on my deeds there was apparently a well in a corner of the dining-room. Not just any old well, but a Roman well. And the great slab-stones, polished like glass all around it, might easily have concealed such a magic as a Roman well.

From the windows, from Ingrid's windows certainly, one looked down over meadows and thickets with no sign of roof, nor chimney, and far away, on the smudge line of the Downs, marking the horizon, you could sometimes see the gold glint of sun on the sea at Shoreham Gap. This was Ingrid's greatest delight. The silence, the cooing of the collared doves gently interrupting, or the wind sighing and riffling through the solitary Scots pine tilted, by past gales, standing at a brave angle at the edge of the ha-ha: it was a healing place.

Sometimes, early in the mornings, I'd see her walking up from the fishponds and azalea garden in the Long Walk, under the candled chestnut trees, bare feet, hair loose, moving her hands about, nodding her head, doing her lines. Sometimes she would stop, throw wide her arms, and embrace the whole world, her head back in silent laughter.

One morning I caught her wearing a blue gingham frock, a

simple sleeveless thing, her hair in an Alice band, and I ran down the lawns to tell her that, once long ago, I had seen a girl in Cyprus in a nightclub trying to do something astonishing.

She correctly looked amazed. 'Do *what?*' she said.

'She did a sort of terrible striptease! As you in *Casablanca*.'

Her amazement was glorious to see. She had never done a strip-tease in *Casablanca*. She was, as always, absolutely literal and fairly humourless. Facts were facts and she did *not* do a striptease, and when I told her about the gingham dress she practically barked a laugh of surprise. 'It was *nonsense*, I suppose? I didn't wear gingham in the film. I had quite pretty things,' she said. 'People are really so crazy for that silly film, we didn't even know how it would all end, and Bogart spent all his time in his dressing-room. I hardly met him. Madness. And this girl does a striptease to all that, in Cyprus?'

I took her hand and we walked up to the house. Dress rehearsal day.

She shrugged. 'I hope to God they fixed the wig, and that Michael knows *his* lines.'

It was a very typical technical dress rehearsal. I went over to the theatre with Claudette Colbert, Ingrid's most loved old friend, and Kay Brown, her agent from New York. We all sat about the empty theatre watching the scene changes and hoping that what we could presently hear we would *not* hear tomorrow evening. Rough, technical, it was.

The sets were tatty, and wobbled about, Ingrid's wig looked like a tea cosy, but apart from that, and a dullish sort of production generally – no *spark* of anything new – it was fairly smooth, and Ingrid's very handsome and successful husband, Lars Schmidt, flew over from Paris and joined us. He was (is) an impresario himself, so we were with a knowledgeable, if rather chastened, professional opinion. It wasn't what you might call a 'magical experience' in the theatre. But, in fairness, it was only the technical rehearsal, and as such passed off 'all right'.

Ingrid was at least word-perfect, and very effective in the sad bits. Afterwards we all went back to Nore, and in the car, a silence, apart from the 'clock ticking', so to speak, I heard Claudette say in a tiny voice, 'Vivien Leigh, perhaps?' wistfully, and we didn't speak again until the corgis met us with their familiar screams of hysteria. Lars and Ingrid, thankfully in a separate car, arrived later and we talked the night away discussing how to get it all really a great deal better. But we all knew, sadly, that discussing would not make much difference, if any at all, and so that was that.

A couple of days later Pia, Ingrid's eldest daughter, arrived to stay from America, and Nore started to rustle with suppressed excitement and worry. The play had two previews, so everyone slept during the day, or else Ingrid would walk alone, as I had seen her, barefoot down the lawns saying Turgenev's lines. Then, on the second of June, a golden day of real English glory, the play opened to a packed, excited house, full of chums from all over the world, fans and curious-surprise-us press. Fortunately they had never twigged where Ingrid was stowed away, so she had managed to stay unmolested all the time.

A very dressy first night. Forwood in his diary says:

The Oliviers, the Cassons, Duchess of Westminster and half Social London present. D. speaks the prologue quite beautifully. The performance of the play is pretty average, I fear. Ingrid is ravishing looking but gives a somewhat patchy performance, but at least she is a *star* which this production badly, badly needs. Reception after, very glittering, well done but boring. All come home and have a *very* long drink.

The reviews the next morning weren't better than that. Some were worse, frankly, and Lars tried to hide a couple quickly under their bed. But she found them, and read them in silence, showing no feeling. Not her style to show disappointment. They all went off after an early lunch and the house tried to settle down again. It had been pretty exhausting for everyone.

Lars and Pia went their ways, Ingrid stayed on at Nore for the run. Our greatest worry was that she would decide to take it into town. She really wasn't very good on the stage, electrifying as Ingrid Bergman, but not really much cop as Turgenev's Natalya Petrovna. She was so beautiful to look at in the role that often tears sprang unbidden to one's eyes. One's heart, however, beat perfectly normally. And that was not perhaps quite enough.

Her beauty was incandescent. Not the incandescence of neon, but that of the old gas-mantle: soft, living, gentle, kind, but at the same time it could be cold, harsh even, or glow gently rose-coloured. It was not brash, not painted, never at all garish or artificial. How you saw it depended entirely on you. It was life-enriching, and she always seemed quite unaware that she possessed it. But, even so, I didn't think it could be enough to save Turgenev from a pretty dire translation and production.

However, after evenings of furious debate in the Yellow Study, and after a lot of Scotch was consumed and hours were wasted, and after I had, quite literally, gone on my knees and begged her *not* to take it in to town and risk what I felt would be certain humiliation critically, and a very long separation from Lars (which he was aware of and dreaded), she went up to her bed and the next morning I found a little note under an empty bottle of Scotch standing on the long pine console table in the Big Hall. 'Dearest Uncle, I have been a very naughty girl. I have gone against your advice. I am taking Natalya to the West End.' Which she did, filling the enormous Cambridge Theatre for eight months solid.

Lars always said that he would never have been able to face the future if he had not allowed her to play, for the first time, in the West End. So she did. And was triumphant, and people fought to see her.

So, in spite of wobbling sets, fairly awful playing all around her, and a terrible wig that always looked like a tea-cosy, 'Tante' won the day. A star blazed. She was right, or at least her bravery was right, and I was woefully wrong. The journey on which she set out from the River Wey in Guildford, and her long walks declaiming her lines along the deep Chestnut Walk at Nore, brought her indeed to clamorous success in the West End. It also marked, sadly, the start of the end of her marriage to Lars.

On the last morning of her stay at Nore (she was catching the midday flight to Paris) we walked, arm in arm, up across the lawns to the house. Behind us the big field was bumpy with plump sheep, the corgis chased imagined rabbits in the hedgerow. She turned and looked back, down over the fields and woods to Shoreham Gap. It was a day of brilliance, gold and blue, still, sweet. Little cherubim of clouds drifted across to the Downs.

'You are so *lucky*! So *clever*!' she said. 'You have made a perfect place to live, *in* a perfect place. Put your roots down, haven't you? That is why it is so secure, so calm, so healing. Oh! . . .' – and she opened her arms to embrace the whole Sussex Weald – '. . . Oh, I shall *miss* you! I shall *miss* you! But I will be back! Be sure, my dear place, I'll be back.' And turning, she took my arm, and we walked on up.

In her own book she has said that her 'entire stay at Guildford was one of the happiest times of my life'. I really imagine that it was; it seemed, apart from ill-fitting wigs and a certain problem with her lines, to be a time of joy and of radiance. Perhaps she brought that along with her? Maybe the days, the sun, the light, the sweetness, and the cooing of the collared doves were all *her* inventions? I would not be in the least surprised. To have someone as glorious as Tante in one's house altered, completely, the meanings of the words 'joy' and 'delight'. Everything, and everyone, shone and beamed, because of her.

It was probably for that reason that I didn't tell her, at any time, that there would be no return to Nore. It was on the market, and while she was fretting and fussing about the 'dreadful Redgrave' and the misery of 'classical theatre', all sorts of strange people were trailing through the house with an eye to buying it.

But I was in no hurry, and she would be far away and gone before the house was finally sold, and I trailed off to a dreary rented house in Ladbroke Grove, with a large garden for the dogs, while I made up my mind to try and leave England, the Shoreham Gap notwithstanding, for good.

We saw each other again, in diverse places, in Paris, in Rome, in New York, in Hollywood, and we wrote constantly: scribbles on her part between takes, longer letters from me because, usually, I had more time on my hands. She envied me, she always said, that I had 'thrown away safety' and could work with 'giants', like Visconti, Resnais, Cukor, with whom she longed to work. But, she insisted, they never asked her because she was considered a ' "Hollywood product". They don't think that I can really *act*! I *must* show them!'

Once, after a wretched lunch at Choisel (their house outside Paris), which she had cooked so badly that Lars stuck a basalt piece of Angkor Vat in the middle of the dish as a gentle rebuff, she admitted, wistfully, that her dream was to live in a small apartment somewhere over a giant supermarket which had a six-screen cinema, so that she could go to a movie every day and eat something 'easy, frozen': 'Just you put in the oven for thirty minutes? So *easy!*' She overlooked the beauty of the park in which their house at Choisel was set, and apparently had forgotten her wild embrace of the Sussex Weald. She was, and remained always, an actress. It was her life-blood, her air, her nourishment. But she was a splendid mother and, when she remembered to forget her work, a good and loyal wife. And above all, perhaps most of all, she was fun, honest, funny without knowing it, a blinding star and blazingly lovely. You can't do much better than that. That adds up to being Ingrid.

She got to work with her 'arty director' eventually in Ingmar Bergman. It was not, perhaps, the happiest experience. She was frightened, uncertain, and behaved badly. But she knew it. And was forgiven, and *Autumn Sonata* was not a giant success. She realized she would have been wiser to stay, as she put it, 'in that bloody Hollywood mould. If you are Cary Grant you play Cary Grant, if you are Ingrid Bergman you play Ingrid Bergman. They have no imagination! None! They say it is what the public want!' They certainly didn't want a dying, ageing Swedish musician. But she was proud to have done it.

And then the bad times came, as they so often seem to do, and the rumours flew around like disturbed bats and were alarming and, wretchedly, correct. I telephoned her one morning when I was over in London. She had moved into a 'very pretty flat, near the river, in Chelsea, come and see me? I'm dying, Uncle, but I won't infect you!'

I had a slight cold, I warned her, and she sighed. 'What I have is bad enough, I don't want any more, you know? The cure is worse than the disease. Much worse. Don't come near me.'

Now, so many years later, whenever I hear 'As Time Goes By' I always remember her immediately, up-front, and, in a blur of nostalgia and distance, a silly, sad, funny little creature called Minouschkin.

Memory, like love, hurts.

A Girl I Knew

Capucine is the French word for 'nasturtium'. It can also be a religious order. In Italian it means a type of coffee drink, 'cappuccino'. Capucine was also the name of the woman I came to love. Properly love, I mean.

She had been a model for Coco Chanel and Hubert Givenchy and others and, one day, got the 'big break' that girls like her always dream about. She was seen dining with a girlfriend (after a punishing day of fittings) at Fouquette by one of the most powerful (and quite the most civilized, handsomest and kindest) Hollywood moguls, named Charles Feldman. He sent his card across to her table and suggested that one day she might like to go to Hollywood and if so this is who he was and where he lived. They nodded politely at each other across the restaurant and, after some weeks of careful deliberation, Capucine decided tht she *might* quite like to go. She had had rather enough of Paris and fittings and the hassle and worry of the fashion world. So off she went. Without a single word of English, no knowledge of the cinema or theatre, nothing apart from the catwalks at Chanel and Givenchy (among others), very unsure of herself, lacking in self-confidence, but determined to try Hollywood before she got too old.

For three years Mr Feldman kept her under wraps. She was taught English, which she came to speak fluently, albeit with a frightful American accent (unless she was careful), and the grooming for world stardom commenced. She was protected at all times, hardly ever seen about. Fascinating and improbable stories developed around this amazing French import who was to be groomed by Columbia Studios to take over from Ingrid Bergman and Katharine Hepburn.

A patrician beauty, remote, elegant, imported. That might have been absolutely splendid except that she couldn't act. Acting classes occupied her days as much as hairdressers and English teachers. The latter did a better job. However, a subject was finally chosen for her in which to make her debut. It was of course tremendously secret. It was also going to be a colossal dollar investment, with vast locations, cast and music everywhere. A super-colossal entrance for Capucine. And I was chosen to be her first leading man. I accepted because I had managed to avoid Hollywood for years, but felt that with such a huge financial carrot I'd be idiotic to refuse yet again. So I crossed the Atlantic on the *Mauretania*. First class.

She was presented to me rather as if she was the latest jewel in the harem and I was the Crown Prince of all Arabia. It was a sumptuous, discreet, very, very distinguished supper party given to mark this special occasion: *Strictly No Press*. She was brought across the room to me, trembling becomingly, by Mr Feldman as if he were handing me a casket of pearls. Which in a way he was – his *personal* casket of pearls. I remember that she was a vision in black net, lavish with black sequins, and one diamond brooch which blazed like a searchlight. A silence fell as 'Liszt' (that's who I was going to play) and the love of his life 'Carolyne zu Sayn-Wittgenstein' (a Princess to boot) were formally introduced. I had a vague suspicion that someone might break a bottle of champagne over one or other of us, or throw showers of rose petals about. Fortunately no one did.

It was all impossibly formal Hollywood and altogether rather alarming. At the elegant table, dressed all about with an abundance of silver and orchids and where each guest was a member of the cinematic *Almanac de Gotha*, I was, mercifully, placed beside Capucine. I say mercifully because she carried a pretty little black lace fan which was to prove very useful in the sticky night air of a crowded room crammed with far too many candles. I was certain that a combination of terror, bewilderment and incipient hysteria (the laughing kind) might bring me to the point of collapse. However, the fan was at hand, and I could see that she needed it too, so I just hissed, 'Fan away for *God's* sake!' and, really, that's how we first met. We were most oddly seated together in the centre of the long table, like a bride and groom at some oriental wedding. Which, although I was blithely unaware at the time, was exactly what the studio had in mind. It was all a dreadful part of the plan to launch their newest acquisition. I asked her if she was called 'Mademoiselle' or 'Madame' Capucine and she said, wearily, that she was simply 'Capucine'. Nothing else. That had been her name when she was a model. She couldn't remember who pinned it on her – Chanel, Givenchy or just a publicist somewhere – but that was her name and the studio was presently in a terrible fuss, wondering if they should leave it at that, just a single name, or invent something glamorous and French instead for the world press release.

Her real name, she said, was Germaine Lefebvre and she came from a small town on the Loire called Saumur, like one of her patrons, Coco Chanel. She murmured that she was getting just a bit fed up being in Hollywood, hidden under wraps, and was quite homesick for Saumur and would like to return there. I pointed out that she probably could in about a year's time, when we had finished the film, but until then what did she want me to call her? Germaine or Capucine? After all, we'd be glued to each other for months. It was essential not to make an error too soon. She said, cautiously, looking over her wagging little fan, that her 'best' friends called her just 'Cap'. The caution in her voice was because she was not at all certain, at that point, that I would ever become a 'friend' let alone 'best', but she was giving it an uncertain try, so I ploughed on as usual and called her a mix of Cap and Capucine. It seemed to satisfy her and she disdainfully sipped a spoonful of soup like a glorious bird of paradise. She was without doubt the most beautiful creature I had ever seen. She already knocked spots off Pinewood stock or any single member of the charm school ladies.

That part they had done tremendously well. She would have quite astonished Paris (and did, eventually). It was just the name which stuck in my craw; I thought it was rather arrogant to use a single name at this stage in her career. Like Garbo but without the experience. She agreed but said that she had no power, and nor did Mr Feldman really, so she let it ride. The only thing was that she detested being called 'Cappie' by the friendly, democratic Americans. She thought that was the pits. However, she belonged to the studio now. They had invested a fortune in her grooming and in the sly, and careful, little slips to the press, to the awful Hedda Hopper and to the terrifying Louella Parsons, both of whom, in those days, could destroy a player instantly with a single small paragraph.

Columbia were trading on her breeding, her elegance and her classical beauty, so that she would eventually hit the screens as real as a fully grown princess. After all, they'd never know the difference in Idaho or North Platt, Nebraska. But 'Germaine Lefebvre' wouldn't quite do for a princess. 'Capucine' was better, aristocratic and more mysterious. They thought. Tough luck for Cap, who, anyway, hated her real name, which she said was about the same as Phyllis Jones in English. And that about wound up that evening's conversation. We never mentioned the subject of our film. I remember that we were both too frightened to. If we mentioned it, it would mean that it was *definitely* going into production. Something which we both had come to dread for very different reasons. *I* dreaded it because, on the *Mauretania*, I had read it from cover to cover in mounting horror. It was perfectly dreadful. I had only given it a quick glance in England, reeled at a few things and had thought, 'Well, I can rewrite that . . .' and took it for granted that I would be able to. But lying on my bunk in the cabin on A-Deck I realized that I simply couldn't rewrite the *entire* script, which was the only possible thing to do with it.

'How in God's name can I say these terrible words! How can I say, "Pray for me, mother!"' I moaned.

'With utter conviction,' said Forwood.

'And there are eighty-five minutes of music at the piano with the camera *on my hands*! It's all marked down here. The *Campanella* . . . the 'Moonlight' . . . the *Hungarian Rhapsody* . . . what do I *do*!'

'Learn it . . .'

I did. I am not going into the film. I have written about that at great length already. Enough now to say that from the initial shock of discovering someone so distant and beautiful, I progressed quite quickly to finding out that we got on tremendously well together.

Capucine needed me as a deflection from her own (very real) terrors, *I* needed her for her companionship and encouragement while I practised, night and day I might add, at the dummy piano. From a brother-and-sister act it sort of grew, over a period of some time, into being 'in love'. Anyway on *my* part. It seemed, at first, to be wiser to remain silent on this score. After all, she did belong to Mr Feldman, and he had given her to me because he trusted me. Otherwise Franz Liszt would have been played by a Hollywood hero who would have been better for the posters, if not the part, and greatly boosted the unknown girl from the Loire. In any case, she lived with, *and* loved Mr Feldman. That anyone could see. She had moved into his splendid house on one of those canyons that run through Beverly Hills. His attractive, and very understanding, wife of some years packed her bags and moved back to New York (which she much preferred anyway), with the utmost grace and sweetness. No acrimony. The Feldmans were far too sophisticated and worldly for that. So Cap became, in a very short time, the chatelaine of the Feldman residence, and was one of the very few unmarried women to achieve such status. No one, at that time in Hollywood, lived with a man *openly* in his house unmarried to him. It was, after all, well over thirty years ago. Things are quite different today.

Apart from her astonishing beauty, Capucine was a marvellous cook and a born housewife and hostess. Very shortly the Feldman residence again became a centre for the top Hollywood people. They have a vicious class system in that town – the British can't begin to compete. A-lists, B-lists and C-lists, and then Unacceptable or Unknown. Cap ran a salon for Feldman on the top rank of the A-circuit. She was as useful to him as he was useful to her. He adored her, full stop. He was a generous and gracious man. He was also *my* agent. There was simply nothing that I could do about anything. Anyway, the falling in love bit didn't start right away – I did have breathing space – and Capucine, although warm, affectionate, trusting and utterly devoted to me, gave me no particular sign that I meant any more to her than the person who was simply her leading man. It helped being European, speaking French and being able to make her laugh.

So I struggled along with dummy keyboards and the ghastly 'Hi! Franz . . . this is my friend Schubert. We're thinking of going to Majorca to see Chopin and George. You want to come along?' It really was as dire as that. I never made any headway with the script, but started to break through on the music, Cap sitting close by, doing her tapestry, day after day when she was not required to be working at something. It was soothing, and she would be as excited as me when I actually played more than six bars in sync. From time to time members of the studio, the Really Big Guys, paid me a visit in my cell at Columbia, cigars in mouth, suits shining, aftershave loitering. They patted my back and kissed Cap,

and said that my costumes had cost over a million dollars, did I
know that? And that the velvets all came from Paris, France, and
we were about to make the first really colossal classical musical film
since the war. 'Just you wait till you hit the screens of the world,
next year. They will just tear you apart! They'll *love* you!'

They didn't.

We reached our first location, Schönbrunn Palace in Vienna, in
May: lilac everywhere, thousands of extras gowned in satins and
laces all waiting to see the adored Franz Liszt – 'He was bigger than
Presley, this guy,' someone said – but *their* Liszt, in the shape of me,
was shaking with terror, and in agony in the too-tight costume, the
pink-dyed (for the Technicolor camera) hair, back-combed like a
mad rocking horse.

It was all quite chaotic and, eventually, disastrous. The extras
playing members of the court, dukes and princes, dressed in huge
costumes in blazing arc-lights, grew hotter and crosser the more
errors I made in playing the 'Moonlight' and by the tenth take they
were ready to mutiny. This didn't go towards helping me one jot.
We had a foul director who screamed at everyone and shook
Capucine like a dead cat, roaring at her to relax. She was as rigid as
a totem pole, her upper lip twitching with abject terror like a
rabbit scenting danger, eyes bulging, two front teeth glittering.
Nothing would make her relax, and certainly shouting at her in a
mixture of Hungarian and Hollywood wasn't going to help. We
ploughed on miserably and then most fortunately, three weeks into
the disaster, the director died of a heart attack in his bed. He was
found there with a distraught extra whose husband was a famous
lawyer in the City and who had been playing in the film 'for fun'.
She had her fun and she was smuggled out of the place, and they
shoved the director down to the back regions of the hotel in a
laundry basket to avoid any scandal.

For a few days we all prayed that the film would be cancelled, but almost as soon as our first director was shipped out by KLM as freight (no other airline would ship a coffin in the tourist season), our new director, the ebullient George Cukor, flew in to take over. He was a Studio man and he came to rescue Columbia from disaster. On we went, less appallingly, but just as wretchedly. It is the most awful feeling to know that you have backed a loser long before it has got anywhere near the winning post. Somehow the awfulness of it all released something in Capucine which I had always secretly thought really *did* exist. She was, under her regality, a perfectly ordinary, funny and adorable creature. Barefoot we ran through the grasses of alpine meadows, climbed trees, paddled in ice-cold crystal streams. We went to Mayerling and saw the secret grave of Marie Vetsera, ate enormous plates of *Bratwurst* and *Rösti* in country inns shaded by ancient chestnut trees. We went to the Opera, dined at Sacher, and I fell stupidly more and more in love with her and grew more and more despairing when I remembered, as I constantly did, my generous agent, Mr Feldman.

If anyone observed these slightly idiotic actions – the alpine meadows and bare feet, the romance of the Opera (fearfully dull most of the time, frankly), the suppers at Sacher – all these simple manifestations of childish affection was *all* they ever saw: affection, properly shown by a player to his leading lady. No more. I didn't, for example, 'declare' myself, as they say, at any time. I merely enjoyed the enormous pleasure which I found in her company. The falling in love part, easily achieved in any romantically minded creature, and that I was, came gradually. It started to glimmer inside, grew stronger as time went on and started to glow fairly brightly by the end of the location on the film. I didn't think that anyone at all noticed anything untoward.

As far as Capucine was concerned it would appear that there was nothing anyway. As far as *her* behaviour would indicate we were just great friends. I caused no ripples, she enjoyed being with me and admired my desperate efforts to master Franz Liszt's music. Not easy. To try and master the *part* was utterly impossible. It was appallingly written, but with Cukor's assistance and a biography of the man by Sacheverell Sitwell we managed to at least make him reasonably human, or human enough. The music was something else and my efforts to master it were deserving of every compliment I got. Cap found it all irresistible. If I was gradually slipping down the slippery slope of affection towards something much deeper, her compassion and pride for, and in, me whenever I conquered some hideous peak only added sticks to my modestly smouldering bonfire. I really didn't think that anyone noticed, and no one did.

Apart from Mr Feldman. He was aware all the time of my growing affection. Never let it show. I was quite unaware of his covert observation and battled on with various pianos and promised myself that as soon as we finished in Europe and went back to Los Angeles for all the studio work I would let myself luxuriate in this developing love, which had rather startled me. I had not expected this to happen. When I mentioned it very, very casually to Forwood he appeared rather uninterested and far more concerned with the withholding-tax forms he had before him. He merely suggested, mildly, that it might be wiser *not* to muddy this particular pond.

So I kept my own counsel and went on behaving excruciatingly correctly – for the time being. We trailed Europe from opera house to concert hall, from piano to piano, from Vienna to Eisenstadt, Munich to Bayreuth, and finally, with a bravura performance of *Rondo capriccio*, at which the entire orchestra were moved to rise and applaud me (to my intense secret gratification), the location work was almost finished and Hollywood loomed. I suppose I should have noticed that Mr Feldman was more in evidence towards the end of the shoot? He arrived from Paris one day and was around for the rest of the time. Genial, affectionate, praising me lavishly, and taking us all out to flamboyant and expensive dinners after work, and Cap back to his suite at the evening's end. Of course that was absolutely as it should be. He had arranged this enormous film all around her, so he had every right to behave as if he was her proprietor. I may have ached miserably inside, but I never let anything show. I decided to bide my time.

I was, at that point, easing myself out of the chrysalis cover of youth. Being thirty-eight cast a slight shadow of discomfort across my path. Shortly, all too soon, I'd *really* be middle-aged. Forty beckoned and could not be denied for very long. So. Anyway. Back to Los Angeles and the studio work ... This was not as dreadful as the piano stuff: at least I was on familiar ground with ghastly dialogue. I was rather more exercised by getting back to *Europe* and sanity once again. Preferably *with* Capucine. But I'd have to be absolutely certain that she was ready to accommodate such a brazen idea.

I never, as it happened, had the chance to begin setting it before her. That was brilliantly taken care of for me by outside sources. Montgomery Clift suddenly, and tragically, failed his insurance medical. His film, to be shot in Italy with Ava Gardner and Joseph Cotton and Vittorio de Sica, was in jeopardy until Mr Feldman slipped swiftly into the game and to my amazement I found myself on a Comet jet bound for Rome before I could actually finish removing Franz Liszt's make-up. Without doing more than lifting a couple of telephones Mr Feldman had severed my immediate chances of pinching his girl. He'd got me out of the way. I was breathless at the speed of it, and only later dimly aware of what had exactly happened. I was far more interested, at the time, by the chance of a second Hollywood film on the heels of the first. And the dollars. But this second 'epic' gradually turned out to be as disastrous as the first. Perhaps Montgomery Clift's failure to pass his insurance medical was the best thing that could have happened to him. At least he wasn't there when the eggs got thrown.

But one good thing was being in Italy, and being in Rome after some long haul in Sicily on cold and filthy locations. We dragged on so long that it inevitably meant that we would spend Christmas in the Holy City. To that end I invited a large party to come out and spend the holiday with me. Everyone accepted. Ma and Pa came over, Glynis Johns, Forwood's ex-wife, caught a flight from Sydney, where she had been filming *The Sundowners*, Irene Howard, Leslie's sister, perhaps my oldest friend at the time and casting director for MGM in the UK, brought Forwood's son Gareth out. He was striding with great self-confidence into adolescence at fourteen. And I asked Cap to come over, and Cap, to my stupefaction and joy, accepted!

I booked everyone into the Hassler Hotel, and tore off to the airport to meet them from their various flights. My heart was lark-gay. I was without doubt making a dreadful film again but the money was good and I had not the least compunction in spending it. The very fact that Cap had agreed to join me for Christmas in Rome was overwhelming. My impatience to see her at the airport was, I imagine, rather absurd to watch. I paced about, waiting for the flight to arrive from New York, up on the observation roof like the proverbial expectant father. I waved frantically at all the windows as the great plane turned into its taxiing position and inched into its place, and felt certain that Cap must have seen me and was waving back. A whole four days in Rome together was almost more than I could believe. Which was just as well. I saw her step down the long, metal staircase, recognized the glorious mink trailing to the ground, and the white chiffon head scarf she always wore to protect her hair. We waved and then my smile must have slipped like melting butter when, elegant and lithe, Mr Feldman followed her down carrying his Louis Vuitton briefcase.

On Christmas Eve (except for Mr Feldman who had appoint-ments at Cinecittà) we all went over to the Forum ruins and walked in the scarlet and vermilion glow of the fading sun. Starlings screamed and wheeled above the dome of St Peter's and our shadows were thrown long and slender across the ancient stones. Under a vast umbrella pine I found a bit of fallen column and pulled Cap down beside me and told her how terribly happy I had been to know that she was coming over, that I had missed her dreadfully. She said wasn't it marvellous that Mr Feldman (only she called him Charley) had so much work to do in Paris and in Rome? That she had fittings with Givenchy for her new film, and that this Christmas just fitted in marvellously well for them both. And I said I *had* hoped she'd come alone, and she said, very gaily, to remember that she *never* travelled alone if she could avoid it, and that now she had to go and buy a Christmas present, for some wretched niece or nephew in Saumur, and I said, 'Cap, you do know, don't you, that I love you? I love you *very* much,' and she kissed my cheek and said she loved me very much too! Why did I think that she'd come all the way to Rome when her duties lay in Paris and Saumur if she didn't love me? Then she got up, because it was getting cold, and she had to get to via Condotti before the shops closed, and she also wanted to go to Gucci and would I take her, and how adorable my parents were, and I said quite calmly and firmly, 'I do *love* you, you know? I really *do*. Very, very much.'

Then she stopped – suddenly – and put a hand on my arm. Behind us the rest of the Christmas party were straggling down to the Forum gates. 'Don't get *heavy*, darling Black Prince [a silly name she used privately between us. I never knew why]. Don't spoil this Christmas. I wanted to come over *so* much.'

So I accepted that, swallowed pride and the holiday was fun, expensive, and glamorous. She and I were never, however, to be alone again, and the day after Christmas (slightly the worse for wear from a long and exotic dinner party at the Hostaria del'Orso and later in the nightclub on the roof called Cabala) they flew off to Paris. That was that. So much for a romantic Roman idyll. The next time we were to meet was at the première of Liszt in London.

I went off to New York after the Italian film was finished, and was given my very first taste of what was then called 'total exposure'. This was to flog the film, the Liszt bio, to the American press. Cap remained, at studio's command, in Los Angeles. In Forwood's meticulous diary it seems amazing that I survived: crossed on the *Flandre*, and was instantly into eleven days of press, one interview every half-hour, including TV and radio. No one mentioned the film much. Enough to say that my 'amazing virtuosity' on the keyboard was 'just breathtaking' and how long had I been a 'piano player'?

Capucine, safely in Los Angeles, sent me a pound jar of caviar and telephoned every evening to find out how things were going. I didn't dare say that no one had voiced a single opinion on our great epic. But she was a bit cast down. No one had, apparently, suggested that I had been playing opposite the 'new' Hepburn or Bergman either. So far, anyway. However, the film opened at Radio City Music Hall in New York, a vast cathedral of a place, and broke *all* records for seven weeks. I was, by that time, happily on my way back to Europe on the *Queen Mary* so I was unaware of our possible success. Just as well. The moment the film went nationwide it died the death.

The studio prayed for better luck in Europe. To that end Cap and I were forced into an ambiguous situation. She had been sent over to assist after the drubbing from the US critics. Alarm bells were ringing at Columbia. The new Hepburn or Bergman was chucked into the fight. The invitation to the London press 'joined us together' by printing on the embossed invitation cards, 'Capucine and Dirk Invite You To . . .' The sheer tackiness of this appalled us both, but to my shame I did not protest. The reception was held at the Connaught, and we brushed all intimate and probing questions briskly aside. It was thoroughly disagreeable.

Cap came down to stay with me in the country. The world press came too: set up tents down the drive, camped in the orchards, rigged platforms in the trees. We spent the whole of two agonizing days locked in the house, curtains drawn (Cap's bedroom looked down the drive out across the park) with the telephone answered only by my valiant press officer, Theo Cowan, or a furious Forwood. We decided, or it was decided *for* us, that we would give *one* interview and *one* photograph to *one* publication. Forwood made the announcement from the front steps and said later that he felt that he had faced Madame Defarge and all her dreadful knitters, who shouted obscenities and shook their fists. Finally we chose *Jours de France*. Cap said it was a pleasant 'family paper': 'Old women in spa towns buy it. It is not malicious.' We spent a miserable afternoon being interviewed (ambiguously all the time) and photographed, locked together in loving embrace in the conservatory, where, I was assured, the 'light was better'. Nearly everyone else, thankfully, packed up and left. *One* paper had now the right to publish, no one else wanted the stuff. After all it wasn't a serial killing. We had not even said that we loved each other.

The première itself was dreadful: crowds and cameras and yelling voices. Cap kept telling everyone who tried to say some tiny polite thing that she, personally, *hated* the film and *looked* hideous, and moaned away until Miss Garland (ever there at the moment of desperate need) dragged her off to the ladies' room and told her, 'Bloody shut up, Cap! Just say thank you! Don't insult people who are *trying* to help you!' A lesson well learned which Cap, more or less, took note of. After all the press and the fuss and awfulness we went back to the country again and tried to relax.

Sitting under a great oak one afternoon, I declared myself fully. I said how much I loved her, how well we got on together, how I was getting on in age and that it was about time I started a family and that I wanted her to share that with me. Would she?

She was wonderfully kind, gentle, kissed me, but said, 'No.' She wanted a career in the movies. Charley had spent fortunes on her training and she liked living the life she lived. Rather more to the point, although she did love me as a friend, a *close* friend, she loved Charles more. Anyway, she didn't at all want children and certainly didn't want to live in Europe again. She missed the sun, the fun, the ocean, her friends (or Charley's friends, really) and I must be sensible and please not be hurt? She adored 'her BP' (shorthand for Black Prince) but not enough to give up her budding career on which so many people had worked so hard. I understood all this, of course I did. I even forbore to tell her that however hard she worked she'd never be any good as an actress. But that was far too below the belt. So I just nodded. But I assume that I looked pretty glum, because after dinner one evening, sitting round the fire in the drawing-room, Ma half asleep in her big chair, ringed hands to her face (I can see her now), Cap lying on the floor covered in the dogs, who loved her, Pa pouring himself a final drink, and me changing records (*Oliver* had opened and Cap was overwhelmed by it), Forwood hunched up at a drum table with maps of Spain, where we would next be working, quite suddenly Pa set his glass down and knelt beside Cap, lovely and glowing in a long pink, silk taffeta housecoat by the fire. Placing his hands together like some elderly monk he said, very sweetly, with a glint of laughter in his voice, 'Please take pity on an old man, Cap, would you be adorable enough to put us *all* out of our misery and marry my son? It really would give *me* the greatest pleasure?'

Cap sat up, reached for his face and pulled his head to hers. '*Darling* Ulric. Thank you, thank you, you make me *very* proud, but we have talked about all this, BP and I, and there is nothing left to say.'

So he smiled, got to his feet and picked up his drink. 'Did my best, my dear,' he said to me. 'Never been on my knees to a woman in my life before. I did try!' He went back to his chair.

'Never been on his knees to me,' said Ma stretching her arms and yawning gently. 'I didn't know he could get down on them . . . Ulric! You might have got stuck down there. You really are mad! Well . . . it's been a *lovely* time, and now I'm off to bed.' She rose and smoothed her skirt. 'He's reading *Trilby* to me. It's really rather boring. So I fall asleep quite quickly. Come along Ulric, darling. Come along. Up to *Trilby*.'

I can remember a sudden clutter of moving figures: Cap got up, the dogs danced round her, Forwood folded his maps. Ma was standing at the door, admiring, as she had done all the week, the jewels which Cap had brought her from Chanel in Paris, faux pearls, and emeralds like gob-stoppers. I put another small log on the fire, I suppose as a deliberate signal of defiance. I wasn't about to be sent to bed. Forwood called the dogs and went off to the kennels, I called goodnight to Ma and Cap who had started, chattering cheerfully, into the hall. Pa drained his glass and set it down. 'Don't drink too much, my dear. You've got a busy day ahead, and don't be *too* miserable.' He unexpectedly ruffled my hair, and said goodnight. I sat by the fire, watching the small log flame and crackle.

Later up in my room, on my bed, I pressed the button on the intercom to Cap's room, a floor below me, and hoped I'd not wakened her? No. She had just taken a shower, was I all right? I told her that I was, and that I understood everything, that I had closed the door on this little episode. Firmly. She was quite free. There was a silence from her end. She didn't know about my corridor-and-door theory, and then she laughed, a sighing sort of laugh, and said that she'd see me in the morning. We said good-night. It was all very civilized. She left for Los Angeles the next afternoon, with six copies of *Oliver* in her luggage.

We never lost touch with each other. Charley shoved her into one picture after another, with a range of pretty varied roles. Well, they would have been varied except that they were always Cap: different hair, wig, clothes, leading men – always just the glittering, aloof, cool Capucine. But she seemed happy with her lot, apart from an occasional telephone call when she seemed to be desperately cast down and unhappy, and loathed Hollywood and everyone in the place, and she was hopelessly depressed in the sunshine. I put this down to the fact that whatever film she was working on was 'difficult', or that she had had a bust-up with a director, or her co-star. I did not know, and did not for some time, that the depression was clinical and would get worse.

As suddenly as switching off the lamps, the sun left the sky for her. The chill winds started and Charley died of cancer. She nursed him bravely and devotedly but her career died at the same time. Without Charley to boost her, without his flair, determination and power, Capucine was absolutely lost. She was made instantly redundant by the cruelty of his death.

He had been a wise and prudent man: I was ashamed, when I knew, how often I had misjudged him. At some time he had bought a luxurious flat at the top of a very expensive block of flats in Lausanne for her. He had furnished it, slung in a brace of Renoir drawings and a couple of other Impressionists, and Capucine was to retire there. He knew, only too well, that Hollywood would turn its back on her the very moment he was no longer there to take care of her. And it did. Her name was no longer the familiar 'Cappie', which she so hated being called, but had easily, and viciously, turned into '*Crap*ucine'.

So to Lausanne she came. We met from time to time at things like the Cannes Film Festival, when, in the early days of her 'widowhood', she was still welcomed and moved smoothly up the enormous staircase in quite glorious robes especially designed for her by Givenchy. She was at all times beautifully dressed and coiffured, mostly in honey, caramel and cream colours. We met sometimes in Paris, dined at Laurent and walked arm in arm, laughing and singing, in the evening lights of the Champs-Elysées. I, by this time, had moved to France to live. She approved the move and the house, and came and cooked and lazed, and read, and one wet afternoon started on a book she had decided to write about the Brontë sisters.

Then there was a long silence. She was suddenly in Kenya living on some safari park. Not alone. But we never discussed it, and from time to time I'd get a postcard of a giraffe, or a lion, and 'love, Cap' on the other side. The close bonds slipped a bit, and dwindled. For a time, some years, we almost lost touch, except for the fact that we never *really* did. Suddenly, from some odd place, Berlin, Klosters, Bath, Nairobi, she would telephone and we'd slip easily back into familiarity. And then, almost without my being really aware, she had gone again. I never asked where. I wrote occasionally to the address in Lausanne, and then someone at dinner one night in Monte Carlo (where else, pray?) said that she was living in England. With a young nobleman. Apparently she was completely besotted with him, and was now marching over Scottish moors, loading guns, and stamping about in wellingtons at local meets.

I have never, at any time, asked my friends with whom they lived, where they lived, who was close, who was distant. Never asking questions of that sort, or ever offering advice unless asked, or passing on scraps from other people's gossip or 'secret knowledge' (a disgraceful habit) has, I think, kept me all the friends I love. The others don't matter. It is a very useful thing to remember. Keep a still tongue, an alert ear, a vigilant eye, you won't go terribly wrong. So with Cap. I never asked her about anyone or anything important, after the death of Charley. The muck chucked up by the tide of malice and jealousy all around her brought all manner of bits and pieces to my beach. There would be long silent gaps. Sometimes it seemed that there never had been a Cap. But eventually she telephoned again. She'd been ill, in some clinic, and how was I? I said well, writing my books, and living on leek and potato soup because it was cheap and nourishing, easy to make, and I was running short of cash. She laughed wryly (she actually didn't laugh much – rather Bergmanish in this *one* respect) and said so was she. She had spent far too much money and did I know there was a marvellous leek and potato packet soup made by Knorr in Switzerland? She would send me some packets to try. Trivia. No serious news, apart from the clinic trips which, I had now come to realize, meant something serious and mental, not physical. She had been warned off her nobleman, by his family, and, it was rumoured, by others higher up. She was liked well enough, but was not considered quite suitable for the young heir. So she went back to Lausanne, a small gold and enamel Peter Rabbit brooch as her only apparent love-token.

Oh, there *was* work. Bits and pieces in German or Italian TV. She had small parts in one or two films where all she was required to do was look remote and goddess-like. She did this awfully well. And then alas the desperate signs appeared. She came more and more often to the festivals: Cannes to Berlin, Venice, with a girlfriend 'minder' and a good wardrobe, desperately determined to be seen around by producers and directors and photographers. This is where ultimate madness lies. No one *ever* gets work from those encounters, and being simply 'seen' in the company of some other star or on someone's yacht has no effect whatever. She had to face it, trying hard to refuse the unthinkable, that she was out of the running. No one remembered her really, and what they did remember did not particularly tempt them to employ her. The appalling fact remained that, however glorious her looks, she simply didn't 'come off the screen', and if you don't do that you might just as well hang up your dancing shoes and become a dentist. There is no hope whatsoever for a *failed* film star in the vicious throat-cutting world of international cinema. You either have it, or you've had it. Cap had had it.

I never, at any time, saw her apartment. I was, somehow, never invited to. But others, who had, said it was very chic, rather more Beverly Hills than Lausanne, yellow and white, the blinds constantly drawn against the sun so that it should not harm her skin and cause wrinkles – her greatest terror. Her friends appeared to be all middle-aged princesses or contessas fallen on hard times living in modest hotels or pensions. She seldom, if ever, ventured out, because she was passionate about her cats, Abyssinian and Burmese, who appeared to run her life. And so it would appear that Charley's Girl was now almost a recluse, surrounded by faux formality at the bridge table, and hustled about by a covey of cats.

I was once in Geneva on business from Paris, called her, offered to drive round the lake to Lausanne and see her. She accepted, reluctantly I felt, but said that we could meet at a certain place she knew well. Not the apartment. The place was a small park under chestnut and beech trees sticking out at the edge of the lake. Perfectly pretty, swans bobbing about, a distant motorboat, water lapping, the white gravel crunching underfoot. We sat on two iron park chairs and discussed absolutely nothing. I couldn't get through the thick layers of protective varnish which she had now applied all over. She almost shone with it, and was brittle if I edged towards any personal remarks. Suddenly she put her hands to her face, drew her skin up towards her temples and, with that gesture, said that she was going into a clinic again, shortly, which was why she had agreed to see me, but not this time for her 'depressions'. I understood instantly what she meant. She folded her hands in her lap and said it was time I left . . . was I staying at the Richemond? She thought the Richemond was rather tacky now . . . I walked back to my hired car, waiting discreetly in the distance. She refused a lift back, said that the walk was just what she wanted. She was finished with her book on the Brontës, and was quite pleased with it, it had been well received by those privileged to read the MS. We kissed briefly, she waved just a finger flick and turned away. I went round the lake, back to Geneva in the gathering gloom of the afternoon, profoundly sad. Things were obviously not at all good.

It was some months later, months of total silence, that the postman came up the track with a packet which was too large for the mail-box. It had a Lausanne, Suisse, postmark. Inside the buff paper and hard cardboard, two large photographic portraits were sandwiched. There was no message, no covering note. Nothing. They were two angles of someone I had never seen before. A gaunt, tremendously elegant and sophisticated woman of about sixty something, maybe seventy? Perhaps a millionaire banker's wife? A vastly rich widow of some oil king? Someone who had obviously spent a small fortune on having her entire face remodelled. Her throat betrayed the real creature below the taut, gleaming, unlined face above. It was Capucine. I just got it in the eyes. All else had been demolished, smoothed out. I tore them up and took them down to the bonfire, I didn't even want them in the waste-bin in my office. I felt that it was essential that, as with the Hindu in India, they should be cast upon logs, doused with paraffin, and burned. I didn't acknowledge them either. I could have said nothing which could have helped her, nothing which would not have betrayed my utter horror at what she had done. Two other friends (we had very few mutual ones) had got the buff-envelope treatment, and had been equally shattered. We agreed to say nothing. It had all been a terrible strain for her and she had, once more, been admitted to the clinic. Lausanne is almost as full of clinics as Blackpool is of sticky pink rock. I didn't know, ever, which one she was attending. I didn't ask. I was not supposed to ask or know.

A silence descended for a time. An obliterating silence, lasting longer than others and during which I was forced to leave France after two decades and return to the UK to restart, a bit late, my life. I sent a change of address card, but there was no response. Still silence, until, late one afternoon, my unfamiliar telephone breached it with a cautious voice from Paris to say that she was dead. Fastidious to the very end, and secretive, she had apparently fed her cats, locked the flat, climbed to the roof and, typically of her, to avoid any distress to others, jumped out over the back of the block and landed sprawled among the dustbins. A slight figure, beautifully groomed and dressed for a lazy stroll round the lake in the afternoon sunshine. She wasn't discovered apparently until later, when the flies had started on her lips.

A Family Matter

I walked down through the high summer grasses, now sun-scorched and seeding, the dogs capering beside me. Any excuse, even in the heat, for a walk. They leapt the terraces in great bounds, I, less agile now that I was over fifty, walked cautiously, the sun hot on my back. Pa was sitting far down at the bottom terrace on a fallen tree-trunk, under a very old olive. He was hatless, secure in the speckled shade it cast, his easel before him held firm on the uneven land by a couple of large boulders. He was totally absorbed and only looked up when I shouted at one of the dogs who was racing along the link-fence of the boundary shrieking at a flock of goats tonkling up to the Chapel Hill.

'Pa! I've come to collect you. Lunchtime. And your beer is ready and cool.'

He didn't look up, went on dabbing, making little swoops at the board before him.

'Your beer, Pa, is cooling!'

He looked up quickly, fearful of missing a change of light which he had just seen. 'Coming,' he called. 'I don't like *cold* beer. Not in the fridge, is it?'

I had reached his side by now and squatted down on a large log beside him. 'Hey! That's good. Really terribly good. You are one cypress short. Intentional?'

He wiped his brush on a bit of cloth. 'Gets in the way. Artist's licence. You probably don't remember the things that old Turner got up to?'

'No. It's not in the fridge, your beer. I know about that. It's out,

167

under the vine, by the time we get there it'll be lukewarm. Just as you like it.'

'No need to be sarcastic, my dear.'

'I wasn't. Really. Making an observation. I am afraid I've come a cropper with Ma.'

He groaned, dipped his brush, mixed a colour on his palette. 'O Lor' . . . what now? You are a devil. Snapping at her again?'

'No, I wasn't. She said I'd watered her bottle of wine . . . she was really angry.'

One of the dogs came slouching up from the road, gasping, sides pumping like bellows, foam flecks dribbling from his open mouth. He crashed with a groan at Pa's side, in the shade.

'Hello, dog . . . silly idiot racing about in this heat! And *had* you?' He was bending closer to the canvas, painting in some tiny detail.

'Had I what? Oh. Watered the bottle? Yes. Yes I had. Henri and I took off the tinfoil, uncorked it carefully, emptied out a full glass and shoved in some water. And did it all up again. It was undetectable.'

Pa leant back, squinting through half-closed eyes at his work. 'Except to your mother. I'll bet she was furious. I would have been, I can tell you.' He unscrewed his eyes, smiled cheerfully.

'Henri was dreadfully shocked, frowning, lips pursed, hands thrust into his apron pocket. Didn't approve of me tampering with wine. Even that muck from Mini-Market.'

Pa started to screw a cap on a tube of paint. 'You own up?'

I pulled a piece of wild fennel and chewed the stalk. 'No. I didn't. Got her another bottle. She can tell. What's the point?'

He slung the capped tube into his box, leant back and surveyed his painting. 'Oh, she can tell, your mother. She can tell. I don't think this is too bad, do you? I've got the other cypress in . . . one, two, three, four. The fifth just doesn't work from this angle, covers the bedroom window.'

'It's better without,' I said. 'It would be a bit "looming" other-wise . . . We'd better go up and face the wrath of God. She's got a decent bottle, well, a *full* bottle, and it's a cold lunch, home-cured ham, tomato and a potato salad. Marie's potato salad, full of chives and garlic, and a touch of white wine.'

My father groaned. 'Oh Lor' . . . don't mention white wine. I presume you gave her white? You know the effect red has on her?' He started collecting together his brushes, washing them out in his little bottle of turps, tying them into a bundle with a strip of cotton cloth.

'Yes. She has her white. It's really pretty hopeless . . .'

'What is?'

'Trying to . . . you know . . . ease the intake. She'll have the lot during lunch.'

'She will. She's got a liver like an Aegean sponge. Absorb a gallon of petrol.'

'It's pretty useless. Trying to cut it down, I do try . . . hence today's row.'

He strapped up his box slowly. 'I've been trying for fifty years, my dear. I shouldn't worry. You'll never stop her. Her father was the same, rather more extreme. He lost his positions everywhere . . . lost his family too, come to that. Will you hold this, carefully? While I fold the easel?' He handed me, reverently, the brilliant rectangle of painted board. I held it between my open palms.

'I don't know how you have put up with it for so long. Was it always like that?'

'Seemed jollier, somehow, when we were young. She was only nineteen, you know . . . it didn't really dawn on me for a month or two. Then I realized that she was, what we now would call "ill". And ill, my dear, she has remained. But she's been a wonderful mother to you all. Can't say other than that. All right . . .' He looked vaguely round the patch in which he had been sitting, patted his pockets. 'Got everything. Let's go up, and face the furies . . .' And we started cautiously up the hill.

As I walked up, slowly, to keep pace with him, he told me how their marriage had almost foundered after four months, but mainly because of a lack of money on his part they stayed together, otherwise he'd have divorced her. He said they had 'managed', just 'muddled through'. He was quite calm about it, just felt I perhaps ought to know. I was so shattered that I asked no more questions and turned the conversation to tell him that I had seen Capucine a few days before he and Ma had arrived.

'You remember Cap? Who I mean?'

'Of *course* I remember Cap, what a funny fellow you are! Saw her here, did you?'

'Down for the Cannes Film Festival. We dined together one evening.'

He stooped to throw a stick for the dogs. 'How did she look? Wearing well? Should do with those bones of hers, marvellous cheekbones.'

I said that she was getting older, we all were, or some other bit of triviality. What I did not say was that, sadly, Cap had become rather tedious, she wasn't very interested in anything but herself and how she looked. And then, as we neared the top terrace, I thought how silly it was to avoid the truth. He'd been blindingly frank with me about his marriage and we were shortly to face my mother. Apart from the wine she was in some degree of discomfort if not pain, having fallen and dislocated her shoulder one evening three weeks earlier. She might not enjoy discussions about Capucine, for she was altogether as self-centred herself, so I suddenly told him truthfully just how boring she had become.

He laughed.

'You have to remember that she was, once, the centre of great attention. When it starts to slip away there is a feeling of quiet desperation. Your Ma suffered it when she gave up the stage, married me and had you and became a mother-figure. Can't altogether blame them. It's a terrible sort of eclipse.'

We had reached the level of the terrace by the water trough. Ma was sitting at the table, her back to us, looking at a *Vanity Fair* album, her arm in a green silk sling I'd bought her from Dior.

Pa set his box and easel down by the concrete basin, dipped his hands into the clear water, flapped them in the warm air to dry. 'I did rather hope that might have been a good thing for you. For you both. Pity. I'd quite like to have had grandchildren.'

'But you have! Elizabeth and Gareth have given you grand-children, you are quite overwhelmed with them!'

He grinned at me, found his handkerchief and wiped his hand. 'Not *yours*. You are the eldest. First born. Never mind.'

We walked slowly towards the lunch table and the motionless figure of my mother.

'Cap wanted to be a movie star, and I wouldn't go to live in Los Angeles. It wouldn't have worked out, Pa. Really. And now, she really is pretty maddening . . . lives in Lausanne with a litter of exotic cats. Plays bridge. It really *wouldn't* have worked, Pa. I know that now. I'm far too selfish, and, frankly, so was she.'

We reached the table and Ma closed the *Vanity Fair* book. Her bottle of wine stood in a basin full of melting ice.

'Who was "frankly" what?' she said, a bright smile on her lips now that we were all together round the table.

'I was talking to Pa about Capucine . . . do you remember Cap? Years ago?'

She waved her cigarette dismissively before my face. 'Silly boy! Of *course* I remember darling Cap. I wear all those lovely bits of jewellery she brought me. The pearls and things. Where is she now?'

And I flogged through the story about dining with her, saying only that she was very well and making a film in Berlin. Ma lost interest almost instantly and asked Pa how his painting was coming on and the conversation became fairly general until Henri arrived with Pa's beer and fussed about hoping it was not too cold for him.

I went down to the Long Room and got a beer for myself from the bar cupboard. As I came up the steps to the terrace, pouring my beer carefully, Ma suddenly said, 'No one seems to have watered *your* drinks, I see. *I* was presented with a bottle of white wine, Ulric, which had been so well watered I could have used it for the windowboxes.'

I sat down at the table. 'Nonsense! One error in a batch of a dozen. It does happen sometimes.'

'It does happen,' said Ma smiling, 'when my son's little fingers get near the bottle! Don't think I'm not aware that you tried to water my wine! I know! I'm not that stupid. I didn't come up the Clyde on a bicycle! You *deliberately* took off the paper and the cork and diluted it. You did! Say you did!'

'Yes, I did.'

There was a moment of utter silence. Somewhere up the hill a dog started barking; my two, at my feet, looked up and bristled.

Ma bristled too. 'Why, pray? Why do something filthy like that?'

I braced myself and said, 'Ma, I think you drink a bit too much, it's not good for you and it makes you miserable.'

She opened her eyes wide in theatrical disbelief. 'I do *not* drink too much ... it does not make me miserable! In the clinic they were sweet to me, I had a half-bottle of wine with lunch and another with my dinner, and they wouldn't have done that if it was bad for me, *or* if it made me miserable! It's the only thing that keeps me sane! *You* try being buried alive in that bloody little house on the common. You try that!'

Pa lifted a gentle hand. 'Margaret dear, it's not that bad, come along now.' His voice was patient and soft.

Ma hit the table top with her good hand. 'I will not be accused of drinking too much! How the hell do you know? You live up here on your mountain in the sun. I'm stuck on a dreary common in Sussex, *and* I can't drive!'

Pa sighed, topped up his glass. Henri arrived and served lunch. The salads and the ham and '*de la moutarde*' for Pa. '*Anglaise!*' he said as if he was producing a rabbit from a hat. I was feeling wretched, decided to play it as cool as possible, and served everyone. Forwood had gone into Nice to see the finance people. Perhaps if he'd been present this ugly little scene would not have taken place. He'd have smoothed things over.

'I do *not* drink too much!' my mother rumbled on like a latent volcano.

I snapped. 'You *do*, Ma. You have always drunk too much. When we were children, Elizabeth and I, we used to call your voice, when you had had a few, "Mummy's Voice". We knew something was wrong, we dreaded it. I still do, frankly, and you have to stop otherwise you'll get terribly ill . . . and it makes you miserable and depressed.'

She flashed a look of fury at me. 'Because I *am* depressed! I *am* depressed! So would you be, isolated, stuck in the country. *And* up here, what is there for me to do? No one comes here, do they? I'm locked away in purdah on this hillside.'

I took her angry hand, she pulled it away roughly. 'You were in the clinic, Ma . . . for three weeks. Because you fell down the stairs . . .'

She finished her glass of wine, poured another. 'And I was far happier there, in that clinic. The nurses were sweet, they laughed at all my stories, and the doctors were adorable. *They* found me amusing, not dull, not drunk! I miss them all. Darling nurses.'

'Well, go *back*! Go back to the bloody clinic! I've done everything

173

I possibly can to make this unfortunate holiday as happy as possible for you, and all you can do is complain. You *do* drink too much, I hate it when you do, and you cause us all terrible embarrassments. So now you know!'

I had gone far over the top, but my anger really had burst the dyke of patience. There was the anguished silence again, just the sound of knife and fork on china as Pa carefully, daintily almost, cut his ham and spread his mustard. I cut Ma's ham for her, into small pieces, asked her if she wanted one of the salads?

She shook her head, her hand clenched in a fist. 'Ulric! Are you going to let him say terrible things to me like that? Not even defend me? *Defend* me, Ulric!'

He placed his knife carefully on the side of his plate, chewed for a moment, took up his beer glass and said, in the gentlest voice possible, 'I can't defend you, my dear. I've been longing to say that to you for fifty years. He's right. You do drink too much . . . it is clinical depression, *I* know that, but that doesn't make anything any better. I know you won't eat anything, but do try? All that white wine on an empty stomach? It won't help you, darling . . . have a little ham? Or the potato salad? Mop it up?'

But she didn't move, and we sat in throbbing silence.

'And I embarrass you all?'

Pa cut a sliver of fat from the edge of his ham. 'You have. In the past. You have. I'm pretty used to it by now. It's just in front of strangers that it gets a bit difficult. Sometimes . . .'

Ma took a good slug of her wine, set the glass down unsteadily. 'I see. Well, thank you both for telling me. I embarrass you both. How absolutely charming.' And she started to weep, half laughing through her tears. 'God Almighty!' she said.

The next time I was beside Pa, he was at my left shoulder, packed away in his simple oak coffin. I was curious to see how 'little' he seemed in the aisle of the village church. Whitewashed walls, smell of bees-wax polish, varnish, candle grease. There was a modest wreath from Ma on the coffin. He had been carried down by friends with whom he had often taken a drink in the Griffin or the King's Head. Ma was at home, Cilla, my sister-in-law, and Forwood sitting with her.

Elizabeth, in a black wide-brimmed hat which hid her grief to some extent, Gareth and I, plus the few members of Pa's office at *The Times*, those who remained and who had come to pay their respects, sat in the crowded pews. He was very popular in the area. I suppose it surprised me a little, and moved me very much. I was dry-eyed. Elizabeth was in front of me, bowed, Gareth at my side. We sat mute with sadness and that swelling sense of loss which arrives.

After the moment of dust to dust, and the wretched trek up the path past the scattered wreaths, through the November mist, we all went back to the cottage where Ma was holding a dignified court. In black, hair perfectly groomed, wonderfully relaxed and welcom-ing, greeting everyone who arrived with evident pleasure and a wide and grateful smile. She really did behave very well. It had been sudden, a massive heart attack in bed while he was reading. She had 'forgotten' the doctor's number. He lived in the village (they were all old friends). It was over an hour before he was summoned. I never quite forgave that. But on that particular day, at that particular moment, I had to do my head of family part in his place. Ma could never, under any circumstances, have played that role, the matriarch, not her scene. But she was admirable, and there was as much laughter, of a discreet kind, in that little drawing-room as there ever had been, as if everyone had delightedly come down to Sussex just for cocktails.

I had managed to get over on the night ferry from Paris, where I was filming. I had to catch the afternoon flight back, to be on time for the next day's work. Elizabeth, red-rimmed eyes, hugged me to her and murmured aloud, 'What happens next?' Ma was sitting in her high-backed chair, grandchildren all round her, people chattering and laughing. She was loving it. Not a sign of distress did she display, or let show. Her actress's instinct had come in to save her from any ordinary humiliations like that.

What *did* happen next is that Elizabeth and her husband George gave up their family home and moved into the cottage. A separate, and attractive, little flat was made for Ma in the attics where Pa had had his studio. It is all very typical. That's what seems to happen to the only daughter in a family of boys: she gets lumbered. It was no good Ma coming out to me in France – I offered and she shied away as if I'd produced a red-hot iron to her face, and pointed out, fairly honestly, that we'd have killed each other within a week. 'We are *far* too alike, you and I?' she said triumphantly.

Gareth had a large family and a small house. So we came to this slightly uneasy arrangement. For a time, a short time, it seemed as if it might work. But one rare day Elizabeth and George, feeling secure, had to go out for one, single hour. On their return Ma was lying at the bottom of the stairs which led up to her little flat with almost every single bone, apart from that in her neck, broken. She had scoffed every bottle on the drinks table, plus a new crate of beer, each bottle of which she had carefully refilled – with water. The extreme, fastidious caution of the secret drinker. Ah well. It happens in the very best of families. It is just terribly difficult to cope with, and the furious denial is always agonizing to understand. But understand one has to.

After months in hospital and physiotherapy Ma was moved to a very pleasant 'Hotel for the Elderly'. Not, as she always insisted to anyone who would listen, a 'Home'. She had her own suite of rooms, her own furniture, pictures, bits and pieces and, to my amusement, some books of Pa's. Elizabeth couldn't be expected to nurse and keep an eye on her at all times, or take the responsibility.

She couldn't now be trusted on her own. Ma knew this and bitterly resented it.

I came over from France as often as possible and Elizabeth went to see her every day. This Ma overlooked, claiming sullenly that she was being abandoned. 'I have been shunted aside like some old goods-wagon!' she said one day. I was pretty certain that this was not *her* phrase. Someone, and there were a number, had told her that. They chattered away sympathetically and all agreed that we had 'turned her out of her own house, and moved in and taken possession of her goods, and dumped her in a *home*'. They wore twin-sets and Gor-ray skirts and spread sympathy and loving understanding about like treacle. They called her 'Maggie' and went to see her regularly.

They were old friends of her village days. Kind, silly people quite unaware of the true situation (helped along by Ma, whose efforts at the truth were minimal). They visited regularly, wrote to Elizabeth and me (sometimes *anonymously*) deploring our 'cruelty' and 'wickedness' in 'stealing her possessions' and dumping her so heartlessly, our 'beloved' mother. She had, they insisted, been 'locked away'. All alone.

After she died the drawers in her dressing-table, and wardrobe, rattled and clattered with dustbinfuls of empty bottles: Gordon's gin, all most thoughtfully supplied, smuggled in to the hotel, by her 'loving and caring' friends, to cheer her up. All they were doing was hastening her death. Perhaps they felt that was their duty? Ma *liked* being cheered up. She bribed (I was later to discover) the local village girls, who came in to wait at table and clean, to bring her secret bottles of booze from the nearest supermarkets (she had a modest allowance). The bribes were all made with the Chanel jewellery which Cap had given her over the years, rare, beautiful, collector's pieces. They must have looked a bit hefty on the Marks & Sparks cotton prints or home knits. However, they, and some other really good pieces, got frittered away in exchange for half-bottles of Gordon's or Booth's. Her modest jewel box was very soon dispersed, except for a few pieces of Victorian stuff which had belonged to my paternal grandmother. These were considered 'too old-fashioned' and not worth the effort. Thus they were saved. But her rooms in the pleasant hotel fairly rattled about with empties. Elizabeth was in agony trying to find somewhere to dump them: in all fairness she didn't want to betray Ma to the staff of the hotel by shoving the lot in the hotel dustbins, so she dutifully carted secret bags of stuff away. Bags of glittering, rattling, green and clear glass bottles were scattered in ditches and thickets all over East Sussex. It is wise to beware of do-gooders. They mean so well and can cause such terrible havoc, especially if they don't know what they are dealing with. To be perfectly fair it was difficult for outsiders to know exactly when Ma had taken a sip too much. She never, at any time, appeared to be 'the worse for drink'. Just rather jolly and eye-flashing. Her speech was never slurred (except when we were children, and got petrified by her voice and the despair), but in company she usually held her drink like a stoker. Probably better. The dreadful repetition of her 'funny stories' gave her away to us, her children. 'Here we go,' we murmured in misery and braced ourselves for the unending spiel which would develop. We'd heard them all so many times that we could prompt her. But never dared. Her 'dear friends' from the village chortled with delight, and squealed with joyful laughter over the oatmeal biscuits and coffee, begging for yet another yarn, apparently quite unaware that their hostess, elegant, groomed, immaculate in her high-backed chair was, in reality, as pissed as a fiddler's bitch. They tactfully rummaged about in their handbags and slipped her a little half-bottle as a token of thanks. Unaware, of course, that she'd already slung back a few from the wardrobe or the chest of drawers before they arrived.

But, as Pa always said, she *had* been the most wonderful mother. Amazingly she managed us all brilliantly. She also had to cope with a young husband who had only just, a couple of years before, left the battlefields of Flanders and was still in a state of appalling shock. Pa was a more-or-less survivor of Passchendaele, the Somme and Caporetto. He did not survive unscathed. He was a man of extreme sensitivity and his mind was filled with terrors which he suppressed. There was no counselling then, you couldn't sue for battle fatigue or the sight of your best friend slipping off the duckboards and drowning in ten foot of mud right before you. You simply had to cope for yourself. In Pa's case his young wife was wonderfully helpful and shielding, treating him, when the images became unbearable, with comfort, soothing him with her love. These attacks were never seen by Elizabeth or me. They were excluded strictly from our lives. We neither saw, heard, nor guessed at anything. Lally knew, with the wisdom of her kind, and kept us strictly away.

But it was always Ma who bandaged our cuts and grazes, kissed us, and smiled pain away, was in charge of the thank-you letters and those of condolence, although I don't remember that we actually knew what we were thanking for or to whom the condolences were sent. Children, anyway under nine, really don't give much of a fig. Our spelling was checked, our table manners, the way we spoke, our general behaviour – all these things were set up by Ma and assiduously followed by Lally later on. She deferred at all times to her husband – they were, after all, among the last of the Edwardians and the rules of the day still applied, even though the war had blasted most of them to bits. The only thing he ever had to do for us was 'the punishment'. This hugely embarrassed him. 'Do I *have* to, Margaret?' and then the uneasy punishment was administered, usually with one of his long-handled paint brushes.

She was gay, laughing, a perfect ambassadress for him when he was obliged to travel abroad, which was pretty often in the developing post-war years. She never managed to come to terms with any language, but it didn't seem to matter much. She learned the addresses where she was staying lest she got lost, '*Vingt-deux avenue Victor Hugo*', or the number of 'Le Nain bleu', a costly toy shop on rue Faubourg Saint-Honoré where she bought us splendid presents. But that was her limit. However, she was capable of spending a couple of hours in some elegant shop chattering away in her voluble French accent (she always used a French accent, with lots of hand waggling and body movement, and convinced herself, therefore, that she was fluent in the language), and with her enormous charm and her looks the shop was in thrall. She knew very well how to 'play the house' and did it *con brio!* Pa said he frequently had to curl his toes, but then he was a very undemonstrative man, though actually secretly amused, and proud. But that was when the world was young. Or, anyway, *they* were.

By the time we hit 1939 things started to slide away. After that nothing would ever be the same. Never again. We'd all be different people with different stresses and strains, different visions, different ideas. Ma never recovered from her absolute delight in the war – she literally thrived in it. With two of us in the services, a husband trapped in London during the Blitz, she bunged poor Gareth, then about seven, into boarding-school and embraced 'her' war with passionate alacrity. She was doing her 'bit' for England. And she loved it. She was needed, in demand, good at it all, and like so many women of her age, with children poised to leave, she suddenly found herself reprieved, not redundant, but thoroughly fulfilled and happy.

But just as they start, rather suddenly, wars seem to end rather suddenly, some people are taken unawares. Ma was. She was overwhelmed by the clashing of victory bells which signalled that her time was over. She was brutally betrayed by the vacuum which came surging about her called peace. She had no idea what to do with all the energy she still had to spend. No one wanted the 'funny stories', the bossing, the hot sweet tea and recipes for carrot cake. No letters had to now be written to mothers and wives, in, say, Seattle or Winnipeg. She was not yet fifty, but she was, at that moment, made redundant to social needs. No one wanted a middle-aged woman. There was no one to listen to her or applaud. Everyone was absolutely exhausted. We, the children, had gone away. Pa was trying to rebuild a newspaper in London. The spring winds could blow across the meadows around the cottage, nodding the cowslips and making tremble the new buds on the beech, but those she didn't see. She just crumbled: and from then on it was very slowly, but quite implacably, down the hill for her.

The strange thing is that, having written all that in detail, the person I desperately miss is Pa. I loved him profoundly. His photograph, a small boy of five in a huge white tam-o'-shanter sitting with a Jack Russell terrier in a Spanish chair, is by my bed. He is the last thing I see when I put out my light. Strange? I don't know the 'mother and father' rules.

It can be pointed out, here and now, that this love was a long time in being reciprocated. He couldn't really forgive me for the, apparently, wastrel life I was leading. Useless at any form of education, which I avoided with all the slipperiness of a sack of eels, showing no chance ever of getting myself into Fettes and, worse still, offering no inclination or possibility ever of taking over his place at the sainted *Times*. This above all things saddened him greatly, I know, and the fact that I even quit art school, where I had clearly made some modest impact, to go to the Old Vic and become a player almost choked him. We hardly ever spoke beyond the mundane things. I drifted further and further away from him, yet all the time longed for his approbation, thoughtlessly doing my best to lose it at every turn. The typical muddle of my life. Never getting it quite right. I wanted his approbation only on *my* terms. But it didn't work like that. The bright afternoon in 1941 when, neat and trim as a nine-pin, brasses, buckles, boots glittering, I marched up the steps at Sandhurst as a brand-new officer, and in the leading rank of three brought that acceptance about. I was as proud as it was possible to be, and he, among the modest throng of devoted parents watching the passing-out parade, suddenly found that he was proud too. Relieved as well, no doubt. But he did give me a very sly smile when we walked together to the station for the train to Waterloo. (We'd all been given a week's leave before our postings.)

In the train, crammed knee to knee, he suddenly leant forward and lightly kissed my cheek. 'Very good,' he said. 'You've made me very happy.' That was all that he said. I'd waited twenty years for those words and now, by dint of my labours, I'd heard them. I was not obvious army material. He was certain that I'd be left gibbering, mad with fear and incomprehension somewhere in the cookhouse for the entire duration of the war. I was pretty certain *I'd* end up barking mad in a cage, rattling my tin mug against the bars, like some demented monkey.

As it turned out we were both to be proved wrong. I slid easily into place. I drove (as I have recounted) my earlier teachers and instructors to madness by my stupidity. I couldn't send SOS in signals and I couldn't learn how to assemble the bloody Bofors gun in the artillery, even if I learned the manual parrot-fashion. But I was very good on the assault courses, gave a very good impression of devil-may-care madness on the battle ranges, chucking hand-grenades and canister bombs about with the abandon of someone who had the death wish. I clambered up and down the sagging nets of enormous ships in Loch Fyne on commando courses, like a latter-day Douglas Fairbanks, cheered by the thought that I couldn't swim and that loaded down with all my gear as I was, I'd soon sink to the bottom should I fall in. I appeared to have no fear. *Appeared.* I had, at all times, an image of a wryly smiling Pa before me saying, over and over again, his warning phrase: 'We are not supposed to fail in this family.' So I dared not. Having failed so much already, I knew I had to win out in this last gigantic opportunity. I did what we had always been instructed *not* to do within the family, which was to draw attention to oneself. *Little boys should not show off.* I showed off like a penny bazaar or a firework display at Crystal Palace, and eventually caught someone's eye and got further than Pa or I had ever dreamt it could be possible for one so maladroit. Then, and then only, did he realize perhaps what he had once most feared would not come to pass: his eldest son was happily *not* a complete dud. A bond was formed between us which would last all his life. It was as deep and profound as any bond of love could possibly be. Impossible to really explain to those who have never experienced it. I loved my father, only rather more intensely, as, for example, I loved Chris, or Hugh, or Forwood. It was a 'male thing': unstated, instinctive, holding.

We were never completely 'apart' from then on. All through the war, wherever I was, he wrote once a week. A sort of bulletin of home news and family stuff – nothing important, apart from his signature every week: 'All love, Pa.' Ma never wrote at all. She scribbled a line at the end of some of his letters – 'Daddy will have given you all the news, love, Ma' – and that was it. I wrote to him constantly, doing my best to be a second Rupert Brooke or Wilfred Owen, not with very much success, as you might guess, but we held the link together, and it never broke, and that's what mattered to me.

Being alone with Pa was one of the greatest pleasures of my life latterly: just sitting, as we so often did, under the olives up on the hill while he painted; chucking bits of thought his way; asking him things that the lost twenty years had denied me in the past.

'You didn't really like me, did you? I mean when I was born. I was a pain in the arse, wasn't I?'

'Your mother say that? I suppose so. Well, yes, frankly. I didn't plan to have a child just then. We were both pretty young, no money. I was working a fifteen, eighteen hour day for Northcliffe at *The Times*. You howled all night . . . it was not the easiest of times. Your mother wanted you, though. She wanted something to play with while I was stuck in Printing House Square. That's all, really.'

'That's why you shut me up in your chest of drawers at night?'

'You made a terrible row always. Screams and yells. I couldn't stick it.'

'Shut me in a bloody drawer! A small baby!'

'It wasn't airtight! I mean, you *could* breathe, didn't suffocate. But it did shut you up.' He mixed some oil and turps on his wooden palette.

'Gave me permanent claustrophobia, that's all.'

'Did it really?' He applied his brush to the canvas before him. 'How curious.'

'That's why I hate flying, and theatres and cinemas and the underground and being in noisy restaurants. All your fault.'

'Well, it doesn't seem to have damaged you permanently really. Probably why you enjoyed your war. All outside. In the open air. You should be very grateful.' He was grinning at his absurdity.

I changed tack suddenly; something had reminded me of a singular meeting, our last together for some years as it happened. 'Pa? Do you remember the time you telephoned me at Medmenham, when I was with the APIS lot. 1944? Remember that?'

He was occupied with his paint and brush. 'Telephoned you once or twice, didn't I? Greenwood [his devoted secretary] used to

"get you on the line", as he said. It always made me think he'd
gone fishing somewhere. What of it?'

'Well, you asked me to meet you in London, that afternoon at
four precisely, I remember that, for tea at the Cumberland Hotel.
Remember? *The Cumberland!*'

'Not really. Seems to be rather off my usual track. The Cumberland? It was a sort of place for Yanks and their girlfriends if I
remember.'

'That's what surprised me. You gave me a present.'

He started to bite the side of his lip. A sign of anxiety, anger or
suppressed worry. 'Did I? What was it?'

'It was a Holy Medal. The Virgin and the Christ Child. There
was a lily on the back, with from D. to D. and the date. Sixth of
June 1944. Remember?'

He shrugged, wiped his brush out. 'Something like that. What of
it?'

'Well. That day at the Cumberland was the *fifth*. The original
Landing Day. We had to cancel at the last minute, because of
weather. The landing was the next day. The *sixth*. How did you
know?'

He looked up slowly. 'I really don't recall. Have you still got it?
Never!'

'I have. Wore it all the time, until the little ring got too thin . . .
but I have it still.'

'Amazing,' he said. 'You'll have to let me have a look at it one
day.'

I did, but the only remark he made was that it was not silver.
Some base metal. He'd not had time to get silver. He never said
why the Cumberland for tea, or how he had got the date right.
Coincidence only? Was the Cumberland Hotel tea-lounge suitably
busy and anonymous? He'd never have been seen there so far away
from *The Times*. But he just looked at me quietly, his face dappled

by the late sun through the gently moving olive branches. 'Oh, my dear boy. I really don't quite remember that far back. However, very glad that you wore it, gave you a bit of comfort perhaps?'

We didn't speak of it again. I was vaguely curious about it all because he never, at any time, spoke of the religion he had denied after his war. His family were all Catholic, his mother a convert, and Elizabeth and I were started off at a Catholic convent but not openly encouraged to be one thing or another. We were, sensibly, left to decide, given the choices before us, which way we should go.

I heard of his death suddenly one morning in Paris. I'd just got off the train from Nice, was shaving, and Forwood called me from his bedroom to say that Pa had died. He held the telephone on his knee, hand over the mouthpiece as if, perhaps, expecting me to cry out or something. But, of course, I did not. We had a full and busy day. Breakfast with someone, lunch somewhere, at Lipp I think, drinks with Yul Brynner. It was a Sunday, he had finished his role in the film, and he was flying back to LA. I remember all that so clearly, except that as the day wore on the pain of loss grew greater and greater, a growing abscess of distress, so that by the time I had got back to the Hotel Lancaster, I could collapse in rage, tears and misery in the (near) privacy of my lavatory. I say 'near' simply because there was a small ventilation window opening into a white-tiled tunnel up to the sky (I can see it clearly now) and my howls of fury and grief thrilled all of Paris. Then an elegant, gold-braceleted hand gently closed the next-door window into the shaft and allowed me to resume my grieving. And, dear God, did I wallow. Just as well perhaps because the next day I had voided all grief and was able to continue working normally. Of course I hadn't *really* lost it all. Grief lies curled beneath the heart like a black dog and, from time to time, stirs itself for a moment or two. Then settles down again. I remember my pain at the fact that he had gone before Ma. In some strange way his children had an unspoken, but fixed, idea that he would outlive her because he seemed to be the stronger. She was frail, and grew frailer every day, so that eventually it was he who did all the cooking, the shopping, even, poor sod, the washing of the 'smalls'. His was, towards his end, not a very jolly existence.

If I suggested, as I did, that they should move into a flat somewhere in Brighton, I was heard out with cold anger. 'Don't try and get me into some bloody flat in Brunswick Square or somewhere. I *have* to have grass under my feet. Be able to feed the birds. Do you know we have fifteen different kinds who come here? I'll end up here, thank you very much.' And when I discovered that you could actually *see the road* under his feet in his ancient little Morris, and sent him down a gleaming new, bright-red Fiat, he was ashen with fury. 'I *do* wish you wouldn't interfere, my dear. I *liked* my little Morris. We knew each other very well.'

'Ma was constantly in danger of being killed. Her door didn't close properly.'

'Well, she learned how to hang on to it. I detest that showy car. Red! A feller just arrived, dumped it, and drove away in *my* Morris! It really was too bad.'

I often wonder, and wondered at the time, just how amused he would have been when I had to kneel before my sovereign and get clobbered with her sword? He might have been pleased, but not nearly as amused as I know he would have been when he saw me try to stride off, an absurdly newly knighted gentleman of the realm to the tune of 'Who wants to be a Millionaire?' played at top whack by the Coldstream Guards.

I talk to him often now, ask why he thinks I am going into a room: 'Ulric. What *did* I come in here for?' Or else, on many an occasion, 'Pa? My glasses? You seen them? Where did I leave them?

Just a little sign? A tiny flash from wherever you are . . .' But I am always left to find things out for myself. That's how he was.

I went over to see Ma for the last time in her pleasant hotel. She was down and sad. We had a disgusting lunch: watery cauliflower, watery mashed potato, dark-brown slices of meat like the soles of worn shoes. Beside her in the very dreary, full dining-room an aged man sat in a blazer, custard stains dribbled down the front, a green eyeshade across his brow, a bottle of mineral water half empty and measured out with a thick line in felt-tip. I didn't wonder at her misery. We sat and talked in the residents' lounge for a while. She chewed away at a piece of gristle from the meat.

'Let me have it, darling. Spit it out?' I offered a cupped hand. There was a modest log fire burning.

'I *like* it. Chewing is very good for the muscles of your neck.' She was defiant, angry because she had been made, in her eyes, to look childish. She chewed on quietly. Furious, lost.

She came with me to the front door; it was in a small glassed-in porch: a pair of wellingtons, some walking-sticks in a pot, a barometer. I kissed her, and she hung on for a second, and then there was a scuffling and two young idiot maids, who waited at table, came up with autograph books, giggling and blushing. I waved them away. I was, after all, saying goodbye to my mother. Surely they could see that? They stood a foot or two behind Ma, nodding and grinning, flapping their wretched books and pencils. Ma's irritation, and my own, was evident – it made not a whit of difference. Careless of others, stupid as a pair of heifers, they hung about and the last I ever saw of my mother was her anguished face behind the glass door of the porch as she waved with one sad hand, and the two idiots behind her waving stick fingers and giggling.

I never say 'Goodbye' on principle, it is always far too final. In this case it would have been, but I called through the door, 'I'll be back, darling!' But I never was.

She died suddenly a few days later. I had only just got back to Le Pigeonnier when Elizabeth called, calm, but distressed. It had been very sudden, no pain. Could I get back? It was Easter week and I couldn't. There was no possible flight I could take . . . one via Zurich and Brussels, a stand-by in Munich. Everyone was terribly sorry, 'But it *is* Easter'. Everything was booked solid. I gave in and wandered about my land, looking to see what was new, if the daffodils had spread, if the big pomegranate was in bud. The sky was clean-washed, not a cloud in sight. The only possible one was that Ma had died, but peacefully. Elizabeth and George said they would cope, and the day before I had hit fifty-nine and was now in my sixtieth year.

A decent age, I supposed, to become an orphan.

On Loneliness

By seven-thirty in the evening, commuter time, the brasserie in the terminus is like an auction in a stockyard, crammed with people, drinking, laughing, eating. If you didn't like the human race much you could mistake them for a seething mass of kitchen cockroaches caught in the light. Waiters push and eel their way, trays held high, shouting, '*Allô! Attention! S'il vous plaît!*', sweat beading on balding heads, down bristled cheeks, white aprons flapping, pencils behind ears. Smoke wreathes and hangs in heavy veils just below the strip-light-cluttered ceiling, amber with centuries of tobacco. It hangs, wavering slightly, a gold and blue aurora borealis suddenly ripped apart when the swing doors by the bar open and yet another body pushes into the crammed space of pillars, mirrors and shiny tiled walls. Across the street, through the gathered folds of grey lace curtains, you can see the red, blue and green zig-zags of neon lights rippling and twisting. Blurs of drifting colour.

Opposite my banquette-table, all down the length of the windows, ran a row of single tables, each with its bentwood chair facing inward. One of them was a clear island, virginal in the sweating crowd. A white paper cover, a bottle of Maggi, salt and pepper in plastic shakers, a paper carnation in a metal thin-necked vase. All were occupied save for this one immediately opposite me. It had a small '*Réservé*' sign stuck on a slant by the Maggi sauce bottle.

Suddenly a waiter, a thick-set, heavily moustached man I knew vaguely from past journeys as Bobo hurried down to the swing-doors, an empty tray banging at his side. He shouted, '*J'arrive,*

Madame! J'arrive!', pulled open the swing-doors as someone slid through and took his hand in quick greeting. He brought her swiftly through the crowd, pushing and parting, but she followed slowly, arms slightly raised before her fending off any possible lurch or stumble which she might encounter.

'Voilà!' he said as she reached the empty table. He pocketed the *'Réservé'* sign as a matter of habit, pulled the table forward to permit her entrance and then clattered away. She moved delicately, gently, as tall, as thin as a stick-insect feeling cautiously through an infestation of killer ants. A long grey cloth coat, scrap of chiffon scarf folded at her throat, grey stockings neatly darned at one heel, a small, absurd, out-of-date hat pierced with a quill like an arrow, on neat white hair. She settled into her chair, placed an old handbag on the table and began to remove her cotton gloves, very slowly. All, clearly, part of an habitual routine. The gloves folded on the bag, she unbuttoned the coat, loosened the thin bit of scarf, let it float over her neatly clasped hands on the white paper table cloth. She wore no rings.

Bobo returned with a bentwood chair, set it before her. She smiled, nodded, looked about her with shy but intense pleasure, her eyes, behind oval rimless glasses, glittering in the striplights, as bright and aware as a blackbird's. Although she was obviously very much at home here, there was, to my mind anyway, a vague sense of loss about her. She seemed to be poised on her chair for instant flight. Temporary. As I was thinking this, she quite suddenly got to her feet, arms outstretched in welcome towards the swing-doors, made a vague fluttering movement with her hand which could have been a wave, indicated the empty chair before her and sat again, adjusting her scarf, smiling now with obvious contentment and pleasure across her table.

At no one.

No one had come through the doors. No one had crossed

through the noisy crowd. No one had pulled out the chair in front of her and sat down. Then quite silently she commenced a long, happy, intimate conversation. With herself. She smiled politely, listened, now and again, nodded in agreement or shook her head at something that no one had said but which she had heard for herself. There was no madness here, no sign of someone unstable. She caused no concern; her whole demeanour was still, gentle and calm. She was having a very pleasant time. Settled now.

Bobo arrived back with a tray, set knife and fork before her, a plastic basket containing two rolls of bread, a portion of cheese, a half-bottle of Badoit, a single glass of red wine. He didn't interrupt the flow of her narrative but he did lean carefully aside to avoid the body of no one in the empty bentwood chair. He was playing her game, something he obviously always did.

Later he returned with a little glass bowl of salad, and a one-egg omelette on a small plate. I know a one-egg omelette when I see one. This at least was *fines herbes*: there was a scatter of chives and parsley in the pallid fold of egg.

She sipped at her water, twisting the stem of her wine glass, paying strict attention to whatever was being said to her by her ghostly companion. From time to time she would nevertheless break the intensity and look up at the big clock over the bar as the big hand staggered stiffly round sending time away with each jerking minute. On the dot of eight-thirty she had finished, opened her bag and counted out the bill, adding a single coin which chinked into the little china saucer Bobo had provided when he brought her '*l'addition*' and a small coffee.

She got to her feet, Bobo in attendance to pull out the table, shrugged into her grey cloth coat, tucked the scarf round her throat, nodded her thanks to him and, still talking silently, more or less animatedly to her unseen guest over her shoulder, clearly following hard behind, she moved, mantis-like, through the 'cockroaches' to the swing-doors. Then she had gone into the winter night. I caught Bobo's eye as he tidied the table and collected the dirty dishes. He smiled thinly, shrugged: '*Elle est comme une mante religieuse.*' I said, '*Parmi les cafards!*' For a moment he looked blank, then got what I had said, and laughed softly.

Apparently this little pantomime occurred every evening between seven-thirty and eight-thirty, and had done so for years, as many as he could remember. She had lost her man during the war. He was taken during a deportation round-up by the Germans for forced labour. He never returned but she went on quietly waiting for years in the bar until she realized in time that she was waiting in vain. She worked in a stationer's shop near by, lived in a small flat alone, then retired. The *patron* and now his son said that her routine should never be disturbed or discussed. Her table was always there, and she arrived punctually, unless she had *la grippe* or some other minor disaster occurred. But the table was empty until seven-thirty always. '*C'est la règle,*' said Bobo and he went to get my coffee. Her man was still her companion.

I wondered if that sort of situation could ever have happened in a vast London terminus. Victoria or Paddington. I didn't think so, honestly. We didn't have that kind of sentimentality or sense of romance to begin with, and anyway, we had never fortunately experienced, or witnessed, a round-up or a deportation. Those obscene items of the German Occupation were, still *are*, woundingly fresh in the French mind today.

Watching her I was aware that I must not stare, merely glance and note. It was just a part of Pa's early training. 'Observe. Notice. Above all, *look* at life.' I observed her with intense curiosity because the feeling of loss and a sad resigned loneliness was just exactly what I must learn, and put to use, when the time came for me to play von Aschenbach in *Death in Venice*. The unknown woman in the terminus bar that evening provided a fount of information with her body language, but above all in that dreadful, contained, aching, mute sense of loss and isolation.

When the time did come for me to play the wretched man I was ready and charged. I knew more or less who he was and how he would behave, basically because of the encounter with the solitary woman. Translating her loneliness to a fictitious character I found extremely interesting. I suppose it is fair to say that I have been called upon to experience many things in this life, and there have been some pretty varied experiences chucked my way, but loneliness has never been one of them. Certainly I have been *alone* frequently. Indeed I have spent a great deal of my life in that state: the old saying 'Alone in a crowd' I know to be patently true. But I have not been lonely. 'Alone' and 'lonely' are two quite different words. 'Lonely' means 'Unhappy as a result of being without the companionship of others', and 'alone' means 'someone who is essentially solitary'. Which seems to apply to me, rather than the former.

I relished being with Chris, with Hugh, with Forwood, with members of my family and so on, but I found it always essential to get away at times and be by myself. The fact is that I am perfectly happy *amusing* myself. I quite like myself. I make myself laugh just as often as I make myself tremble with hopeless fury at my own brands of stupidity. But I don't at all mind being on my own. I have never (but perhaps I will, there is still some time left) experienced the desperate misery of Ma who could only truly exist in the companionship of others. She would happily travel miles to be with 'amusing people', to be surrounded with people who found her enjoyable and flattered her, or laughed with her. It made no difference to her really if they were unpleasant or, *au fond*, 'ugly' people. As long as they didn't overtly show those sides to *her*, she would flourish. But on her own, or even sometimes with her close family about her, she was secretly wrenched with longing to be somewhere else. With 'the crowd'.

I resemble my father greatly. Pa and I both agreed that we liked our *own* company best of all. Naturally there are times when the company of others can be amusing. But generally I avoid being among large groups of people. I had enough of that in barrack-rooms and troopships to last me a lifetime. I have, for example, rarely stayed away from my own home overnight if I can possibly avoid it. The last time was at Rex Harrison and Kay Kendall's house in New York when he had opened in *My Fair Lady* and it was impossible for me to catch the last train home. So I stayed, perfectly contentedly, in their house for two weeks. That's the only time, apart from being on locations or promotions somewhere and living in hotel rooms (or even on extremely rare holidays) and a couple of hospital trips, that I have ever stayed away from my own bed. Even if getting into it for an hour was all I could manage.

I think that the years spent at the school in Glasgow trained me pretty well in self-sufficiency. I had to have myself as a 'best friend' because there was absolutely no one else who could even remotely comprehend my desperate desire to be alone. It was considered unhealthy. I should be playing games, swimming, going to the gym, joining teams, all the general things that boys of my age did. To encourage me I was dragged off to football matches at Ibrox Park by my uncle, who, during the incomprehensible games, grew ever more excitable: screaming, spraying excited spittle, waving a striped scarf and thumping me until my eyes rolled with his hysteria. I found it all cold, wet and extremely embarrassing. It was even worse at the Alhambra with the D'Oyly Carte Company – that too was sheer agony *and* incomprehensible. Worst of all was the Orpheus Choir chanting away robed in long white shifts and whooo-hoooing and nonny-nonnying for hours on end, usually in Gaelic. I'd long for it all to end so that I could retreat to the womb of my room with the peach sateen bedspread on the Put-U-Up, the Valour Perfection stove throwing wavering shadows on the low ceiling. Here, in these dismal surroundings, I was perfectly happy and contained within myself. I had a diary (a vast ledger, cloth-covered and with a shiny black spine, which I crammed with useless information), my paints, my books (few, but mine), and I could 'imagine' myself away. I was never lonely.

To begin with I always had the image of the Ovaltine Lady shimmering before me. There she was by the railway line, the huge basket of eggs on her arm, offering, with gleaming, giant white teeth, her huge jar of Ovaltine. She indicated that I was (going south anyway) only about half an hour from Euston and sanity. Going north was, as I have said, quite another matter. However, her beaming image lent me delight and strength. I felt strong enough to even withstand my aunt's badminton matches.

Every Thursday was ladies' evening with Mrs Mackenzie, a broad-hipped Australian lady, her hair iron-barred with kirby grips. I had to keep the score while these two lunatic women, my aunt and she, leapt and slid about the wooden floor in pleated skirts, crying and grunting as they whacked a handful of feathers at each other over a high net. All around there were other ladies watching – a dusty smell of talcum powder and 'Evening in Paris' rose up – all wagging their heads from side to side like elderly metronomes.

I used to sit high up on the varnished pine seats to keep apart from those below, but also, I thought, to get a better view of the game. This was naturally considered rude and aloof. But I didn't really care. I'd soon be back in my ugly room (well, they couldn't play *all* night), printing the number on the top of the page in my ledger, marking off the days quietly until my release to the arms of my waiting lady with her Ovaltine icon at Leighton Buzzard, or wherever. I am extremely grateful today that I had to endure such an existence. It was far more use to me than any boarding-school. It really did force me, like rhubarb or endive under a flowerpot, to grow strong and firm, which was, after all, just what was wanted of me. There was *not* a great deal of scholarly brilliance, alas, which was the basic reason for those three years, but I was armed, or armed myself by strength, to face a pretty bumpy journey ahead.

There were to be a few 'satin cushions and barley sugar twists' on the trip for me to be sure, but an awful lot of reverses and pitfalls. Had I known it, bright, young, determined, ignorant and keen, the 'good times' were really then: without any responsibility except to myself. The fact that I had the strength to deny loneliness didn't make my life plain sailing. Out of the sheer terror that I might fall ill, and not make my journey south, I developed a pretty dire form of hypochondria (to which I am still prey) and an acute anxiety complex. I once caught German measles a *day* before joining my Lady by the Railway Line and was forced to lose an entire holiday – a solid year from summer to summer, missing the Christmas break, which nearly killed me. From then on I became a hypochondriac, brutally torn with anxiety. However, as always, I did my best never to let that show – just got on with things by myself, counted myself lucky, and continued writing the numbers on the top of my pages in the ledger. Filled with hope. But marking days off my life at the same time.

We left Saint-Paul for Venice at four-thirty a.m., the dog, Labo, wedged into a space on the back seats between two blue suitcases and a record-player. He was to stay there for some time. He didn't mind. Like Forwood, who was driving, he was a car-freak. In the pre-dawn sky, flushed softly by its approach, there hung a great sickle moon, and moving slowly towards it, so slowly that we were almost abreast all the time between Nice and Menton, a giant comet sped, leaving a plumed trail of scarlet and yellow stars behind in a haze of turquoise-blue light; a giant comet which faded away, a hard, blinding diamond, as the sun rose and we reached the Italian frontier at Ventimiglia, and the night sky was washed clean, flooded with the light of a new day. The fact that it happened also to be April the first didn't particularly alarm me. I am not superstitious. Perhaps I should have been.

'A comet!' I cried with unerring obviousness. 'That *is* a comet! It might have been Halley's comet. Do you think so?'

Forwood was fighting the racing traffic which had suddenly appeared the moment we reached Genoa. The Italian driver is not a cautious fellow. You have to *fight* for your rights.

'Do you think it could be Halley's comet? Pretty rare, isn't it?'

'I don't know if it's Halley's bloody comet. I have a double-tanker up my arse and fifty-five lunatic Fiats ahead. Let me get through Genoa and then we can have a happy astrological conversation. But not at the moment. Unless you'd like to take the wheel?'

I mumbled apologies and he coaxed his new Maserati through the Fiats. Later he explained patiently that Halley's comet had last been seen in 1910; it swung round every seventy-five years or so, so perhaps I'd like to work it out for myself? I just shut up. I got the point. He always made his points neatly. Anyway, *I* took it for a comet and as a sign of good luck, a sort of portent, momentous rather than disastrous.

We were driving to Venice to begin work on *Death in Venice*. I had rented, through the good offices of Luchino Visconti, Ca' Leone, the summer house on the Giudecca of the Volpi family. It had been an effort. Visconti disliked being asked favours.

'Look, Luchino, I can't sit about in hotels on this film. I hate hotels, and I'd have to be in the place for six months at least. Also I have a dog. I am not leaving him in kennels in Italy for months. I need a place of my own, somewhere I can work on von Aschenbach. I need the solitude. I am working *every* single day on this film, I am being paid a pittance, and you know it, so I must find a little apartment in the city where I can be self-contained . . .' and so I whinnied on.

Eventually he saw some sort of reason behind my pleas for 'privacy' and 'solitude' and I got his friends' rather neglected little house set in one acre of gardens on the south side of the Giudecca facing the Lagoon, for a reasonable rent. It was walled all round, a small canal, the Rio della Croce, on one side (the only entrance to its front door by boat) and on the other side, smothered in huge domes and pinnacles, the majesty of Palladio's wondrous church of the Redentore built in 1577. The gardens were green and dark, spiked with cypress trees thrusting through groves of ilex. My garden had a wealth of municipal flowerbeds filled, presently, with red salvia, orange canna lilies, the borders fringed with scrawny 'Mrs Sinkins' pinks. But it was still, silent. The house with its tall Venetian chimneys and ochre-painted walls smelled of years of damp and neglect. It had been flooded almost every winter to a depth of up to two feet. You could see the oily marks where the water had reached various levels. But none of this bothered me. It was secluded, calm, just the place in which to indulge myself in discovering 'loneliness' and 'loss', and to explore in depth the man I had been engaged to play.

It might be wise, at this stage, to admit that everything which is to follow I have taken from the private diaries of my manager, Anthony Forwood. I destroyed all my own when I left Provence, so I have had to pillage here and there. It is not at all a pleasant feeling reading through someone else's private papers. It is akin to listening on the stairs, or steaming open someone's mail. Sooner or later you are bound to read something about yourself it would have been pleasanter not to know. However, that is the risk.

I suppose it is fair to say that I was terrified by the opportunity Visconti had offered me. I knew that I was considered by the trade, and in the salons, as far too young. Even though I was teetering on the edge (the very edge) of fifty, I didn't much look like it, and there was no dialogue to deal with, to flesh out the exceptionally complex character of von Aschenbach. Thomas Mann didn't go in for a great deal of chatter in his characters. But every time I had ever asked Visconti for a meeting to discuss the character and how he wished me to play him, he raised one glacial eyebrow and asked how many times I had read the book. When I said about twenty, he advised another twenty. Or until I had understood the character ... I never got nearer than that, and we never spoke about anything all through the film. Once or twice (never more) he would murmur (to me, no one else) '*encora*' and we just went all over again. *Without* explanation, just a slight nod to the camera. It was so seldom that it surprised the crew as much as it surprised me, but I was happy because I was quite aware that somewhere I had offended my *own* taste. I felt somehow that I was doing what Visconti wanted. So I just went along with courage on my own railway line.

I lived a fiercely solitary life. It was absolutely no fun living with me in Ca' Leone. As well as the dog, Labo, I had brought my faithful married couple from the UK to look after me, Antonia and Eduardo. They were not, as you might guess, English. They were Spanish and had decided, when I left the UK, to come with me, take pot luck, and settle me in to wherever it was that I might decide to live. They joined my caravan cheerfully. They were perfectly happy in Venice. Church bells rang all day, and they could flop into mass or confession at any old time, it seemed, and the secluded house pleased them. They made friends with the guardian, Giovanni, and his wife Maria, who lived in a cottage by the stables, the latter stacked with the furniture and stuff rescued from repeated floods. I soon had that sorted out, and Ca' Leone became once again a house filled with flowers, elegance and sunlight dancing in from the Lagoon. So we were pretty well off. Provisionally.

I sat in the garden in a loggia by the water, all on my own, nursing myself in the fat eiderdown of von Aschenbach and 'being' him. I was coming more and more to understand him as the days progressed. Understanding him and, what was far more important, trying to make him comprehensible to an audience. Who, for heaven's sake, is going to give a fig for a prissy, fastidious, ugly, lonely old German composer? That was my job. Wrapped in the eiderdown – or perhaps ectoplasm is a more apt word? – of the man, I soon moved and even spoke like him. Unnerving if you didn't know what was happening, interesting (to a degree) if you did. Most did, so I was comforted. The tiny details I had garnered from my encounter with the woman in the Bar Terminus were put to good use. Sitting in the little loggia with just the gentle slap of the Lagoon along the tiny strip of sand beyond the filigree iron gate, the wheeling swifts, swooping like commas high above the dome of the Redentore, and the distant bells of the city drifting across the Lagoon from Venice, all mixed with the bumble of pollen-heavy bees nudging into the white and pink discs of holly-hocks beside me, eased stress, and left my mind completely open, unencumbered by any other thoughts so that I was able to make myself wholly available for the arrival of my prissy playmate. I grew to hate, as well as pity, him and I was completely possessed by him. I hated who he was, his intelligence terrified me. It was not mine. I was simply the vessel used to carry him into life. I had no choice but to let *him* dictate the way we went. I was intellectually incapable of fighting him. It was the oddest, most fearful experience. I turned into someone else altogether.

According to the diaries I was at all times polite, distant, forgetful, on another plane. I ate only boiled fish, usually the little sole you could get from the Lagoon, with two boiled potatoes. No butter, no vegetables, a chunk of bread and, on occasion, a bit of cheese. I ate the same every day. How I managed (I who delight in food) I no longer remember. Dinner was a bowl of pasta or a plate of thinly cut ham. Again with boiled potato.

Hardly surprising that I lost weight, and went down to seven and a half stone. Hypochondria swung into the battle for misery-eating whenever I wore the crumpled white suit or my white baggy trousers for the beach sequences. I *knew* there were no replacements, *ergo* I was on the brink of psychosomatic diarrhoea for practically the entire film. I dared not eat anything, therefore, which might even suggest a stomach upset. Scampi, wondrous sauces, spider-crab, butter-drenched tagliatelle and so on were banished from my mind and my meagre body. This was a pity because Harry, at Harry's Bar, kept me a far corner table throughout the entire seven months. Except for Sunday, when I didn't have to work, or a holy holiday. I ate to rule, however, and Harry, beaming with delight at his offer of some glory set before me, and refused sadly, became bewildered and cast down.

Forwood, however, I gather had a perfectly splendid time. The main reason that I had a permanent table at Harry's Bar was that our shooting hours were so peculiar. Visconti wanted the 'light of the sirocco', that is, a pale, still, pearl light. So we shot at dawn. My call for wardrobe was always four-fifteen a.m. We would start to shoot just as the sun rose above the steel water of the Lagoon and before the city awoke, on the very lip of dawn and before the businessmen had been gathered from their hotels for the first flight of the day. We only had a couple of hours to work. Then the tourists arrived, the shops started to open, and modern day obliterated 1910 with roaring *motoscafi*, *vaporetti* and rattling shutters. Until then we had the city to ourselves, but by seven a.m. work was no longer possible, so it was over to Harry's for a coffee, and croissant, and back to Ca' Leone to sleep until two o'clock. Work began again, for the night-shooting, at five. It was a bizarre way of life, controlled all the time by the light. I rather think now that it was perhaps starvation and exhaustion which were responsible for the 'loneliness' and 'sense of loss' for which I strove so hard and was beginning to achieve. Plus lack of sleep. It's difficult to sleep during a brilliant summer day, with all the blasted bells clanging across the water and the novice monks in the gardens of the Redentore jumping up and down in their brown cassocks, at the far end, to tinny transistors playing 'Volare!' or Piaf blasting out her lack of regret. However, one took another sleeping-pill, crashed out and then blearily went to work by *motoscafo* across to the Lido. The little cabin on my boat had four plastic armchairs, a tiny table with a vase of paper daisies on a lace doily and, above the doorway, alerting one to instant decapitation, unless one ducked, a glossy lithograph of Jesus Christ baring his flaring heart and pointing, warningly, upwards.

It was about four kilometres across to the Lido, and for that time I was splendidly, and amazingly, myself. Jeans, t-shirt, flip-flops. I even managed a cigarette, knowing with increasingly sickening lurches that von Aschenbach was waiting ahead, ready to enfold me in his Germanic misery. It was the only really happy moment of the day, with Umberto at the helm, and the spray of the wake scuttering diamonds into the fading sunlight. I loved that part – didn't last long, but just enough to refresh me to greet the others in Make-up: Silvana Mangano in her wig, wearing jeans and doing a crossword, the girls sitting in sullen misery while their hair was dressed for 1910, and Björn Andresen, our Tadzio, playing his transistor, the room rocking agonizingly to the American Forces in Europe.

'Hi yah, man!' he'd wave, and I knew I was back with Thomas Mann and von Aschenbach, his complex creation: well, to be fair, partly mine also. No one else, as Visconti pointed out, had ever presented von Aschenbach to public gaze. We were the first. So it *had* to be correct. Everyone, he said, had a vision of their *own* von Aschenbach. We must not disappoint them. How he imagined that what we would present to the world would satisfy everyone I never dared ask. I just depended on myself and the woman in the grey cloth coat in the Bar Terminus. Later, one day, there would be an opera and even a ballet. But we had gone first. I like to think, but can't of course be certain, that with that crumpled white suit, the brim-tilted panama hat, the pink rose and Mahler's adagio from the No. 5 Luchino Visconti will be remembered.

Although it might appear that I lived in a house completely surrounded with loving, attentive people, plus dog, I truthfully hardly ever realized it. So much of my time was spent on the 'set' and keeping myself apart that I suppose I took everyone for granted. You could say that I was *not* alone, never could have had a sense of 'loss' or isolation, couldn't possibly know how to produce that for the character. But you can be amazingly isolated in a football stadium jammed with thousands, or crammed up against the sour body odour of rush-hour commuters strap-hanging their way to Cockfosters or Morden, and I was just as isolated at Ca' Leone.

But, according to the diaries, while I was trailing about the back streets of Venice in search of True Beauty and Purity, Ca' Leone welcomed a whole host of jolly people. Rex Harrison came on his yacht with a new wife, David Bailey arrived with cameras, Penelope Tree with black nail varnish, Kathleen Tynan to do a piece for *Vogue US*, Patrick Lichfield with more cameras than a pawnbroker, Alain Resnais with his new script for me about de Sade, Peggy Guggenheim, Patrick Kinross, Alan J. Lerner and *his* new lady – and various counts and countesses and others spill from the pages. I seem to have spent, with sickening regularity, most of my time in bed. 'D. sleeps all day' is a constant entry. So I missed many of this glittering array, and they were forbidden to come on the set.

Visconti, detesting the press, had closed Venice. It didn't bother me in the least, I couldn't have handled any of them, so they got carted across the canal to Harry's Bar while I sat glumly on a distant beach eating my boiled sole.

One Sunday evening Forwood called me in from the loggia where I had been sitting, reading a week-old London paper. He had been trying to put into English some of the impossibly flowery Italian that Visconti had written for me to say at some point. I can't remember it all now, but one line sticks in my mind like a shard of glass: 'I am ready to open my heart to all the world!' Try it in English. Italian, or French, makes it slightly easier, but he had a hell of a job trying to make it reasonable in English. In the end, I remember, I *did* say it. Visconti simply could not be made aware that it was too florid in English, any more than he could tell an American accent from an English one. We often had some grave problems there. However, I went into the hall to the telephone, terrified that it would be cut off (usual in Italy at that time) before I got there. I was fearful that there might have been a 'problem' at home with Ma or, more alarmingly, with Pa.

It was Capucine from Rome, and my heart lifted. Sank a little at the thought that she might want to come down and stay for a while. But she didn't.

'It's your day off, am I right? Sunday?' Her voice was clear, bright, there were no crackles on the line.

'And alone! Amazing. No one here this weekend. Where are you?'

She was in Rome. She had been doing some stills (which I knew she adored doing) and some post-synching for a film she had just finished. She didn't ask about my film, but told me all about her wig.

'It's amazing, B.P.! It is *gigantesque*! Really *so* marvellous! It's silver and green with sort of snakes writhing about. It weighs a ton, I can tell you, and in the heat! *Mon Dieu!* I think it slightly makes my nose too large? I fight and fight, but they won't listen. Anyway I'm covered in grey and silver make-up. *Covered!*'

'Are you playing Medusa?'

A silence of incomprehension, then a snort of laughter.

'No, *dear* B.P., I am playing a goddess, what do you think! I am a goddess from the sea, or something. But it is so uncomfortable. It's the heat, you know. I envy you being in Venice. Rome is a furnace.'

I told her Venice wasn't much better but didn't elaborate on the calm of my garden in the Giudecca, fearful of her taking the train down or a plane. But that was not the point of the call.

'And how is *your* film? Are you having a ball with Luchino Visconti?'

'Not exactly. It's a toughie this one . . . worse than the Liszt bio . . .'

'And how is Madame Mango? Is she being *sensational*?' This was the reason for the call. Madame Mango was her name for Silvana Mangano, whom she detested at this point.

'She's hardly worked. She's very nice. Shy. She looks glorious, of course, in the costumes.'

'Of course, my dear. Is she *thin* enough now? She used to be so awful. So fat! I hear she has arrived in Venice with her gigolo. A cockney. *Very* young. Is this true? It's all over Rome. So stupid at her age. She could be his mother.'

'I honestly don't know. I haven't seen anyone. She keeps apart. Rather like me. We don't mix much on this film. It's all very serious. You know . . .'

'What I *do* know, darling B.P., is that you are a lousy friend. That is the one part I just *longed* for. The Countess –' Suddenly she covered the receiver with her hand and spoke, in a muffled voice, to someone in the room: 'And bring some ice! A big bucket. I'm half dead with this heat, eh, *cameriere*! *Subito, capisci?*' Then back to me. 'They are so *thick* in this hotel . . . But you *are* a lousy friend!'

'Cap, darling. I tried. I did try. I suggested you the moment I read the treatment, but he'd already cast it in his mind.' (True.) 'He wanted Silvana from the start.'

'Visconti is a shit. At least *I* was trained to wear those clothes, I know how to move in them . . . She's just an actress, great at playing peasants.'

'Not any longer, darling.'

'She must have changed quite *amazingly*.'

'She probably has. Anyway, I did try, he was very sweet . . .'

He hadn't been sweet at all. When I spoke to him about Capucine, and I did at the very start of negotiations, he snorted, remembered that we had worked together and had, as he put it, been *copains*. But she wouldn't do. She had 'a 'orrible voice, American' and 'too many teeth'. He was otherwise polite. I pressed on lamely: 'But, Luchino, the Countess never speaks in the film, never opens her mouth.'

'You fight for your friend, that is it?'

'Well, it just seems the right part for her. Chanel-trained. She can wear clothes.'

I remember that he snapped his fingers at a waiter and opened his wallet to pay a bill. 'And that, dear Bogarde, is all that she can do. A mannequin. I already have my Lady of the Pearls. No more, eh! *Basta!*' And that was that. Until we got to the glass door of Alfredo's, when he quietly turned to me, adjusting the wallet in his inside jacket pocket, pulling his scarf round his throat. 'Like a *'orse*. She looks like a *'orse*. A *beautiful* 'orse, I know that. I was trainer, I know all about 'orses. But I do not want a *'orse* for my Lady of the Pearls. *Capisci?*' Hating him, I did.

'Well,' Capucine said dryly, 'as long as you tried. Now tell me: you have a very pretty house, eh? The Volpi house on the Giudecca? They used to keep their mistresses there many years ago. Did you know? It is called the Whores' House. Everyone says it was once beautiful. Maybe I'll come down to see you?'

'Maybe. Why not? It's not so far' – my heart staggering with anguish. 'I fear you won't be seeing much of me. I am on set all the time, or in my little beach hut.'

She laughed. I knew that she had instantly got the message. 'Ah ha! You are taking this all *very* seriously? I am correct?' It was said very sweetly. She *had* seen me at work, after all.

'Correct,' I said. 'I am almost dead.'

'Well *I* must go back to Lausanne. There is a German man from Hamburg TV who is coming next week. There might be something for me. And my cats! I can't leave them for very much longer. Kennels are so expensive. Anyway! Supposing I met Madame Mango. *Quelle horreur!* I best keep away. I could go to Paris, just for a few days. Look about. See if there is anything happening, work-wise. I do, after all, "speak the lingo", as you say.'

'How was Kenya?'

'I haven't spoken to you since then? You got my cards?'

'A giraffe and an elephant, I think. All right?'

'Kenya is divine. And my "friend" is well. He has gone back to LA with his ever-loving wife . . . and so, and so, and so . . .' Her voice changed scale. 'My ice has arrived, darling B.P. . . . I'll drink your health . . .'

She had only called to be certain that Mangano really was cast. Now that Charley was no longer around, and she was stuck in Lausanne, the pickings were lean on the ground. I went out into the late afternoon. The sun had started to throw long shadows across the municipal flowerbeds. The diary says that 'D. seemed very down after talking to C. How times change.'

How indeed. Walking slowly back to the loggia on the corner I remember little needles pricking my eyes. It's a really shitty profession, this.

Luchino was at lunch in the local Gasthof when I was ready to leave. No one told me. I'd had my hair cut off, the suits wrapped up and bound with what looked like binder-twine. The boots were labelled and chucked with all the rest into a large skip and, finally, von Aschenbach had gone. For ever.

Luchino looked up vaguely (he was eating alone), indicated a chair and that I might sit. 'I am driving back to Roma immediately. We are finished! At *last* we are finished! It is difficult to believe, eh? After all the nonsense with Mr Ferrer, the weather, the money men, the so terrible Warner Brothers. You go now to France? Your new home? I wonder if you will like? To change your country is a big thing to do, no?'

I said no, I was happy to leave, and I hoped I'd done a decent job for him in the film. He assured me that I had, kissed my cheek (to my astonishment) and bade me farewell. We just drove away. I didn't say farewells. We were all too close on the film for that, and we were all of us absolutely exhausted as well. It had been even tougher on the crew (the night and dawn shooting) than it had been for me.

So we left, drove slowly down the twisting mountain road from the little place in which we had done the final shots, down to Bolzano, along to the *autostrada*, down to Cremona, Genoa and, eventually, Le Pigeonnier. I was pretty well whacked. The five months had taken a certain toll, not least of my shaky confidence. Just before starting work it transpired that we didn't own the rights to the story. I had bragged to Ingrid Bergman in a letter. She had told her agent, Kay Brown, and she had informed my agent that the rights belonged, and had done for a time, to Jose Ferrer. Panic, of course. Anguish so near the start. Cancellation of costumes and (in some cases) salaries. Mr Ferrer was finally induced to accept half of our budget and give up his dream of playing, directing and producing Mr Mann's story. But it left a wretched feeling. Now we were poor, Warner Brothers stepped in to help us but took all the distribution for the world market, leaving us only Italy. It was a mucky business and I thought, exhausted but safe, in the car to the frontier, that now I'd pack it all in. Filming was for mugs.

'I'll stop now. No more movies. I've done fifty-five or six. Quite enough, and I don't like it enough. This is the finish for me, I *really* don't like it. It's for kids.'

'I see. How do you expect to live if you don't work? No theatre? No films?'

'I don't know. I do know I've reached a kind of peak. A summit. I don't have to go any further. I can't go *on* trying to prove something.'

'Well, one does. Usually. I'd say you'd reached a *plateau*, not a *summit*, and when you are less tired you'll let the mists clear and find another peak, which you will feel impelled to climb.' Forwood sounded light but serious. 'I *know* you, mate.'

'You really mean that?'

'I really do. I can't see you just sitting about, or dead-heading roses, for long.'

'Will you hang on, here in France, for a while? Until I get settled?'

'Fine. Until you do.'

'There may be a film with Resnais. I'd do that. Promised already. But not till next year . . . I'd need help . . .'

The traffic had got heavier, near Genoa. Just like the journey up with the big comet.

'Speak to me again when we clear the frontier,' he said. 'I have to concentrate now.'

So I sat still. Thought about Chris and my first clearance for take-off . . . Another one ahead. A new start, a new journey. I had been twenty-four then in the pines and birch wood at Lüneburg Heath. Now I was almost fifty, racing through the rush-hour traffic of Genoa.

No comet this time but it did sound better to say a 'plateau' rather than a 'summit'. A summit did mean there was no where else much to go. You'd got to the top. But on a plateau you *could* catch your breath. Have a look round, wait for the mists to clear. See what lay ahead.

I had no idea then, that afternoon, that what lay ahead were to be the happiest years of my entire life. All twenty of them.

Touch-Down

It seemed to me that the removal men, the builders and the ladies who hung the curtains had only just left the wretched little Doll's House in Kensington (which I'd had to swap for Le Pigeonnier in a hurry), when the undertakers arrived at dawn one morning and carted Forwood away, down the too-narrow staircase, bumping him wincingly on the steps in a black plastic body-bag. I heard the door slam. I'd kept out of the way and left the 'finals' to his son, Gareth, and stared out of the window into the gardens of the monastery opposite. Now I *was* quite alone. This time there was absolutely no theoretical nonsense. Alone I was, but still not lonely.

As the hearse slid away with tactful silence, so as not to disturb the neighbours of 'leafy' Kensington, up whirred the milk-float. A bill owed. I heard him knock, whistling 'Puppet on a String', clink of bottles, another cheerful knock. 'You owe me for four pints, Mr B. I'm not worried, mind you. And some other stuff. Orange juice. Nurses ordered it, hadn't got no change.' I asked how much I owed him, he told me, and said he'd 'forget the penny'. Went off whistling. I called after him to say that we wouldn't need so much milk again. Just a pint a day and a bottle of Evian. 'Will do!' he called. He didn't ask why.

So life goes on. Well, it has to. One death from cancer doesn't bring the whole world to a stop. A small portion of a world, maybe, but not all of it. I was so tired that I could hardly drag myself round the house, but I did. I sort of pulled myself up on things, ageing, hoop-backed, lame in my right leg (from a stroke). It was too much of a hassle to get to the top of the stairs and reach the pleasant sitting-room. So I just sat where I was, back to the wall, feeling absolutely drained and lost. I didn't 'know' this empty, silent house; I'd never liked it. After Le Pigeonnier it was brutally small and imprisoning. No quick step out on to the terrace. No view of smudgy mountains in the slate blue of summer distance. No rustle of the vine or scent of lemon blossom.

There I was. Stuck halfway up the stairs, sitting on the disgusting pink-fitted carpet (fixtures and fittings) on to which I had sprawled not so long ago when my modest stroke felled me with a surprising viciousness. Looking up at the landing and the white banister rail through which, with amazing dexterity, I had somehow managed to weave my legs, I thought how astonishingly clever nature was. I could never have arrived in that situation had I tried, by myself, for a week. Nature did it in a second.

I can't now remember how long I stayed on the stairs. Not long. I didn't bother to try and get down, bumping on my backside, to the kitchen in the basement. I had whined away to Forwood, when we first saw the house, that there *were* five floors. Kitchen in the basement, and if he ever got flu, he'd have to struggle all the way down to refill his hot water bottle. *I* wasn't going to do it. But it wasn't flu that he got – he had Parkinson's and cancer of the colon, and *I* had to go down to the bloody kitchen and make the tea and boil the awful junk in plastic bags for our meals. 'Let's have a flat? Something on one floor, somewhere you can get to, and I can get to, easily. Not this dotty house on five floors.' But he liked it. It was old, it was elegant, it was probably Queen Anne, and it would doubtless prove to be lethal. It did. Suddenly I realized that it was I who had to be boss. We had changed places. But he had made the decision to buy the house. It was like being in the country, he thought. If it pleased him, and I knew that his time was limited, he'd better have it. So he did. Leaving me sitting, stroke-struck, on the staircase.

Eventually, oh, ages later – I know it must have been ages because dusk was falling and I had heard various bells from the monastery clanging away – I started to move. I didn't know then, don't know now, what the bells signified. Mass? Prayer? Grub? Whatever. They came at intervals and I judged the passing of the day in that manner. However, in the dusk I crawled up the stairs and got into the 'quite pleasant' sitting-room. It was pleasant because it had most of the bits and pieces from Le Pigeonnier which had not been completely destroyed during the move across the Channel by the English removal firm (who, to my horror, are still in business). So, surrounded by familiar things, some of which I'd had since Chester Row days, with the familiarity of pictures and the few bits of china which I had saved, I opened a new bottle of Scotch, poured myself a quarter-litre, slumped on to a chair and, as another wretched bell clanged dolefully across the garden over the road, burst into tears. Something I hadn't done for years. They were copious. I know that they streamed down my face and filled my mouth and I know that my mind said, 'Good! That's right! Have a good old blub, get it all out of your system.' Or something equally inane. A left-over of Lally-training. I wasn't weeping for the hideous sight and indignity of a fifty-year-old friendship being bounced awkwardly down the stairs in a black plastic bag. I was just weeping openly and without restraint, for *myself*. A whacking great bout of self-pity. Something I can't endure in others and found even more reprehensible in myself. But somehow I knew that I had to let rip. The tears, I mean. I'd seen this before, in battle, after Belsen, and when Chris had, eventually, told me about the appalling death of his co-pilot on Malta. Men do cry. But only when really pushed.

And, that evening in the Doll's House, I *was* really pushed. What on earth would become of me? I know that I got very drunk, sitting in a heap, staring into the darkening room. I know that

someone telephoned me – I remember that because the sudden shrill
sound so frightened me that I jumped, inert or not, and spewed
whisky all over me and the hideous carpet. I can't remember now
who it was. A woman's voice. Perhaps Elizabeth? Maybe my best
friend in London, Maude? Whoever it was asked if I was all right.
And I said 'Fine!' and crashed off the chair. Happily, carefully. I
picked myself up and got gingerly back on the chair. The voice at
the other end asked cautiously what had happened. And I said I'd
fallen off the chair. I was drunk. It told me, gently, to go on up to
bed, or should it come over and help?

I went up to bed. There was no hurry, I knew. There was
nothing to do tomorrow and no one was coming. No nurses, no
doctors, no urine bottle to wash, no bedpan to scrub, no sheets to
change, no anything. Not even a pleasant night nurse who would
want to see the re-run of her favourite TV programme: *Neighbours*.
I wouldn't have to find the right buttons to press, I wouldn't have
to do anything. There was nothing, nothing, now to do.

Passing Forwood's room on my way up, the bed neatly made by
Nurse, the curtains drawn, I saw, on his bedside table, the last
magazines he had been able to look at weeks ago. A *Country Life*,
something called *Blitz* and *Car* magazine for April. I still have
them. I didn't particularly keep them: they just seem to have
stayed around. But they didn't give me a clue as to what I should
do next. Where did I go from here? Home, back to France, was the
obvious answer. But I'd sold up there, I was lame now, and couldn't
drive. I was stuck. I felt trapped, like an alien in an alien land. What the
hell would I do? Fortunately I was so hopelessly drunk I just managed
to clamber on to my bed and black out. It was the bloody bells again
which woke me: but by then it was a new day.

A new day in an empty house. No food. The milkman came again
and I bought a bag of potatoes and a loaf. He asked if I wanted to

open an account and I said no, not yet. Then the man next door started to play his saxophone. I thought it was a bit early, so I banged on the kitchen wall and he shut up. He was a kindly creature with glasses and a beard. He had nowhere else to practise, but I wasn't keen that he should do it at dawn in my kitchen. As near as, anyway.

With some butter left over by the nurses I made a sandwich, scraped some Marmite on to the bread, and the door bell rang and there was a tall, smiling woman, grey hair in a bun, trim tweed suit, glasses and a clipboard and pencil. She shoved the pencil at me brightly.

'Good morning! You're new in the area, am I right?' Bleary-eyed, badly hungover, unshaved, holding my Marmite sandwich, I admitted that I was. 'Well, I won't keep you a jiffy. Just sign there . . . at the end of the list . . . Your name.' I asked what I was signing and she looked rather cross, as if I should know, or had already agreed to something and was now reneging. 'For the *bells*! The *bells*! Oh, *silly* me! *Not* for the bells! To *stop* them . . . Just sign there.' I asked again what this signature was for, and she said crisply that it was to have the bells in St Mary Abbots silenced once and for all. It was driving everyone mad in the area. I said I rather liked them. They were comforting. And she said it was quite clear that I had no family, no children. I admitted to this crass error, and she said, well, if I had I'd know how difficult it was to get them off to sleep with those frightful bells clanging away. I shook my head, and repeated that I did honestly like them, I actually *doted* on them. They reminded me of sheep and fields, the country, and that was that. She withdrew in loathing and went away and I went slowly up my stairs and got the beastly Doll's House put on the market. When it was sold (pretty quickly), I bought a small, high-up, all-on-one-floor flat far across the park and out of sight and sound of St Mary Abbots. The determination to continue to exist, somehow or other, was forced on me by the bell-woman. I wanted no part of communal civic life. That was out. So was her 'area'.

Thus all the furniture was moved once again, pictures rehung. The flat was so small that a mass of stuff had to go to auction and eventually, stripped down to the bare essentials of what I needed and what would fit into the lift, I started off at sixty-seven on a new life. Well, if you have to, somehow you do. I reckoned I'd manage until I was seventy. If I got there, fine. If not, equally fine. I didn't really care; frankly, didn't give a tinker's gob.

There isn't a very great deal that an ageing, lame, very-out-of-touch player can do if he has already chucked the theatre and turned his back on the cinema, the two areas in which he could work. If I was to continue to exist on this earth, and I had not the least, remotest thought of suicide, I'd better have a think and find something to do to earn a bit of money to tide me over the generous allocation of time I'd decided would be mine to enjoy. I'd sold the only good painting bought years ago as an investment and there was precious little left in my account. I wasn't paid all that much in the cinema days, and night and day nursing cost a small fortune; so did the scans, doctors and the rest of the paraphernalia that accompany serious illness.

So I began, pretty late in the day, I confess, to take financial things seriously. This had always been Forwood's province. He worried away with solicitors, accountants and all the rest of it, while I planted out my dianthus and heliotrope. Fair exchange? Except that I was financially illiterate. I started to try and read through my bank statements. It seemed a sensible way to start and not before time: I had never seen one before. Well, not with any interest. Now I was avid to learn but ignorant. I was rather depressed by this ignorance, and had to call my patient solicitor, Lawrence Harbottle, to ask him what the worrying OD at the end of each page implied. He told me carefully, in such a way that my incipient hysteria was held at bay, but the idea of finding some form of employment throbbed like toothache. What on earth could I do?

Le Pigeonnier had occupied me fully. Now I had a narrow terrace and four flowerpots. Added to this dismal scene I knew that there was no possibility of ever returning home. The idea of repacking the furniture and moving back to France was more than I felt I could endure. I had now got a limp, moderate but painful, I had sold up completely and knew no one now in France, apart from the few chums in Paris, and they all had their own lives to live. The plain fact was that I had to stay where I was and try very hard to come to terms with a completely new kind of lifestyle. No longer the happy peasant-lad. No bare feet. No tieless shirts – jackets and pressed trousers seemed to be the average pattern in my area. So, regretfully, deeply regretfully, I resigned myself and started to face a new life. Apparently I was now available to all and sundry, and although at the time I felt as raw and hashed as a dish of steak tartar, I was chivvied into accepting a present for my contribution to world cinema. This seemed a bit pompous and silly to me, but I was assured it was a great honour. So I reluctantly had to face my first, in over twenty years, major public engagement. With no dinner jacket, no black tie, a mouth as dry as pumice dust, I appeared in a vast cinema before a mass of my peers and found myself doing a kind of *This is Your Life*. For real. It was agonizing.

As soon as that hurdle was over I began to consider my anxious present. What benefits had I got so far? How best to use them? Well, I had a small flat, all on one floor, and also a tiny room which would offer space for a desk, the few files which remained and a typewriter. Whatever I did now I had to do sitting down. I could no longer run or sprint about – it was bad enough trying to climb the stairs (when the lift was out of order) without clutching heart and banister rail. Among other delights I now had asthma and wheezed like a bellows. What to do to occupy the dead days? Lace-making was out, dried-flower arrangements fairly detestable, knitting was not for me, and the elderly gentleman's absorbing hobby of tapestry filled me with horror. Terrible remembrances of my Scottish aunt doing her lazy-daisy sprang to mind.

I could do jigsaw puzzles of course. But did anyone make money from doing them? In any case, I didn't care for them. As a child recovering in bed from some minor ailment I remember sitting hunched in a wealth of thousands and thousands of squiggly blue bits which, according to the picture on the box, were a view of Lake Lucerne under a sunny sky. All blue. It so panicked me that I heaved it all aside, rather like the pack of cards at the end of *Alice*. The only thing which I felt I might reasonably do was write. I had, after all, written a few books which had been kindly received. I had vastly enjoyed the work. You could do it all sitting down. This was exactly what I should now perhaps do. I had no intention of sitting about the flat with a tin of lager for the rest of my allotted time. So I unpacked the typewriter. There were a few bits and pieces of stuff which had somehow survived the move and my own destruction of my papers earlier: file upon file of legal and financial matters which no longer applied to me in the UK; some letters to a Mrs X in New England; and three chapters of something which appeared to be the start of a novel to be called *Jericho*. I had not the least idea what this was all about, remembering only that I had started it in the gaps of anxiety waiting for Forwood's X-ray results and scans in France. The letters, however, were easier – most had been shredded; just a fraction remained, but perhaps I could start on them? They would make a modest book, with a few scribbles to fill out the pages. They did constitute a personal, if blinkered, picture of my life in the early sixties. My agent, Pat Kavanagh, considered them and gave me the green light. So did my publishers. I was starting again. Ice was cracking. I was beginning to hack a new path through the apparent wilderness. Better by far than limping round Brompton Cemetery looking for a plot. Someone told me it was full and closed anyway, and I'd have to go to Putney Vale or Golders Green, which seemed too far out. So I went on typing. Which, as it has turned out, was really a sensible thing to do.

I remember, as a child, that there was a thing which we got at Christmas in our crackers. It was called the Magic Shell, a small, grey-speckled shell, perfectly ordinary and dull, just a shell, with a bit of paper with 'JAPAN' printed on it. Put in a glass of water it exploded before one's eyes into the most amazing water-garden you can possibly imagine. From this dull, common little shell, a great cluster of glorious flowers began to blossom, opening slowly in vivid colours: pink, scarlet, blue, yellow, every colour imaginable. And there they'd be wavering gently in the trembling water on thin strings of cotton. They didn't last terribly long, but while they bloomed their magic was dazzling. And all from a perfectly ordinary, unnoticed (normally) little shell.

Well, it seemed to me that I had a grey shell in the hollow of my palm. Unnoticed, until released, it began to offer me a wealth of glories I'd never have dreamed of before. Instead of flowers there were words. I began to see them and use them as I had never done before. No longer just 'something to do in the long winter evenings', they were to be my life-line from now on in. First came the book of letters, a modest success; then telephone calls, invitations to dine from people I'd known before but who had rather 'let me slide'. Deliberately. Well, I do see why. I was a poor guest and a bad conversationalist. Also, when I said I did not possess a dinner jacket, pressures eased off. The dinners, suppers, soirées I was asked to attend were tedious simply because after living abroad for so long I knew little, if anything, about the English arts. I hadn't seen an English play or film for over twenty years, I knew very few writers, read only those books I bought in a bundle once a year when I came to London. I never watched television, and heard the BBC only for the world news at seven. A limited world, to be sure.

So at these elegant supper tables, with strange names bouncing like ping-pong balls across the Sheraton and Blind Earl with sickening familiarity, I was hopelessly lost. I knew absolutely no one, in France, who had ever read an English author. Perhaps I might have had I lived in Paris or Lyons, but no one in my village had ever heard of one. I think that the nearest anyone ever came to knowing an English author was the local doctor, and he thoroughly enjoyed his Agatha Christie. As for television, I was completely lost; no one much ever even watched it where I lived. Oh, Florette Ranchett did sometimes 'enjoy a good *policier*', a detective story, on the telly, and she also enjoyed a perfectly dreadful show called *Champs-Elysées* which was the top variety show in France, and I know that Madame Bruna had it on in the evening when she was ironing her giant laundry. She said that hearing other people working at that hour made her less fed up with her lot, ironing other people's sheets and underpants.

But I had no contributions to make myself at those dinners. You can't get far in SW1 or even 3 if you talk only about beekeeping, cheesemaking, olive-pressing, lambing or the agony of a summer crop destroyed in a minute of hail: it's not to most people's taste. But I had been classified as an agriculturist, and that is as far as I was going to go with these people. They, some of the old friends, were still talking about exactly the *same* subjects which they had been talking about when I left, over two decades ago. Nothing seemed to have changed. They were pickled in aspic really. Who was dead, who had died, who was about to 'fly off the twig'. Who had lost '*the* most glorious role' in some play or film, had got married, divorced, changed sex, or run away with whoever, or who was 'simply dire' in something, or 'utterly brilliant' in some other new version of the Bard who was still, monotonously, being played. It seemed that new plays got put on in scout huts or public houses. Odd. I found it sad and depressing, really. This was, of course, my Old Lot, not the New Young. I didn't know any of them, alas.

But sometimes, when I had left one of these gatherings early, using the fact that I was lame still, and my leg tired quickly, I used to go away relieved but haunted, as if I had just missed boarding the *Titanic*. It seemed to me on reflection that my lot were all marking time on the one spot, easing themselves slowly, inexorably, into the mud of the past, and it was not going to happen to me. I had missed 'embarkation' so to speak, and I was going to strike out on my own. Alone, afresh. A new life altogether.

I started with the letters to Mrs X, and went on to the unremembered *Jericho*. That filled in a good, solid year of work. However, the parties which I had attended provided a warm bed of compost for gossip to breed. And it wasn't very long before there were chirruping little telephone calls, and correct little letters, suggesting that perhaps I might like to let them have 'say, about 1,000 words' on 'My Life in Provence' or 'The France You Don't Know' or even 'Bogarde Blasts Britain!' Why? I hadn't. Or worse still, 'How to Restart Your Life'. Why the hell should I tell *anyone*? The originality of it all quite stupefied me. Anyway, at that time I was also writing reviews for the *Daily Telegraph* so I hid behind that to avoid giving offence. I was very careful to keep my head far below the parapet of social life.

But then I got caught. My fault entirely. I was asked to do an important show for the BBC. Very good, proper, no danger, almost dull, really. Would I be tempted? Oh! *Do* agree! Well, I had done this particular programme years ago; it was bland, popular and pleasant. I felt for a 'first outing' it would be all right to do: I couldn't make a cock-up, it was so benign, and it might help the modest book of letters, just out, to Mrs X, so I accepted. On condition that no *personal* questions were asked. It was emphasized that this was 'not that kind of programme. It is for Radio 4!' But alas it wasn't quite. I suppose that because I had been unavailable for two decades the temptation to question me was too great. The avuncular presenter of the early years had, alas, died; now a young woman was in charge: perfectly nice, ambitious for her programme, anxious to ease my anxieties. It all went well, until we got, inevitably, to the personal questions, which threw me rather, although I did my best to remain calm. I scare easy. Then I heard the gentle, honey-and-Mars-bar voice say, 'So, is there *no* love in you to give?' I was so astonished by this question, asked before a couple of million listeners, that I was uncertain what to do. Behave well, was all I could think of, and finally, it was all over. I dragged myself through corridors and up steps and vowed never to return to Broadcasting House. I felt rather gutted. But, of course, some time later, when my anxieties started to crumble a bit, and the drawbridge of resistance started to lower, a brisk North-country voice set before me a suggestion for a new method of 'sedentary work'. Would I, Janet Whitaker asked brightly, be interested in doing the narration to a twenty-something series on the *Forsyte Saga* for Radio 4? I could do it all on my own in a studio? It should take three days at most? I said, in principle, fine, and she sent a *truck* round with the pile of scripts (this alarmed me, but it was all right) and we started work together and did it all in two and a bit days. Working with Janet was marvellous. She opened a whole new world for me: the world of radio and the spoken word. I was learning again, and she was a brilliant teacher. I could do radio! You didn't have to appear anywhere, or join a happy crowd of players. All alone! Janet in the control room guiding carefully, a mike, the scripts and you, just sitting on your bum. Quite splendid!

Just relax, and play with words. Beautiful words written by master craftsmen. This was a revelation. But all was not exactly as it seemed. Miss Whitaker might be my producer and indeed director; she was not, however, responsible for publicity.

Some long time after the series was finished, long after I had gone on my way and forgotten, I was cajoled to come to a 'party to meet *all* the cast'. It was after all the first time we'd have met, and I 'really *had* to be present'. So I agreed, a car was sent for me, and we drove to some private club on the King's Road. No one, at that time, had mentioned the dreaded, for me, word 'press'. The BBC are either maddeningly, or touchingly, however you look at these things, inept at entertainment of this kind. They may be whizz-kids running the World Service or *Woman's Hour* but they can't run a drinks party in Chelsea. If you have a cheese straw in one hand and a glass of warm Chardonnay in the other, they reckon you are well 'looked after'.

I had agreed, privately, that I would give a short interview to one *single* newspaper. *The Times?* The *Telegraph?* I can't remember now and it is of no consequence. In the chattering, laughing crush I eventually met my journalist and we found a settee in a quiet room away from the jolly circus around us. It was an extremely deep, squashy settee, the kind that gets hold of you so that you feel like the shrimp and the anemone: sucked down. I was jammed tight, backside wedged into huge cushions. The journalist was far more sensible and sat on a coffee table, pad in hand. He opened it up and said, I suppose, about five words of greeting, looked up, went white with shock, muttered something, closed his pad and fled. I never saw him again. Wedged as I was (trapped is better), I started to flail about to go off with him, but was stopped by a high voice which cried, 'Oh! *What* luck! He's finished!' Now this fellow was pretty tall, so I was stuck peering up at him. He wore a sort of sandy toupee, rather like a bit of Weetabix, on his head, and before he took his place on the abandoned coffee table he summoned together a little flurry of young women, who were possibly trainee journalists. Anyway, he was in control, and sat them around us, pads and pencils at the ready, opened his own pad, crossed his long legs, nodded at the girls to indicate, I suppose, that they were to be ready to catch any little crumbs which might perhaps fall from his, or my, lips. Sweet little dustpans: they are usually to be found at minor events drifting about with their pads and pencils and swooping in to ask some trite question which 'will be of interest to our readers'.

So there we all sat, me jammed in my smothering settee, the chief on his coffee table, his little flutter of ladies poised. I was dry-mouthed. 'So!' he said brightly. 'After *all* these years! Got you at last! You *are* a little recluse, aren't you? Haven't seen you about for *years*, have we? That lovely villa in the South of France! Lucky old you.' I mumbled something, and tried to move. Instead I seemed to crouch even deeper into the recesses of my settee, a terrified toad. I knew without doubt that I was about to be journalistically humili-ated. I had seen it done to others. Now it was my turn and I was helpless, and isolated, since I had chosen to move into the little room apart from the general gaiety. I had no 'minder'. There was no one about to help, and I couldn't summon aid. Couldn't move.

'Oh don't try to go away! I suppose things must be *difficult* for you now? Working for the BBC. You *must* be broke? They don't pay a fortune, do they? And *no* car? Have you a car in dirty old London?'

I think I shook my head. One of the little girls said brightly, 'You had lots of lovely Rolls-Royces once upon a time, didn't you?'

I shook my head again, not daring to speak.

'No car!' cried the chief, writing briskly. 'We *have* come down in the world! Still, not much use in this traffic . . . and I suppose you are still inconsolable about the death of your "*partner*"? He did *everything* for you? Didn't he? It must be simply *awful* to have no one . . . and' – he turned a page of his pad swiftly – 'and where do you live now? In tatty old London?'

I heard myself say, as if from the bottom of a well, 'A flat. I have a flat.'

He raised his eyebrows, looked round the girls. '*What* a pity! A *flat*! After that lovely villa in the sun.'

I tried to explain that I didn't live in a villa, but gave up. It was useless to even try to speak. A girl said how high the prices were for a flat now, and the chief said, quite kindly, that I perhaps had a *basement* flat? They were *much* cheaper. I suppose that I again tried to lever myself out of the situation, because he waved me back to my squashed position. I slumped back, spilling a little of my drink. He instantly fastened on this – 'What are we drinking, orange juice?' – and laughed happily, grabbing my glass and sniffing. '*Scotch!* I do declare! It's whisky! Tut! Tut! Bit early in the day for spirits, isn't it?' He nodded brightly round the girls to take note.

Suddenly a woman in black with a vast false pearl brooch sped into the room. 'Ah! There you are,' she cried brightly. 'All finished are we?'

The chief remarked through clenched teeth that no, *he* had only just started. 'How do you find London now, had time to look around a bit? So tatty and dirty. So many . . . strangers about . . . *black*, you know? It must be *hateful* for you, don't you agree? So lonely? You must *often* feel quite suicidal?'

There was no Forwood, no Theo Cowan, the lady in black from the BBC had obviously thought all was well and had gone off to do her 'mingling' with the enormous cast. I was absolutely stuck. Panic-stricken and tight-wedged. I was incapable of dealing with this situation until a sudden burst of terror-stricken energy forced me to my feet in a scatter of cushions and surprised lady journalists.

I dragged myself up and like a mad crab scuttled wildly through the laughing throng to try and find the way out. The BBC lady saw me but didn't interfere. I reckon she twigged that the situation was something she couldn't, or preferred not to, handle. The Guest of Honour was in the shit, pursued by a cluster of eager press people, and seemed to have lost his cool. All that I was doing, I knew perfectly well, was pushing through people and nodding in agreement at everything I was asked.

I got to the front door, and the BBC lady cried, 'Oh! Don't go yet! You haven't met darling Alan Howard. *Do* stay . . .' But I slammed myself and the front door into the King's Road. Shaking. There are *real* people here. The sun is out! Ordinary, kind people are going about their business, real people, just walking along, oblivious to the terrors behind the shiny black door. There were trees somewhere. I saw them filigreed against the afternoon sky.

I walked towards them and found myself in a square, away from the crowds: a few trees, trodden grass, some laurel bushes. I was seeking invisibility, pulling back into my shell, like the hermit crab I'd often thought I might resemble. It didn't work, of course. You *can't* just suddenly dissolve in the middle of the King's Road (or a square off it). Anyway, the kind of hermit crab I was pretending to be, or wishing to be, was usually naked and seeking an empty shell. You can't pull into an empty shell and hide if you are tarted up in your one best Aquascutum single-button two-piece. Walking round the square, I saw beneath my polished shoes the dirty cracks in the pavement and remembered my feet bare in the red dust of the stony track down to Madame Meil's cottage, the plastic bag of kitchen refuse for her goats swinging about in my hand, throwing a shadow like a great melon in a net. No bleat of goats here, no bell tonkle-tonkling, no scent of crushed oregano under my bare feet, no need to curl my toes against the warm softness of her dust-and-pebbled path. I was in London.

At the far end of the square the hired car drew up and parked. I told the driver to leave me, that I'd walk back to the flat. He said it was quite a way, did I know how to get there? I tipped him generously and said I'd get there, that I needed the air, which I did. I was, initially, terrified to walk among the crowds. I hadn't done it for years and years – of course, in the village or the local town, even, on occasions, Cannes or Nice. But never naked and alone, so to speak, in London. I found that I was still shaking from my session in the settee: I was rattled. I realized that I had become quite paranoid. And have regrettably remained so ever since that day. After my life up on the hill, in solitude and calm, among people who didn't give a toss about 'celebrities', as they are now called, I had forgotten the hurt and intensity of the pain that press curiosity could cause.

I got back to the flat, walking head bent, God knows why, through the cheerful throng of quite unimpressed people. Once inside, door shut, I more or less relaxed and then remembered that I must, no matter what, telephone the family and warn them that I had behaved idiotically at a press gathering and that they must expect some ugly piece in the papers the next day. I really was in such a panic that I was certain I'd make headlines. Thus paranoia can grab you. Elizabeth said, 'Oh! What a pity. Why didn't you have someone with you? You *know* how silly you are when you get into a panic.' My brother was even less concerned and just said that no one in his household read the comics and wished me good luck. So I just sat in a heap of misery, had a couple of stiff Scotches and then, the next morning, found myself facing a deathly photograph of myself, which the art editors had obviously got from the obituary people, plus a simple story about how I was now 'ageing', 'broke' and living in a 'basement flat' drinking 'bottles of Scotch' because I was inconsolable after the death of my 'close partner' and 'forced' to play 'bits' for the BBC. Heavy implications on the Fall of the Handsome Young Doctor in the House. Oh well. I couldn't fault them for invention. No one seemed to have read anything when I bravely ventured out to get some bread and frozen-fish pie. Perhaps they hadn't even seen the not very large pieces? At any rate no one chucked stones, or pointed accusing fingers. I honestly don't know what I expected them to do. They did nothing. Life was as usual, until I got back to the flat and got my first ever 'foot in the door'. Some pallid man conned the housekeeper by saying that he was my cousin and had a book to give me. So she, quite rightly, let him in and up he came. Fortunately I had the chain on the door, and when his black Russell and Bromley toecap thrust into the gap, I stamped on it. Rather brave, I thought. Shortly after another arrived and said that he was actually my *brother*, and I then had to tell the housekeeper that if she ever let *anyone* in I'd get her sacked instantly. Not her fault, poor lady. She didn't understand the problem that I posed in her building, but we had a little talk together and got things sorted out. Now no one on God's earth can get to me unless I speak to them first. Comforting.

In time the unease and real distress created by that unhappy afternoon faded, just a little.

Among the magic flowers I wrote about earlier, one remarkable and glowing one was when the French Government promoted me to Commandeur des Arts et des Lettres. This award, rarish for foreigners, gave me the greatest joy. I really did feel that I had accomplished something for my beloved adopted country. It was a modest night. I took Kathleen Tynan along with me to the ceremony to hold my hand, and we all drank champagne and my medal was put round my neck and they said, did I know, we had a new Prime Minister in Great Britain, a John Major. And we all looked suitably astonished. It had just come via the TV apparently. Anyway, Kathleen and I went off to the Connaught and had more champagne and a lot of caviar – not ounces, *a lot*. An award such as mine and a companion such as mine deserved no less. Much later, after the Queen had given me permission to wear my green and white ribbon (why?), I received one morning a buff envelope with 'Secret' on it and a Government stamp. I was requested to tick the appropriate box. 'Yes' or 'No'. My reply was expected in Downing Street as soon as possible. I ticked 'No', and got a gentle, but firm, reprimand from a very pleasant Scots lady somewhere in No. 10. I did realize, she said kindly, that I was behaving with the greatest discourtesy to the Prime Minister? This was his first Honours List, the first of his Term. It was also, she added sweetly, insulting to HM the Queen. I protested that I really didn't want a knighthood. It was the *last* thing I wanted. It had taken me almost fifty years to get my name clear of English prejudice (I kept hearing Hugh's gloomy concern over the name in the sitting-room at Hasker Street. A nice *English* name, he had said . . .) and sticking a 'Sir' before it would cause great ridicule. It didn't fit. *Please* accept my ticked box? She heard me out with enormous patience, asked me to send her a signed photograph, preferably in colour, for her office, and said I could have until Monday to make up my mind, to call her at the number she would give me exactly at nine o'clock. It was a very private number. I asked, facetiously, if I should perhaps eat it right away? I knew my decision. And she said that I was to take this seriously. 'Knighthoods', she said with great wisdom, 'don't grow on trees, you know.'

It was a fairly miserable weekend. No one to turn to, and I then got into a mild panic and thought that perhaps, when the list was submitted to her, the Queen, or someone else, would grab a Biro and cry 'Oh! God! *Not him!*' and strike me off. That would be a terrible humiliation, but I consoled myself glumly that only I, the Queen, the Prime Minister and the pleasant Scots lady at No. 10 would know. I could nurse my wounded ego alone. Late on the

Sunday night, rather relaxed on my Scotch – well, not exactly relaxed: clear-headed – I ticked the wretched box for 'Yes'.

I thought of Pa, frankly: his huge pleasure at Sandhurst when I marched up the steps as a new little officer wearing his old Sam Browne. The fact that I was marching behind the Duke of Gloucester on his enormous white horse up on the marble steps gave it a great impact, I suppose. Especially as the horse defecated hugely on the very top step and the first thing that I had to do, leading my brave fellow officers, was to take evading action. But I remembered Pa's pleasure at my performance, his eldest son – the dunce. And thought that he might, wherever he was, be very much more amused by my appearance in the Throne Room at Buckingham Palace. So for him, no other reason, I ticked my acceptance.

Elizabeth came with me, in a new suit and a terrific hat with a feather, Ron Jones bought himself a new cockade for *his* cap and polished the car to glass, I bought a black suit and a grey tie, and we all went off together.

I remember climbing the great staircase, the white and gold, the pillars and crimson swags at the top of the large sign which stated simply, 'Final Lavatory for Gentlemen', with an arrow pointing to the right. Quite enough to cause me, of all people, to flood. However, I managed to contain myself, even to kneel and rise without falling over. Alec Guinness had warned me to be very still and not budge an inch at the investiture lest HM should miss her aim. But she didn't and I limped away to selections from *High Society* clutching in my hand my insignia with the pride of a child who had won first prize in the egg-and-spoon race. To dodge the press and all the photographers we found a side door and slipped out that way, triumphant. Except that the battery to Ron's sparkling car was flat. Flat as a pancake. Hastily, discreetly, two other cars moved towards us and exchanged power, feeding our battery, so that we were finally able to drive bravely through the hordes of screaming Japanese with their flashing cameras. Elizabeth gave them all a number of stately waves and they screamed even louder.

We made the turn round the Victoria Memorial and up the Mall. Elizabeth began brushing imaginary lint from her skirt. 'Well. I thought that was *very* nice. Very nice indeed.' She was happy. 'Mind you, it was a very long sit, wasn't it? Two hours. Are you all right?' I nodded urgently. 'The chairs were terribly hard, I mean, *numbing* . . . and I was rather stuck in a corner. Didn't see all that much honestly. Well, enough . . . but it *was* rather tucked away. A jolly bossy man told me to sit there, so I did. I mean he was some sort of official. But it was very nice. All those happy faces, and the policemen from Hong Kong, they were so proud. Quite small, the Queen, isn't she? Really quite little.'

Ron turned into St James's. 'Mind you, you were a bit mean, just shoving us through that side door. I know why, of course. But still. *I'd* quite have liked a photograph. My hat. I never wear a hat. Oh well . . . never mind . . .' Ron turned and said he was very sorry about the battery, he'd no idea why it had gone flat, it was fully charged last night . . . anyway, the 'transfusions' were very helpful . . . very lucky they were there. I told him not to worry about it, everything was splendid and we'd dodged the photographers.

Suddenly I saw Chris. Sitting under the birch and pine trees years ago on Lüneburg Heath. He was as clear as clear. 'You're cleared for take-off,' he had said. Well, fair enough, I'd tried. It was fairly bumpy, a bit white-knuckled as they say, some wretched bits of turbulence, but at least I'd done it. I'd risked the flight. It had taken rather longer than I imagined, that was all. As we turned towards Carlos Place it seemed to me that we were really on our descent to touch-down. So far it looked quite good.

I felt a silly surge of joy and leant across and kissed Elizabeth on her cheek.

'Oh! You *are* stupid! Do be careful! My *hat*! You could have knocked it off . . . I am glad *you* didn't wear a top hat and all that outfit. You'd have looked like a bookie . . .'

I didn't reply. I was thinking how fortunate it was that the Queen, or whoever, hadn't actually struck me off the List with her Biro. I was almost quite enjoying myself. Suddenly Elizabeth said in a low, private voice, 'Are you all right? Do you want to "go"? I mean *really* terribly?'

I nodded hard. 'Busting. Simply *busting* . . .'

She calmly smoothed her long leather gloves. 'Well, we won't be long now, almost there. Aren't we, Ron? The Connaught? Almost there?'

And Ron, still a bit flustered by the flat battery, said, 'Yes, Madam. Any minute now, there it is, just ahead.'

So that was all right.

London
March 1995